Ref

D0893696

SOCIOLOGY

Recent Titles in
Reference Sources in the Social Sciences

American Military History: A Guide to Reference and Information Sources
Daniel K. Blewett

Education: A Guide to Reference and Information Sources
Nancy Patricia O'Brien

Northern Africa: A Guide to Reference and Information Sources
Paula Youngman Skreslet

Sports, Exercise, and Fitness: A Guide to Reference and Information Sources
Mary Beth Allen

SOCIOLOGY

A Guide to Reference and Information Sources

Third Edition

STEPHEN H. ABY, JAMES NALEN, AND LORI FIELDING

Reference Sources in the Social Sciences

LIBRARIES UNLIMITED

A Member of the Greenwood Publishing Group

Westport, Connecticut • London

Library of Congress Cataloging-in-Publication Data

Aby, Stephen H., 1949-
Sociology : a guide to reference and information sources / Stephen H. Aby, James Nalen, and Lori Fielding—3rd ed.
    p. cm. — (Reference sources in the social sciences)
    Includes bibliographical references and index.
    ISBN 1-56308-947-5 (alk. paper)
    1. Sociology—Reference books—Bibliography. 2. Sociology—Bibliography.
3. Sociology—Electronic information resources. 4. Social sciences—Reference
books—Bibliography. 5. Social Sciences—Bibliography 6. Social sciences—Electronic
information resources. I. Nalen, James. II. Fielding, Lori. III. Title. IV. Reference
sources in the social sciences series.
Z7164.S68A24   2005
[HM585]
016.301—dc22   2005040708

British Library Cataloguing in Publication Data is available.

Library of Congress Catalog Card Number: 2005040708
ISBN: 1–56308–947–5

First published in 2005

Libraries Unlimited, 88 Post Road West, Westport, CT 06881
A Member of the Greenwood Publishing Group, Inc.
www.lu.com

Printed in the United States of America

The paper used in this book complies with the
Permanent Paper Standard issued by the National
Information Standards Organization (Z39.48–1984).

10 9 8 7 6 5 4 3 2 1

CONTENTS

ACKNOWLEDGMENTS

Many individuals contributed to the completion of this bibliography. Specifically, we would like to thank faculty members in the Department of Sociology at the University of Akron for some helpful suggestions, both for the previous edition and the current one. The staff at Libraries Unlimited, especially Martin Dillon, has been professional, supportive, and extremely patient throughout this project. Finally, we want to thank our spouses for their support and encouragement. Thanks to all of these individuals, this bibliography is better than it otherwise would have been. However, the remaining mistakes, whether of omission or commission, are our responsibility alone.

INTRODUCTION

Scope and Purpose

This third edition of *Sociology: A Guide to Reference and Information Sources* provides undergraduate and graduate students, faculty, and librarians with descriptions of 610 of the major reference sources in sociology, its subdisciplines, and the related social sciences. Indexes, bibliographies, handbooks, databases, World Wide Web sites, dictionaries and encyclopedias, and other print and electronic reference and information sources published from 1997 through early 2004 are cited. Works that precede this period are also selectively included if their coverage is historically important or not historically bound, as in the chapters on sociological theory, retrospective sociology bibliographies, and sociology dictionaries and encyclopedias. The sources are in English, and works from the United States, Great Britain, Australia, and Canada predominate, though some other important international sources are included. With the new cutoff dates for inclusion, and the addition of many more Web sites than in the previous edition, this third edition has approximately 325 new titles and electronic sources. Also, many newer editions and updates of previously cited works are included, making this a substantial revision of and complement to the previous edition.

Entries follow *The Chicago Manual of Style* bibliographic format and are descriptively annotated with occasional evaluative comments. Annotations range in length from approximately 60 to 250 words, except in the descriptions of journals, organizations, and World Wide Web sites, where the annotations are often briefer. Virtually all sources have been examined and annotated by the compilers.

Organization

The organization of this edition is modestly different from the second edition. There are now three major parts of the book instead of the previous four. The first chapter, subdivided according to the type of reference source, includes those titles of use to all of the social sciences, but particularly to sociology: social science guides; bibliographies; indexes, abstracts, and databases; handbooks and yearbooks; dictionaries and encyclopedias; statistics sources; directories; and biographical sources. Within these categories, entries are arranged alphabetically by author or editor, or lacking this, by title; this arrangement is used throughout the book. In a few instances, for well-known titles or works with supervisory editors, title entries are used. Now also included in these categories are entries drawn from what was part 2 in the previous edition, "Social Science Disciplines" (i.e., "Anthropology," "Economics," "Education," "History," "Political Science," "Psychology," and "Social Work"). For example, dictionaries and encyclopedias from all of these fields are now filed together in the dictionaries and encyclopedias chapter, along with more general social science dictionaries. The intent here was to reduce the number of places the user might have to look for relevant sources of that type. All of these reference sources should potentially be relevant to researchers in sociology. Entries for indexes may cite either print or electronic versions, with the other available options mentioned in the abstract. The citations, however, include Web addresses for more complete descriptions of the particular print index or database as provided by the publisher.

Chapters 2 and 3 comprise the most important and largest sections and include reference sources dealing specifically with sociology and its subdisciplines. Chapter 2 includes general sociological guides; bibliographies; indexes, abstracts, and databases; handbooks and yearbooks; dictionaries and encyclopedias; general sociology World Wide Web sites and organizations; journals; and directories. Research centers, which had received a chapter of their own in the previous edition, are now integrated with Web sites into the various subject chapters to which they relate. Similarly, entries for organizations are now included as a subsection of the chapter on sociology Web sites. As before, the number of centers included is very selective, listing primarily centers that are either mentioned in the book's citations and abstracts or that recur in searches on the topic. For a much more thorough listing of potentially useful centers, one should consult the *Research Centers Directory* (Detroit, Gale Research). The number of World Wide Web sites has been expanded, and entries for new and previously included sites have been updated in terms of their Internet address (URL), the date last accessed, and the description of the site. Additional Web sites can be found through the general sociology sites or search engines mentioned in this section. Selective lists of Web sites for the specific subdisciplines in sociology are located in those particular sections in Chapter 3. These, too, have been updated and expanded since the last edition. Finally, the titles selected for the chapter on sociology journals comprise a core list and were sifted, in part, from suggestions by sociology faculty and graduate students. Only one new title has been added since the last edition. A selective list of major indexing sources accompanies each journal entry. New to this edition are Internet addresses for each journal, as well as the date these sites were accessed. Virtually all journals have publisher Web sites now that describe the journal, its editorial policies, its subscription prices and, often, the tables of contents of recent issues. There may also be descriptions of and links to full-text services for the journal.

Chapter 3 covers reference sources in specific sociological fields, though some specializations are not covered due to the paucity of appropriate reference sources. Within each subject area, entries are arranged first by type of reference source, then alphabetically by author/editor or, lacking this, by title. Most of the standard subdisciplines within sociology are represented in this section, though we have changed some of the subdiscipline names to reflect current usage and practice (e.g., "applied sociology" is now "sociological practice"). We have also added a new chapter on social networks and social support. Overall the chapters include: sociological practice; criminology, law, and deviance; sociology of education; marriage and the family; gerontology and aging; social indicators; medical sociology; research methods and statistics; social change, movements, and collective behavior; social networks and social support; sociology of organizations and groups; population and demography; social problems; race and ethnic relations; sociology of religion; rural sociology; socialization, social psychology, and gender roles; sociology of sport; social stratification; sociological theory; urban sociology; women's studies; and sociology of work. In some cases, subdisciplines are combined into one section when their subject matter is closely related or where the number of entries is modest. Examples of this are the combining of criminology and the sociology of law, and the combining of social psychology, socialization, and gender roles. No slight is intended, nor are the valid distinctions between the areas minimized.

The section on social problems is a collection of works on specific problems, such as drug abuse, alcoholism, violence, suicide, rape and sexual harassment, and homelessness. While this is not an exhaustive list of social problems, it does represent some major problems currently treated in reference works. Many other problems, such as poverty or child abuse, are covered within other subject sections and are further accessible through the subject index.

The section devoted to race and ethnic relations includes general sources as well as sources on particular racial and ethnic groups. For reasons of space, only African Americans, Native Americans, Asian Americans, and Hispanic Americans are included. For sources on other racial or ethnic groups, the indexes, abstracts, databases, and other reference works in the general sources section should be consulted.

Women's studies is an interdisciplinary subject that is included here because some of its reference works address concerns that are central to a number of sociological areas. These include the roles of women and men in society, social inequality, the feminization of poverty, marriage and the family, and more. In fact, one could easily argue that there are few areas in sociology that are not illuminated by the growing literature in feminism and women's studies.

Throughout the book, the citations include information on the author(s), title, publisher, location of publisher, date of publication, paging, indexes, series, price (if in print), and ISBN. ISSNs are included for serial publications. Prices are included, wherever possible, for books in print and for serials, though generally not for online databases and government documents. Book prices were taken primarily from *Books in Print* online. Prices for serial publications were drawn from the sources themselves, from their Web sites, and from *The Serials Directory* online. Journal prices are for institutional subscriptions and, as with books and index prices, are subject to change.

The arrangement of the book by subject and type of reference source should make locating titles fairly straightforward. However, additional access to the entries is provided by the author/title and subject indexes.

General Social Science Reference Sources

Chapter
1

Guides

1. Herron, Nancy L., ed. **The Social Sciences: A Cross-Disciplinary Guide to Selected Sources.** 3d ed. Greenwood Village, CO: Libraries Unlimited, 2002. 494 p. ISBN 1-56308-985-8.

　　Intended as both a reference work and a teaching textbook, this third edition includes approximately 1,000 reference sources in the general social sciences and its subdisciplines. The annotated entries are organized into four parts comprising twelve chapters, each written by one or more subject librarians specializing in that discipline. Part 1 covers sources in the "General Social Sciences" that should be of use in all of the social science disciplines. These are further subdivided by the standard reference categories, such as guides, handbooks, indexes, dictionaries, directories, and so on. Part 2 has specific chapters for reference works in political science, economics and business, history, law and legal issues, anthropology, and sociology. Here again, reference works are cited under traditional reference book categories. The "Sociology" chapter includes eighty-nine reference tools for accessing the literature, with good coverage of basic indexes, abstracts, and reviewing sources. Part 3 provides similar coverage of disciplines that have a "social aspect," specifically education and psychology. Part 4 covers the disciplines of geography and communication, which are noted as having "recognized social implications." Each chapter begins with an essay orienting the reader to the discipline and its scope. Author, title, and subject indexes are provided.

2. Li, Tze-Chung. **Social Science Reference Sources: A Practical Guide.** 3d ed. Westport, CT: Greenwood Press, 2000. 495 p. $119.95. ISBN 0-313-30483-1.

1

Originally designed as a textbook for a course on reference sources in the social sciences, this new edition is a "substantial revision" of the second edition and provides an excellent overview of 1,600 reference sources in the social sciences. Only reference works with publication dates between 1980 and July 1999 are included in this edition. Beyond that, there are hundreds of new digital resources and Web sites included, as well as a new listing of periodicals that provides various kinds of bibliographic information, among other changes. Overall, the guide is written in bibliographic essay style and is divided into two sections. The first section covers the social sciences in general and is comprised of seven chapters: reference sources in an electronic age (e.g., search engines, Web sites, online databases); research resources in the social sciences (e.g., online library catalogs, printed catalogs); access to sources (e.g., bibliographies, indexes, and abstracts); sources of information (e.g., encyclopedias, handbooks, dictionaries); statistical sources; periodicals; and government publications. The second section includes reference works that specifically address the subdisciplines of the social sciences, including cultural anthropology, business, economics, education, geography, history, law, political science, psychology, and sociology. The section on sociology identifies 116 titles in this edition. For each of the subdisciplines, references sources are divided into those that provide access to sources (e.g., bibliographies, indexes, abstracts) and those that provide sources of information (e.g., encyclopedias, dictionaries, directories, biographies). Appended are a list of cited URLs, a name and title index, and a subject index. As with earlier editions, this well-written work's bibliographic essay style lends itself to a comparative evaluation of sources.

3. Martinez, Rey C., and Carol Lea Clark. **The Social Worker's Guide to the Internet.** Boston: Allyn & Bacon, 2000. 180 p. index. $26.00. ISBN 0-205-29735-8.

The focus of this guide is the navigation of the Internet for specific social work information. The guide covers the development of the Internet and what the Internet has to offer to the field of social work. Connecting to the Internet, using electronic mail, subscribing to Internet discussion groups and listservs, reading and posting to newsgroups, and using chat services, among other things, are also discussed in depth. "The Social Work Tour" chapter focuses on numerous Web sites of interest to social workers. Other chapters focus on creating Web pages, file transfer protocols, and telnet services. The guide concludes with an appendix of World Wide Web resources for social workers; this list provides myriad annotated Web sites and Web addresses. Within each chapter there are numerous examples and visuals, chapter-specific Web sites, a chapter summary, and questions for discussion. This is a clear and easy-to-use guide for anyone interested in exploring the basics of Internet searching for social work research purposes, and it also provides useful information on the basics of more challenging Web applications such as file transfers and creating Web pages.

4. O'Brien, Jacqueline Wasserman, and Steven R. Wasserman, eds. **Statistics Sources: A Subject Guide to Data on Industrial, Business, Social, Educational, Financial, and Other Topics for the United States and Internationally.** 25th ed. Detroit: Gale, 2001. 2v. ISBN 0-7876-3603-7.

This regularly updated source includes approximately 100,000 citations for data sources focusing on the United States and foreign countries. The arrangement is alphabetical by subject, with a significant number of subject headings devoted to countries. These, in turn, are broken into subtopics. While most references cited are publications, some are statistical offices that may have unpublished data. The guide is much stronger in its coverage of Western or industrialized countries. Data sources for Eastern European countries are still somewhat uneven. Sociologists and other researchers interested in development issues and social indicators may find this source most useful. However, there are also citations for data from states, as well as data on interesting social issues. Without a detailed table of contents or subject index, or even cross-references to preferred terms, the user will have to do more searching to determine if their topic is covered.

5. O'Brien, Nancy P. **Education: A Guide to Reference and Information Sources.** 2d ed. Englewood, CO: Libraries Unlimited, 2000. 189 p. index. $40.00. (Reference Sources in the Social Sciences). ISBN 1-56308-626-3.

This second edition is a well-organized and clearly written update of the first, including 488 items published between 1990 and 1998 and a selective number of earlier titles. Excluded are entries for organizations or associations, for children's and young adult literature, for general social science sources, and for bibliographies, which can be more readily assembled through database searching. This edition also includes a larger number of journal entries and Web sites. The book is organized into fourteen chapters: general education sources; educational technology and media; early childhood, elementary, and secondary education; higher education; multilingual and multicultural education; special education; adult, alternative, continuing and distance education; career and vocational education; comparative and international education; curriculum, instruction, and content areas; educational administration and management; educational history and philosophy; educational research, measurement, and testing; and educational psychology. These chapters, in turn, are arranged by type of source, which can include dictionaries and encyclopedias; guides, handbooks and yearbooks; directories and almanacs; World Wide Web and Internet sources; statistical sources; and journals. Though there are only a handful of titles explicitly related to educational sociology, numerous databases, Web sites, journals, and chapter categories (e.g., educational psychology, history of education, philosophy of education, comparative education, multicultural education) have relevant entries. The citations are clear and suitably detailed, and the abstracts are descriptive and well written. There are author, title, and subject indexes.

Bibliographies

6. **International Bibliography of Economics.** Vol. 1– . London: Routledge, 1952– . annual. index. (International Bibliography of the Social Sciences). ISSN 0085-204X.

Thousands of articles and books from the economics literature are cited in each volume, representing items from dozens of countries and in many languages. There is a detailed classification scheme for organizing the references. Among the sociologically relevant subject headings are those dealing with income and income distribution, the organization of production, social economics and policy, and public economy. Subheadings are included for topics, regions, and countries. There are author and subject indexes, with the latter being in both French and English. The *International Bibliography of Economics* is available online and on CD-ROM as part of the *International Bibliography of the Social Sciences* (see http://www.lse.ac.uk/collections/IBSS/Default.htm for details).

7. **London Bibliography of the Social Sciences.** Vol. 1–Vol. 47. London: Mansell, 1929–1989. annual. ISSN 0076-051X.

These volumes comprise a subject index to the major social science collections in London. Most titles are from the catalog of the London School of Economics. Many of the works date back to the early 1800s. While the subject coverage is wide-ranging, there are aspects that would be particularly useful to sociologists. The retrospective coverage allows a historical study of earlier approaches to and explanations of social problems and issues (e.g., crime, inequality). Another advantage is its international coverage; works from the United States, Great Britain, and Europe are cited, thus facilitating comparative study. There are author indexes in volumes 4, 5, and 6, providing coverage through May 1936. However, there is a lack of author access in subsequent volumes. More recent supplements list additions to the holdings of the British Library of Political and Economic Science and the Edward Fry Library of International Law.

8. Wepsiec, Jan. **Social Sciences: An International Bibliography of Serial Literature, 1830–1985.** London: Mansell, 1992. 486 p. index. ISBN 0-7201-2109-4.

For researchers trying to identify periodical titles from the recent or distant past, Wepsiec has compiled an historical list of social science periodicals and arranged them alphabetically by title. For most serials, there is information on: (1) the beginning date and volume, (2) an ending date and volume (if it is no longer being published), (3) the name of the publisher and issuing body, (4) the journal titles it has superseded or been continued by, (5) the index title that indexes the journal's articles, and (6) the frequency of publication. *See* references direct the user from unused names or acronyms to correct or preferred ones. There is also a list of index and abstract abbreviations with full titles and starting dates. The appendices discuss the composition of the social sciences and provide brief histories of each discipline. A subject index is included.

Indexes, Abstracts, and Databases

9. **ABI/INFORM Global.** [electronic resource]. Ann Arbor, MI: ProQuest. 1971– . Available: http://www.proquest.com/products/pd-product-ABI.shtml (Accessed: March 15, 2004).

The *ABI/INFORM Global* database indexes and abstracts more than 1,600 business and management publications, including 350 international English-language titles. Articles from more than 700 of these publications are available in a variety of full-text formats—text, text-and-graphics, and pdf. The database covers a wide variety of social science topics, in addition to its coverage of companies and industries, including organizational behavior, work, labor relations, organizational development, corporate culture, and group dynamics. *ABI/INFORM* is also available on CD-ROM and as Dialog File 15.

10. **Abstracts in Anthropology.** Vol. 1– , No. 1– . Amityville, NY: Baywood Publishing, 1970– . quarterly. $515/yr. ISSN 0001-3455.

Over 700 articles from approximately 150 journals are abstracted in each issue. They are classified by subject under major subject categories: archaeology, physical anthropology, linguistics, and cultural anthropology. The section for cultural anthropology may be of most interest to sociologists. It has subheadings for social policy, family organization/marriage, medical anthropology, minorities, social organization, sociocultural change, symbol systems (e.g., religion), and urban studies, among others. There is a list of the periodicals indexed in each issue, as well as subject and author indexes. Major topics and journals from sociology and the other social sciences are well represented here, making this much more than a tool just for anthropologists.

11. **Alternative Press Index.** Vol. 1– , No. 1– . Baltimore, MD: Alternative Press Center, 1969– . quarterly with annual cumulation. $400/yr. (institutions). ISSN 0002-662X. Available: http://www.altpress.org/ (Accessed: December 11, 2004).

The *API* is a subject index to approximately 300 alternative, critical, or radical periodicals, both scholarly and popular. Entries are arranged by subject heading (including proper names), then alphabetically by article title. Periodical titles are abbreviated in many of the bibliographic citations. A periodical list translates these abbreviations into full titles and includes addresses and subscription prices. It also lists the specific volume and issue numbers indexed in that issue of *API*. Book, film, theater, record, and television reviews are cited by author/artist or film/play/program title under headings for the type of review. Biographies, autobiographies, and obituaries are listed by the name of the person. The annual cumulation includes selective abstracts for a small percentage of the articles.

Like *The Left Index*, this index covers a broad range of sociological subjects from a critical perspective. These can include topics such as gender, racism, social policy, social theory, inequality, feminist theory, postmodernism, socialism, organizations, urban studies, crime, communities, social change, and the family. This title indexes more periodicals than does *The Left Index*, but it provides only subject access. Though the periodical titles covered overlap somewhat, each index has enough distinct titles that the two should be viewed as providing complementary access to critical literature. The *Alternative Press Index* is also now available online through OCLC FirstSearch, and over forty titles are available full text through a related service.

12. **America: History and Life.** [electronic resource]. Santa Barbara, CA: ABC-CLIO, 1964– . Available: http://serials.abc-clio.com/ (Accessed: June 28, 2004).

For historical research into the United States or Canada, this is the single best source to consult. It includes abstracts of articles from more than 2,000 journals, as well as citations to book reviews and dissertations covering from prehistoric times to the present. The database covers many topics of interest to sociologists including politics, crime, education, social groups, culture, health and medicine, and science and technology. *America: History and Life* is also available on CD-ROM, in print, and as Dialog File 38.

13. **American Statistics Index: A Comprehensive Guide to the Statistical Publications of the U.S. Government.** Bethesda, MD: LexisNexis, 1973– . monthly, with quarterly and annual cumulations. ISSN 0091-1658. Available: http://www.lexisnexis.com/academic/3cis/cise/AmericanStatisticsIndex.asp (Accessed: December 11, 2004).

There are two related volumes in this index to government statistics. To locate data, one must look in the index volume to find a code number for a statistical publication. By looking up this number in the accompanying abstract volume, one finds a bibliographic citation and abstract of the document. The citation is usually accompanied by a government document number, which is used to retrieve the document that contains the data. Sociologically relevant data cited here include demographic data, population data, vital statistics, educational data, and more.

The index volume permits searching by a number of routes: subjects and names, categories (geographic, economic, and demographic), titles, agency report numbers, and Superintendent of Document (SuDoc) numbers. This source is also available online in the *Lexis Nexis Statistical* database.

14. **Anthropological Index.** [electronic resource]. London: Royal Anthropological Institute. Available: http://aio.anthropology.org.uk/aio/AIO.html (Accessed: June 28, 2004).

Similar to *Anthropological Literature*, the *Anthropological Index* is produced by the Anthropology Library of the British Museum. It primarily indexes the nearly 900 journals received by the Anthropology Library. Date coverage is

1957 to the present. Subject coverage includes the traditional subfields of anthropology (physical, archaeology, cultural/social, and linguistic), as well as sociology and human ecology. The database is available online as an RLG Citation Resource (see http://www.rlg.org/cit-rai.html); other subscription options, including a nonproprietary version of the database, are described at http://aio. anthropology.org.uk/aio/AIO.html.

15. **Anthropological Literature.** [electronic resource]. Cambridge, MA: Harvard University. Available: http://www.rlg.org/en/page.php?Page_ID=162 (Accessed: June 28, 2004).

Anthropological Literature is produced by Harvard University's Tozzer Library. Subscriptions to the online version are available through RLG (see http://www.rlg.org/cit-anl.html for more information). The database indexes research published in roughly 900 international journals, along with reports and monographs. It incorporates *Anthropological Literature: An Index to Periodical Articles and Essays*, which has been published quarterly since 1979. Additional records in the database date back as far as the nineteenth century. Subjects covered include demography and sociology, as well as the more traditional fields of anthropology.

16. **ASSIA: Applied Social Sciences Index & Abstracts.** [electronic resource]. East Grinstead, West Sussex: Cambridge Scientific Abstracts, 1987– . monthly updates. ISSN 0950-2238. Available: http://www.csa.com/csa/factsheets/assia. shtml (Accessed: January 13, 2004).

This indexes social science journal articles from over 650 journals from the United Kingdom, the United States, and sixteen other countries. It also now includes relevant Web sites. Currently, there are some 300,000 records in the database, with approximately 1,500 items added each month. The emphasis is on applied aspects of the social sciences and the focus includes such sociologically relevant subject areas as criminology, geriatrics, family, marriage, race relations, ethnic studies, health, industrial relations, unemployment, and religion, among others. This database is the online counterpart to the print source *Applied Social Sciences Index & Abstracts: ASSIA* (ISSN 0950-2238).

17. **Book Review Digest.** Vol. 2– , No. 1– . New York: H. W. Wilson, 1906– . monthly (except February and July), with annual cumulations. service basis. ISSN 0006-7326. Available: http://www.hwwilson.com/sales/printindexes.htm (Acccessed: December 11, 2004).

The *Book Review Digest* provides both an index to and brief excerpts from book reviews appearing in almost one hundred periodicals. To be included, a title must have been reviewed two times (for nonfiction) or three times (for fiction) in journals covered by this source. A number of important sociology and sociology-related review sources are included, such as the *American Journal of Sociology*, *Contemporary Sociology*, *Journal of Marriage and the Family*, and *The New York Review of Books*, among others.

Arrangement of the entries is by author. The complete citation for the reviewed book includes the author, title, publisher, date, price, Dewey decimal number, LC number, ISBN, and subject headings. This information is complemented by a brief summary of the book. The accompanying excerpts from reviews are generally a paragraph long and include a complete reference to the review source. Subject and title indexes are appended. This index can also be searched online through the EBSCO, SilverPlatter, and OCLC database equivalents, as well as on CD-ROM. Wilson's own WilsonWeb database service also provides access to *Book Review Digest Plus*, which supplements the original source with added reviews cited in Wilson's other databases (e.g., *Social Sciences Full Text*).

18. **Book Review Index.** Vol. 1– , No. 1– . Farmington Hills, MI: Gale, 1965– . 3 issues/yr. or annual cumulation. $330/yr. ISSN 0524-0581. Available: http://www.gale.com/servlet/BrowseSeriesServlet?region=9&imprint=000& titleCode=BRI&edition= (Accessed: December 11, 2004).

Covering reviews in over 600 publications, the *Book Review Index* arranges citations to reviews alphabetically by the author of the reviewed book. These citations include the review's source, volume, date, and pages. There are also, in some cases, abbreviations indicating whether the reviewed work is a reference book, periodical, children's book, or young adult book. A title index is also provided; it cites an author's name, which can be cross-referenced in the author index for the list of reviews. Reviews of sociological works are traced not only through *Contemporary Sociology*, the American Sociological Association's reviewing journal, but also through related social science journals such as *Families in Society*, *Society*, *Sociological Review*, *Policy Studies Journal*, and *Social Service Review*. This index is available via the Dialog database service, such as DialogWeb, as File 137.

19. **British Education Index.** [electronic resource]. Leeds, United Kingdom: British Education Index, 1976– . quarterly updates. Available: http://www.leeds. ac.uk/bei/bei.htm (Accessed: April 18, 2004).

This is the electronic equivalent of the printed *British Education Index* and the *British Education Theses Index* (on microfiche). The first source is covered from 1976 to the present, while the second is covered from 1950 to the present. The database covers approximately 300 education journals from Britain. Any number of important topics in the sociology of education and educational policy are covered. Education theses from United Kingdom and Irish universities and polytechnics are included. Its contents are also included in the *International ERIC* database, as well as Dialog (via DialogWeb, Dialog OnDisc, and Dialog Classic). It is also searchable in the Education Literature Datasets, which includes *ERIC* and the *Australian Education Index* (Available: http://www. jisc.ac.uk/index.cfm?name=coll_bei&src=alpha).

20. **Business Source Premier.** [electronic resource]. Ipswich, MA: EBSCO Publishing, 1999– . Available: http://www.epnet.com.proxy.ohiolink.edu:9099/ academic/bussourceprem.asp (Accessed: May 2, 2004).

This includes full-text articles for 3,800 business-related journals and magazines out of a total of 4,600 indexed titles. Relevant articles from numerous sociology journals are included as well. In the advanced search mode, users can search with up to three terms, each of which can be searched in a number of searchable fields. One can also limit the search to peer-reviewed or full-text journals, date, publication type, document type, and more. Any number of sociology topics are included here within the fields of sociology of work, organizational sociology, leisure, social psychology, gender and work, emotions, social support, and much more. Full-text articles come in HTML text, pdf format, or both.

21. Combined Retrospective Index to Book Reviews in Scholarly Journals, 1886–1974. Evan Ira Farber, ed. Woodbridge, CT: Research Publications, 1979. 15v. ISBN 0-8408-0157-2.

As a retrospective index to book reviews, this is an invaluable source. Twelve of the fifteen volumes comprise an alphabetical index of authors of reviewed books. Each reviewed title is listed separately, followed by the journal title, volume, year, and page(s). Volumes 13–15 comprise the alphabetical title index. The title is accompanied by a *see* reference to the author; by looking up the author's name in the author index, one can find the review citations. Reviews for many of the classic works in sociology can be found here, and therein lies its value for sociologists doing historical research.

22. Combined Retrospective Index Set to Journals in History, 1838–1974. Annadel N. Wile, ed. Washington, DC: Carrollton Press, 1977. 11v. LC 77-70347. ISBN 0-8408-0175-0.

Part of the Combined Retrospective Index Series (CRIS), these eleven volumes provide subject and author access to articles in world history. The first nine volumes comprise the subject index. Under each major subject category, articles are located by keywords in the title. Each citation includes the abbreviated title, author, year, volume, journal number (translated in the front of the volume), and page. Volumes 10 and 11 are the author index; citations are identical in format to those in the subject index. Biographical information can be found in volume 6.

23. Comprehensive Dissertation Index, 1861–1972. Ann Arbor, MI: University Microfilms International, 1973. 8v. LC 73-89046.

24. Comprehensive Dissertation Index. Supplement. Ann Arbor, MI: University Microfilms International, 1973– . annual. ISSN 0361-6657.

For locating dissertations by either author or subject, these sources are useful, though electronic versions of *Dissertation Abstracts International* are much faster. To find dissertations by subject, one first must locate the volume for the discipline. The cumulative volumes for 1861–1972 and 1973–1977 are devoted to specific disciplines, whereas the supplements for 1978 on are labeled either "Social Sciences and Humanities" or "Sciences." The latter supplements are subdivided by discipline. Within disciplines, dissertations are arranged by as many title keywords as apply. Thus, there should be multiple subject access points for each dissertation.

Citations include author, title, date completed, university that awarded the degree, pages, order number, and *Dissertation Abstracts International* citation. The last item allows one to locate the abstract in *DAI*. There is also an author index that includes the same citation information.

25. CSA Worldwide Political Science Abstracts (WPSA). [electronic resource]. Bethesda, MD: CSA. 1975– . Available: http://www.csa.com/csa/fact sheets/polsci.shtml (Accessed: December 11, 2004).

The *WPSA* database was formed in 2000 through the merger of ABC-POL SCI and *Political Science Abstracts.* Though ostensibly an index to journals in political science and government, *Worldwide Political Science Abstracts* also indexes a significant number of journals in sociology, law, and economics. Among the nearly 1,500 journals currently covered are major sociological titles, such as *American Sociological Review*, *American Journal of Sociology*, and *Social Forces*. Also included are important journals in the area of social policy that should be of interest to policy sociologists. The coverage of these journals, along with related social science titles, makes this a valuable index for current awareness.

26. Cumulative Subject Index to the Public Affairs Information Service Bulletins, 1915–1974. Ruth Matteson Blackmore, ed. Arlington, VA: Carrollton Press, 1977. 15v. LC 76-50520. ISBN 0-8408-0200-5.

Given the number of years the *PAIS Bulletin* (now the *PAIS International in Print*) has been issued, this index is quite a time-saver for historical research. Sociologists interested in tracing the way social and policy issues were analyzed and addressed over time should find this useful. Subject headings are broken down into subheadings and sub-subheadings. Consequently, finding materials on one's specific topic is relatively easy. The index uses *see* and *see also* references for used and related terms. Citations include the year, page, column (left or right), and numerical position of the article in the *PAIS Bulletin*.

27. Current Contents/Social and Behavioral Sciences. Vol. 1– , No. 1– . weekly, except last week of December. Philadelphia: Institute for Scientific Information, 1969– . $860/yr. ISSN 0092-6361. Available: http://www.isinet.com/ products/cap/ccc/editions/ccsbs/ (Accessed: December 21, 2004).

Current Contents is a guide to the tables of contents of over 1,600 journals, including numerous sociological journals. As such, it is a great current awareness service for scholars interested in scanning the social and behavioral science literature for relevant references. Of course, not all journals are covered in each issue. However, those that are included are listed in the front of the index and subsequently grouped under broad social science headings (e.g., law, psychology, social work and social policy, sociology and anthropology). Each issue of *Current Contents* has an author and address directory, a title-word index, and a directory of publishers. A cumulative journal index comes out triannually, and a complete publisher's address directory is issued twice yearly. Also included in each issue are the tables of contents of three or four multiauthored new books. This source is also available in the Dialog database service (as *Current Contents Search*, File 440). All of the seven print versions of *Current Contents*, including the one for the social and behavioral sciences, are covered by this Dialog database. An advantage of this collective version of *Current Contents* is that it also includes the medical and life sciences journals, which may be of interest to medical sociologists. The database is also available from SilverPlatter, Ovid, and Information Access Company. ISI also markets its own diskette and CD-ROM versions and provides Web access via Current Contents Connect.

28. **Current Index to Journals in Education.** Vol. 1– , No. 1– . Phoenix, AZ: Oryx Press, 1969– . monthly, with semiannual cumulations. ISSN 0011-3565.

Part of the ERIC "family" of reference publications, *Current Index to Journals in Education* (*CIJE*) and *Resources in Education* (*RIE*) index materials on a wide range of educational topics, including the sociology of education. For example, one can find literature on the production of educational inequality, the sociology of school knowledge and the curriculum, and educational policy analysis. The *CIJE* indexes articles from upwards of 1,000 journals, with the citations and abstracts arranged under the broad topical areas of the sixteen former ERIC clearinghouses. In *Resources in Education* the focus is on the indexing of research reports, conference proceedings, books, manuscripts, and so on. Both sources have a subject index, which uses subject headings from the *Thesaurus of ERIC Descriptors*, as well as an author index. They also provide descriptive abstracts, with the abstracts in *RIE* being substantially longer. The *CIJE* includes a "journal contents" index that lists all of the indexed articles from each journal; *RIE* has supplementary "institution" and "publication type" indexes. The content of both indexes is available in the ERIC database, which can be searched via the Web, on intranets, on CD-ROM, and through online database vendors such as Dialog.

29. **Directory of Published Proceedings: Series SSH-Social Sciences/Humanities.** Vol. 1– . Harrison, NY: InterDok Corp., 1968– . quarterly, with annual and four-year cumulations. $395/yr. ISSN 0012-3293. Available: http://www.interdok.com/html/ssh.cfm (Accessed: December 11, 2004).

Along with *Index to Social Sciences and Humanities Proceedings* (see entry below), this provides access to published conference proceedings. Its main section provides a description of each proceeding, as well as information including the date of the conference, an access number, location, conference name or publication title, conference acronym, conference sponsor, proceedings title, series or serial information, editor, publisher, and acquisition information (i.e., cost, LC number, ISBN, number of pages and volumes, date of publication). There are supplementary indexes for subject/sponsor, editor, and location. Proceedings can focus on such sociological topics as social movements, gerontology, sociology of education, policy studies, race relations, urban sociology, social psychology, and more. Future conferences can be searched freely by subject in *Mind: The Meeting Index*, which is available online at the same Web address.

30. **Dissertation Abstracts International.** Vol. 30– . Ann Arbor, MI: University Microfilms International, 1969– . monthly, with annual author index. ISSN 0419-4209 (pt. A); 0419-4217 (pt. B); 1042-7279 (pt. C). Available: http://www. umi.com/products/pd-product-disabsint.shtml (Accessed: December 11, 2004).

For those involved in advanced research or thesis and dissertation literature reviews, this is an essential source. The author-written abstracts are organized into volumes by broad topics: the humanities and social sciences (part A), the sciences and engineering (part B), and worldwide (part C). Within volumes, abstracts are classified by broad subject (e.g., sociology) and more specific subjects. The subcategories for sociology are: general, criminology and penology, demography, ethnic and racial studies, individual and family studies, industrial and labor relations, public and social welfare, social structure and development, and theory and methods. Abstracts are then arranged alphabetically by author.

Citations include author, title, date of completion, institution, pages, dissertation director, and order number. Further access is provided by a keyword title index, which cites dissertations by every keyword in the title. There is also an author index that is cumulated annually (except for part C, the worldwide abstracts volume). Part C, *Worldwide Abstracts*, is a sequel to the previous title, *European Abstracts,* which began in 1976. It includes titles in the original language along with English translations; the abstracts are usually translated into English.

Coverage back to 1938 is provided by *Dissertations Abstracts* and *Microfilm Abstracts*. *DAI* is also available online through database vendors such as ProQuest (ProQuest Digital Dissertations), Dialog File 35, and on CD-ROM (e.g., from SilverPlatter). Digital Dissertations facilitates the online ordering of dissertations in various formats, including pdf, paperback, hardbound, and microfiche. Abstracts of older dissertations are only available through the print version of *DAI*.

31. **EconLIT.** [electronic resource]. Pittsburgh, PA: American Economic Association, 1969– . Available: http://www.econlit.org/ (Accessed: March 15, 2004).

EconLIT is a database comprised of the print publications *Journal of Economic Literature*, *Index of Economic Articles*, and *Abstracts of Working Papers in Economics*. The database indexes and abstracts working papers, journal articles, books, articles in collective volumes, dissertations, and book reviews. Of particular sociological interest is its coverage of the sociology of economics, political economy, collective decision making, health, education, welfare and poverty, organizations, and more. EconLIT is also available from numerous online vendors, including EBSCO, Ovid/SilverPlatter, OCLC FirstSearch, and CSA.

32. **Education Index.** Vol. 1– , No. 1– . New York: H. W. Wilson, 1929– . monthly, except July and August, with quarterly and annual cumulations. ISSN 0013-1385. Available: http://www.hwwilson.com/dd/edu_i.htm (Accessed: May 4, 2004).

This identifies articles in over 500 journals in the field of education, with numerous articles and journals addressing issues in the sociology of education.

It also cites yearbooks and, as of late 1995, books in education. It is a straight name/subject index arranged alphabetically. There are ample *see* and *see also* references to preferred and related subject headings. There is also a separate section for book reviews in the back of each issue; video, motion picture, and computer program reviews, as well as citations on law cases, are filed with their subjects. The book reviews are arranged alphabetically by the book's author or, when no author is available, by title. As is true of other Wilson indexes, this one is easy to use. It is also available on CD-ROM, online through the WilsonLine database service, and on many computerized library systems. The *Education Abstracts* and *Education Full Text* database equivalents go back to 1983 and the latter includes full text for a high percentage of recent articles. All are available at the WilsonWeb online database service.

33. **Educational Research Abstracts Online.** [electronic resource]. London; New York: Taylor & Francis Group. monthly updates. Available: http://www. tandf.co.uk/era/default.asp (Accessed December 11, 2004).

This is an international guide to research on education, and the sociology of education is one of its six primary areas of focus. Among other sources, the database includes the contents from the print *Sociology of Education Abstracts*. Overall, some 30,000 abstracts are included, with updates monthly. Since 1995, there are links to full-text versions of articles, as well as to a document delivery service. In all, over 500 journals are indexed here.

34. **ERIC.** [electronic resource]. Washington, DC: U.S. Department of Education, 1966– . Available: http://www.ericfacility.net/teams/Login.do?action=7& userName=guest (Accessed: May 4, 2004).

ERIC is the database equivalent of two printed indexes, the *Current Index to Journals in Education* and *Resources in Education*. It includes all of the journal article and ERIC document references and abstracts going back to the beginning of the print indexes in 1966. Approximately 1,000 education journals are indexed and abstracted, including a number from Australia, England, and Canada. The database provides excellent coverage of topics in the sociology of education. Currently, numerous commercial companies provide online and CD-ROM versions of ERIC, including Ovid, EBSCO, National Information Services Corporation (NISC), Dialog, OCLC FirstSearch, and Oryx. The Department of Education has selected a new provider for the ERIC database, and it is scheduled for release in September 2004. However, users can anticipate that commercial versions of the database will continue to be offered.

35. **Historical Abstracts on the Web.** [electronic resource]. Santa Barbara, CA: ABC-CLIO,   1955– .   http://www.abc-clio.com/products/overview.aspx? productid=109712&viewid=0 (Accessed: December 11, 2004).

The companion abstract to *America: History and Life*, this covers world history from 1450 to the present, excluding Canada and the United States. Abstracts of journal articles and citations for books and dissertations are included.

The database covers many topics of interest to sociologists including social and cultural history, religions, and science and technology. This source is international in coverage, drawing citations from more than 2,000 sources in approximately 90 countries and 40 languages. However, titles are translated and abstracts are in English. The database is also available in print, on CD-ROM, and as Dialog File 39.

36. **Human Resources Abstracts.** Vol. 1– , No. 1– . Thousand Oaks, CA: Sage, 1966– . quarterly. $968/yr. (institutions). ISSN 0099-2453. Available: http://www.sagepub.com/journal.aspx?pid=104 (Accessed: December 11, 2004).

Approximately 250 books and articles are abstracted in each issue. Topics covered span the social sciences, with many subjects of interest to sociologists. These subjects include work life and environment, education, industrial and labor relations, workplace crime and violence, stress, organizational theory and research, aging, health, social services, and more. Entries are arranged alphabetically by author within the subject categories. The paragraph-long abstracts include subject headings so that one can find related articles through the subject index. An author index is also provided, as is an annual source list of titles consulted. There are cumulative author and subject indexes in the final issue of each volume.

37. **Index to Social Sciences and Humanities Proceedings.** Philadelphia: Institute for Scientific Information, 1979– . quarterly, with annual cumulations. $2,055/yr. ISSN 0191-0574. Available: http://www.isinet.com/products/litres/isshp/ (Accessed: December 11, 2004).

This indexes published proceedings, with coverage including such subject areas as sociology, demography, criminology, urban studies, religion, and ethnic group studies, among others. Included are the "most significant" (p. v) proceedings, which may be available as books, journal issues, preprints, or Institute for Scientific Information (ISI) reprints. The main body of the index is the conference proceedings section. Entries are arranged by conference number, and information is provided on the conference title, location, date, sponsor, title, and availability of proceedings (in books or journals), ordering address, titles of papers, and more.

Access to these proceedings is provided by a number of indexes: category (broad subject), permuterm subject (to papers/conferences, books), sponsor, author/editor, meeting location, and corporate (arranged by an author's geographic location and organizational affiliation).

A large number of sociology and related social science conference proceedings are cited. For tracking down additional conference papers, one should consult those listings in *Sociological Abstracts* or the *Directory of Published Proceedings* (see above). There is also a CD-ROM version of the database, updated quarterly, and it is also available online via ISI's *Web of Knowledge* subscription database service.

38. **International ERIC.** [electronic resource]. Mountain View, CA: Knight-Ridder Information, 1976– . quarterly updates. Available: http://www.dialog.com/sources/ondisc/intl_eric.pdf (Accessed: May 4, 2004).

Available as a Dialog OnDisc CD/DVD resource, as well as online through Dialog's Internet/intranet services (Dialog@Site), this database includes the contents from the *British Education Index*, *Bibliography of Education Theses in Australia*, and the *Australian Education Index*. The education literature from these countries has made a major contribution to the field of educational sociology. The earliest developments in the "new" sociology of education from the early 1970s originate with British education writers, among others. Hundreds of journals are indexed, with coverage back to 1976, making this a tremendous international resource for research in education and educational sociology.

39. **International Political Science Abstracts (IPSA). Documentation Politique Internationale.** Paris: International Political Science Association, 1951– . bimonthly, with cumulative subject index. €408/yr. ISSN 0020-8345.

Political science is construed broadly in this index and includes many references of interest to sociologists, particularly in the areas of policy sociology, political sociology, social groups, research methodology, and theory. Each issue abstracts about 1,200 articles from major international journals. While the articles may be in any number of languages, the titles are in both the original language and English. Abstracts are either in English or French, and source abstracts from the journal are used whenever possible. The citations and abstracts are arranged under broad categories for methods and theory, thinkers and ideas, institutions, political process, international relations, and national and area studies. There is a supplementary subject index, as well as a list of periodicals indexed. *IPSA* is also available on CD-ROM (see http://www.ipsa.ca/en/publications/abstracts.asp for more information).

40. **The Left Index: A Quarterly Index to Periodicals of the Left.** [electronic resource]. Baltimore, MD: NISC, 1982– . monthly (online); quarterly (CD-ROM). $80/yr (institutions). LC 82-5102. ISSN 0733-2998. Available: http://www.nisc.com/factsheets/qli.asp (Accessed: December 11, 2004).

Formerly a print and electronic source, *The Left Index* is now published entirely online (via NISC's BiblioLine service) and is also available on CD-ROM. Sociology students and researchers interested in finding articles written from a critical or conflict perspective should find this index useful. It cites over 120,000 articles from approximately 774 indexed sources, including journals, books, chapters, reviews, radical periodicals, and more. Web sites are also now included, as are links to full text for some 10,000 documents. Full-text journal articles are linked in many cases and available freely on the Internet or through commercial providers (e.g., EBSCO) that may be available through one's library. Sociological topics are well represented, including social movements, social classes, social theory, work, criminology, race, sex roles, and more. One can also find entries on specific theorists, such as Antonio Gramsci, Jurgen Habermas, Émile Durkheim, Hannah Arendt, and Louis Althusser. This is a valuable index to critical analyses of social issues.

41. **MarciveWeb DOCS.** [electronic resource]. San Antonio, TX: MARCIVE, 1997– . Available: http://www.marcive.com/webdocs/webdocs.dll (Accessed: January 22, 2004).

This is the online equivalent to much of the content in the *Monthly Catalog of United States Government Publications*, covering such documents from 1976 to the present. The subscription database provides express browsing and keyword searching of titles, authors, and subjects, based upon words typed in the simple-search window. The database also provides searching through various number indexes, including SuDoc, technical report, stock number, GPO item, monthly catalog, and OCLC. Subscribers will see holdings for various documents retrieved, including for their own local institution. The database also offers a combined-search option in which one can search multiple index fields at the same time, including title, author, subject, notes, format, and much more. One can also browse some of the searchable fields, including format, date, language, and GPO item. A CD-ROM version is available under the title Marcive GPO CAT/PAC.

42. **Monthly Catalog of United States Government Publications.** Washington, DC: GPO, 1895– . monthly, with semiannual and annual indexes. ISSN 0362-6830.

This is the most comprehensive and definitive print index to government publications. It offers a variety of access points in the cumulative indexes, including author, title, subject, keyword, series/report, contract number, and stock number. The indexes provide entry numbers, which are used to look up the citations. These citations generally include a government document (SuDoc) number, by which the documents are arranged in library collections.

The U.S. government publishes a great deal of information and data of use to sociologists, including data on population, aging, health, crime, income, educational achievement, and more. This index is also available through online database services such as Dialog (File 66, *GPO Monthly Catalog*), on CD-ROM (MOCAT, MARCIVE) and, for new records, on the Internet. Available: http://www.marcive.com/webdocs/webdocs.dll (Accessed: December 11, 2004).

43. **PAIS International in Print.** Vol. 1– , No. 1– . New York: OCLC Public Affairs Information Service, 1991– . monthly, with cumulations every fourth issue and annually. $590/yr. ISSN 1051-4015. Available: http://www.pais.org (Accessed: December 13, 2004).

PAIS International in Print indexes and briefly abstracts books, articles in over 700 journals, government documents, agency reports, and other materials relating to public affairs and public policy. It has a subject arrangement and includes a number of topics of interest to sociologists, such as crime, poverty, group behavior, family, work, women, culture, race relations, social status, evaluation research, and policy sciences. Coverage of state and federal publications on these subjects facilitates social policy analysis. Comparative analysis is made possible by the selective inclusion of foreign language publications in French, German, Italian, Portuguese, and Spanish. This title continues the earlier *PAIS*

Bulletin, which can be searched using the *Combined Retrospective Index to the Public Affairs Information Service Bulletins 1915–1974.* An online archive of the *PAIS Bulletin* from 1915 to 1976 will be available in 2004.

PAIS is also available online through database services such as OCLC FirstSearch, Dialog File 49, *PAIS International,* Ovid, and EBSCO, and on some library online catalogs and networks.

44. Professional Development Collection. [electronic resource]. Ipswich, MA: EBSCO Publishing. Available: http://www.epnet.com/academic/profdevcoll.asp (Accessed: April 18, 2004).

This database provides indexing and abstracting for almost 800 education journals, and full text for over 500 journals. Some 350 of these journals are peer reviewed, and the database allows one to limit the search results to full-text and peer-reviewed articles only. There are both basic and advanced search modes, and the advanced mode allows the user to search on multiple terms at once. Furthermore, searches may be limited by the full-text and peer-reviewed options, as well as by date, document type (e.g., pamphlet, periodical, book), available images and more. Full-text articles may be in either HTML or pdf formats and can be read, printed, or e-mailed in their entirety. The database also allows the user to refine searches, view the search history, print that search history, save searches, and more. Searching on "educational sociology" as a subject term retrieves almost 350 articles, including items in such notable journals as the *Oxford Review of Education* and the *British Journal of Sociology of Education,* among others.

45. ProQuest Digital Dissertations. [electronic resource]. Ann Arbor, MI: UMI, 19— . Available: http://www.umi.com/products/pt-product-Dissertations. shtml (Accessed: December 23, 2004).

Digital Dissertations is a database of approximately two million dissertations and theses found in the *Dissertation Abstracts International* print source. It allows one to search the most recent two-years-worth of dissertations for free. Libraries and institutions with subscription access can search the entire database, which includes entries back to the nineteenth century (e.g., one can find a reference for Thorstein Veblen's dissertation from the turn of the century). Furthermore, institutions that contribute titles to the database get free, full-text download access to their institution's dissertations. The database allows one to search for dissertations using up to three search windows, each of which can be tailored to search one of thirteen search fields. The database facilitates the online ordering of dissertations in various formats, including pdf, paperback, hardbound, and microfiche. This is an excellent source not only for dissertation literature reviews, but also for identifying the use of research instruments and the findings from quite specialized research topics.

46. PsycARTICLES. [electronic resource]. Washington, DC: American Psychological Association. 1987– . daily. Available: http://www.apa.org/psyc articles/facts.html (Accessed: June 18, 2004).

This database allows for full-text access to articles in fifty-two journals published by the American Psychological Association (APA), the APA Educational Publishing Foundation, the Canadian Psychological Association, and Hogrefe & Huber. Of particular interest to sociological researchers may be the *Journal of Personality and Social Psychology*, *Journal of Educational Psychology*, *Journal of Family Psychology*, and *Journal of Psychology, Public Policy, and Law*. Full-text articles are available for purchase through PsycARTICLES in both pdf and HTML formats, the average turnaround time for the electronic full text to be made available in the database is about one week after the print issues are mailed. A helpful feature of this database is the free e-mail alert service that can be setup to notify researchers when the next issues of PsycARTICLES journals are available, this service will also allow subscribers to see tables of contents for newly added issues. Furthermore, numerous vendors carry the full-text content of this database, for complete access information please visit: http://www.apa.org/psycarticles/facts.html.

47. **PsycINFO.** [electronic resource]. Washington, DC: American Psychological Association. Historic 1840–1967. Contemporary 1967– . weekly. Available: http://www.apa.org/psycinfo/products/vendors-all.html (Accessed: June 18, 2004).

This is not only the major guide to journal articles, books, book chapters, and dissertations in psychology, but also a useful source for sociologists and social psychologists. Articles are drawn from approximately 1,900 journals, with journal abstract records making up 77 percent of the database, PsycINFO contains more than a staggering 1.9 million records. Records are classified under 22 major subject categories and 135 subcategories. Of particular interest to sociologists may be topics such as: social processes and social issues; social psychology; health and mental health treatment and prevention; and industrial and organizational psychology.

The database makes use of a hierarchically arranged thesaurus, *The Thesaurus of Psychological Index Terms*, which contains more than 7,000 controlled terms and cross-references; both major and minor terms are assigned to each record. It is important to note that all the records published in the print *Psychological Abstracts* are now in PsycINFO, with *Psychological Abstracts* now being termed as the print version of the PsycINFO database. There are more than 335,000 historic records in PsycINFO; however, these records do not contain the descriptor (thesaurus term) field, and the classification categories for these entries are broad only. Other database coverage includes dissertations, 12 percent of the database; book chapters, 7 percent of the database; books, 4 percent of the database; and reports, 1 percent of the database. PsycINFO is international in scope, including publications from more than fifty countries and journals written in twenty-four languages. To further enhance researching capabilities more than 9.8 million indexed and abstracted article, book, and book chapter references are included in PsycINFO. This database is available electronically from numerous vendors, for complete database access information see: http://www.apa.org/psycinfo/products/vendors-all.html.

48. **Public Opinion Online (POLL).** [electronic resource]. Storrs, CT: Roper Center for Public Opinion Research, 1936– . weekly updates. Dialog File 468.

Included in this full-text database are public opinion surveys and results from major polling companies and news gathering organizations. Roper, Harris, Gallup, and Yankelovich polls are covered, as are surveys conducted by major newspapers and broadcast networks, among others. Coverage is from 1936 to the present, though there is selective earlier coverage. A wide range of social policies and issues are covered.

49. **Resources in Education.** Vol. 1– , No. 1– . Phoenix, AZ: Oryx Press, 1966– . monthly, with annual cumulations. ISSN 0098-0897.
See *Current Index to Journals in Education.*

50. **Social Sciences Citation Index.** Vol. 1– , No. 1– . Philadelphia: Institute for Scientific Information, 1973– . 3 issues/yr. with annual cumulations. $5,920/yr. ISSN 0091-3707. Available: http://www.isinet.com/products/citation/ssci/ (Accessed: December 13, 2004).

This is an invaluable reference work in the social sciences, covering some 1,700 journals in the social sciences and, selectively, 3,300 journals in the sciences. It is really four indexes in one: a citation index, a source index, a corporate index, and a subject index. The citation index indicates who has cited authors and their particular works. After using the citation index to find who has cited a work, one can look up that person's name in the source index and find a complete reference to their article. The corporate index is an alphabetical list of institutions accompanied by a list of authors affiliated with those institutions. Finally, the permuterm subject index is a sophisticated index to combinations of all significant terms in the title and subtitle of an article. This is useful if one remembers only parts of a title, or if one wants articles relating certain concepts.

This index is issued three times a year, with an annual cumulation. There is a cumulated index to the years 1976–1980. An online equivalent is available through ISI's *Web of Science* database, which provides access to all of its citation indexes. This could be invaluable for searching topics, such as medical sociology, that cut across the different subsets of the database. Another version, *Social SciSearch*, is available through the Dialog File 7. There are also CD-ROM versions, with or without abstracts, for retrospective information.

51. **Social Sciences Index.** Vol. 1– , No. 1– . Bronx, NY: H. W. Wilson, 1974– . quarterly, with annual cumulations. service basis. ISSN 0094-4920. Available: http://www.hwwilson.com/sales/printindexes.htm (Accessed: December 13, 2004).

Like other Wilson indexes, this is an easy-to-use author and subject index to English-language social science articles in over 550 periodicals published worldwide. Virtually any sociological specialty will show up as a subject here; *see* and *see also* references direct the user to preferred and additional subject terms. A separate section at the end of each issue cites book reviews alphabetically by book author or title.

The major sociological journals are indexed here, as are the journals representing the various specializations, making this a good source for representative, current articles on sociological topics. This source is also available online from various companies, such as UMI's *Social Sciences Plus Text* (via its ProQuest service) and H. W. Wilson's *Social Sciences Index* and *Social Sciences Full Text* (via its WilsonWeb database service). This version can also link to full-text articles in either HTML or pdf formats. A CD-ROM version, *Social Sciences Index/Full Text*, is also available from H. W. Wilson. The index is also available from the Dialog database service (*Wilson Social Sciences Abstracts*, File 142).

52. **Social Work Abstracts.** Vol. 1– , No. 1– . Washington, DC: National Association of Social Workers, 1965– . quarterly. $115/yr. (institutions). ISSN 1070-5317.

53. **Social Work Abstracts Plus.** [electronic resource]. Norwood, MA: Ovid/SilverPlatter. 1977– . quarterly. Available: http://www.ovid.com/site/catalog/DataBase/150.jsp?top=2&mid=3&bottom=7&subsection=10 (Accessed: December 30, 2004).

Social Work Abstracts Plus is the database equivalent of the print *Social Work Abstracts* and the *Register of Clinical Social Workers*. The database abstracts articles from over 450 social work and related journals and is updated quarterly with approximately 450 article abstracts. Topics of most interest to sociologists may include children and families, addictions, aging, criminal justice, health care, mental health, and social policy. Entries include full citations, paragraph-long abstracts, an address for the lead author, and subject headings.

54. **Wilson Business Full Text.** [electronic resource]. Bronx, NY: H. W. Wilson, 1982– . Available: http://www.hwwilson.com/Databases/business.htm (Accessed: May 2, 2004).

Wilson Business Full Text is closely related to two other Wilson products: *Wilson Business Abstracts* includes the same indexing and abstracting but does not include links to full-text articles; *Business Periodicals Index* features the same indexing but includes neither abstracts nor links to full-text articles. All three products are available online and on CD-ROM; only *Business Periodicals Index* is available as a print publication. (A related product *Wilson Business Abstracts Full Text* is available as Dialog File 553.) The database indexes and abstracts more than 600 publications back to 1982; full-text links to articles are provided for more than 350 of these titles back to 1995. While the database primarily focuses on company and industry research, it also covers articles dealing with work, health care, social class, power, social role and role conflict, sex role, socialization, organizational behavior, organizational structure, and more.

Handbooks and Yearbooks

55. **American Reference Books Annual (ARBA).** Vol. 1– . Englewood, CO: Libraries Unlimited, 1970– . annual. index. ISSN 0065-9959.

With more than 1,800 books reviewed in each volume, this is one of the major reviewing sources for new reference books. There are broad subject headings for general reference works, the social sciences, the humanities, and science and technology. Each of these is extensively subdivided by subject area and type of reference source. Sociology regularly includes subsections on aging, the family, community, social welfare, and more. Other major social sciences covered include anthropology, education, history, political science, psychology, and law/criminology.

While new scholarly books can be found in reviews and bibliographies, new reference books can prove to be more elusive. *ARBA*'s annual compilation of signed, evaluative reviews provides scholars and librarians with information on important new reference titles. Each volume includes thorough author/title and subject indexes.

56. **Books in Print.** New York: Bowker, 1948– . 9v. annual. index. $510/set. ISSN 0068-0214.

These volumes provide bibliographic and ordering information for new and old books that are still in print. The set is made up of two related four-volume sets covering authors and titles, as well as a supplementary volume on publishers. For both sets, arrangement of entries is alphabetical. Bibliographic information includes not only the author(s) and title, but also number of pages, date of publication, publisher, price, edition, and ISBN.

The ninth volume provides lists of symbols and abbreviations, a name index, and a variety of information on and indexes to publishers, distributors, and wholesalers. Subject access is provided through the four-volume companion set, *Subject Guide to Books in Print* (see entry below). All of the information in the print volumes of *Books in Print* is also available online through Bowker (http://www.booksinprint.com/bip/) and via Dialog File 480.

57. **The Condition of Education.** Washington, DC: National Center for Education Statistics; distr., Washington, DC: GPO, 1975– . annual. ISSN 0098-4752.

Begun in 1975, this annual provides a statistical overview of the current state of and trends in American education. Major topics covered span elementary/secondary education and higher education. Data are arranged into six major topical sections: participation in education; learner outcomes; student effort and educational progress; contexts of elementary and secondary education; contexts of postsecondary education; and societal support for learning. Each section begins with a three- or four-page summary discussing the data and their trends, and each table within the section has a half-page or more explanation of the table and its implications. Throughout, there are data of sociological interest relating to equity, educational inputs, student attitudes and behaviors, educational outcomes, and differential student achievement. A subject/name index is provided. Data from recent editions can be found online at the National Center for Education Statistics Web site (http://www.nces.ed.gov/programs/coe/).

58. **Cultural Anthropology Tutorials.** Available: http://anthro.palomar.edu/tutorials/cultural.htm (Accessed: March 8, 2004).

The *Cultural Anthropology Tutorials* Web site is maintained by the Department of Behavioral Sciences at Palomar College. The site currently features twelve individual tutorials: human culture, language and culture, patterns of subsistence, economic systems, social organization, nature of kinship, sex and marriage, process of socialization, ethnicity and race, anthropology of religion, medical anthropology, and culture change. Each tutorial is concise and aims to convey basic information about the topic at hand. The tutorials feature links to related Web sites, as well as glossaries of key terms; some parts of each tutorial are also available in audio format.

59. Diagnostic and Statistical Manual of Mental Disorders: DSM-IV. 4th ed. Washington, DC: American Psychiatric Publishing, 1994. 886 p. index. $49.95. ISBN 0-89042-062-9.

60. Diagnostic and Statistical Manual of Mental Disorders, DSM-IV-TR: Text Revision. Washington, DC: American Psychiatric Publishing, 2000. 943 p. index. $83.50. ISBN 0-89042-024-6.

This is intended to give clinicians, researchers, and statisticians empirically supported, diagnostic criteria for mental illnesses and disorders. The descriptions of these disorders are arranged into chapters according to their type. This includes such categories as substance-related disorders, anxiety disorders, sexual and gender disorders, disorders diagnosed in infancy/childhood/adolescence, personality disorders, and dissociate disorders, to name a few. There are many more specific disorders identified within these broad categories. For example, the category of disorders diagnosed in infancy, and so on, includes learning disorders, mental retardations, and attention deficit/hyperactivity disorder. "Learning disorders" is broken down further to include reading, mathematics, and written expression. For most disorders, there is at least information on the diagnostic features, associated features and disorders, prevalence, specific culture/age/gender features, course, and differential diagnosis. There is extensive supplementary information in the manual, including a user's guide, a glossary, and an annotated list of changes from the *DSM-III R*, an alphabetical listing of diagnoses, a subject index, and more. Sociologists studying health and mental illness, family systems, or social support/networks may find this useful.

There are a number of relatively current supplemental works that enhance and accompany the *DSM-IV*. Although widely accepted as the standard resource used in diagnosing mental disorders, due to the listings of particular mental disorder characteristics the DSM manuals have often met with controversy and the *DSM-IV* is no exception. The revised text edition, or *DSM-IV-TR*, includes changes in diagnostic criteria for Tourette's disorder, exhibitionism, pedophilia, and voyeurism among other mental disorders. The *Case Book* features real-life accounts to illustrate the material covered in the *DSM-IV-TR*, with each case example including a discussion of the *DSM-IV-TR* diagnosis. This resource is organized into sections including adults, children and adolescents, and historical cases. The volume of the *Case Studies* is arranged with the same organization of the *DSM-IV-TR*, and includes examples of the more frequently encountered disorders. The next installment, the *DSM-V*, is scheduled for publication in 2010.

61. **Digest of Education Statistics.** Washington, DC: Department of Education, Office of Educational Research and Improvement, National Center for Education Statistics; distr., Washington, DC: GPO, 1975– . annual. index.

The *Digest* selectively assembles data from both public and private data sources to "provide an abstract of statistical information covering the broad field of American education from kindergarten through graduate school" (2002 ed., p. iii). The 2002 edition includes 428 tables organized under seven headings: all levels of education, elementary and secondary education, postsecondary education, federal programs for education and related activities, outcomes of education, international comparisons of education, and learning resources and technology. These categories continue from year to year. Of particular interest to educational sociologists might be the data on educational attainment, educational achievement, opinions on education, and educational expenditures. Appended are a guide to sources, a subject index to the tables, and definitions of key educational terms. This is arguably the single most important print source for educational data and very likely the first place an educational sociologist might check for data of interest. The recent 2003 edition can also be found full-text online at the NCES Web site (http://www.nces.ed.gov/programs/digest/d03_tf.asp (Accessed: December 30, 2004).

62. Frances, Allen J., and Ruth Ross, eds. **DSM-IV-TR Case Studies.** Washington, DC: American Psychiatric Publishing, 2002. 386 p. index. $66.50. ISBN 1-58562-0491-1.

See entry for *Diagnotistic and Statistical Manual of Mental Disorder, DSM-IV* (above).

63. Keyser, Daniel J., and Richard C. Sweetland, eds. **Test Critiques.** Austin, TX: Pro-Ed, 1984– . $89/vol. ISBN 0-9611286-6-6.

This ten-volume handbook provides descriptions and critical overviews of standardized tests and research instruments in psychology, education, business, and related disciplines. For most instruments, there are four categories of information: an introduction to an instrument's development; an overview of its practical applications/uses; a review of its technical aspects, including validity, reliability, and related data; and a critique. The entries also include a list of references and an indication of who owns copyright on the tests. There are test title, test author/reviewer, and subject indexes in each volume that are cumulative for all of the volumes to date; an index to test publishers is also provided. The subject index lists tests alphabetically by title under the three major subject categories (i.e., psychology, education, business) and a handful of subheadings. Sociologists in social psychology, sociology of work and organizations, marriage and the family, and educational sociology may be particularly interested in the subtopics of "marriage and family" or "personality" (under "Psychology"); "academic achievement and aptitude" or "student attitudes and personality factors" (under "Education"); and "interpersonal skills and attitudes" (under "Business"). Along with sources like *Mental Measurements Yearbook* and *Tests in Print*, this is an invaluable guide to existing research tools.

64. Kinship and Social Organization: An Interactive Tutorial. Available: http://www.umanitoba.ca/anthropology/kintitle.html (Accessed: March 8, 2004).

This tutorial on kinship is maintained by Dr. Brian Schwimmer of the Department of Anthropology, University of Manitoba, Canada. It features numerous illustrations of kin systems drawn from the ethnographic literature and explains how these and other systems operate. A glossary and bibliography are also included. This site should appeal to sociologists of marriage and the family wishing to gain an understanding of the different elements of kinship.

65. Mental Measurements Yearbook Database. [electronic resource]. Norwood, MA: Ovid/SilverPlatter. 1989– . semi-annually. Available: http://www.ovid.com/site/index.jsp (Accessed: June 18, 2004).

See entry for *The Fifteenth Mental Measurements Yearbook* (below).

66. Michie, Jonathan, ed. **Reader's Guide to the Social Sciences.** London; Chicago: Fitzroy Dearborn Publishers, 2001. 2v. $285.00. ISBN 1-57958-091-2.

This handbook truly is a reader's guide. It includes hundreds of essay-length entries that provide overviews of social science topics and, most prominently, the key texts that one should be familiar with on that subject. In fact, each essay begins with a bibliographic list, arranged by author, of the key texts. The essay that follows highlights those works in the discussion, with the authors' names appearing in capital letters. *See also* references to related terms are often noted at the end of the entry. Most of the essays are approximately a page long, with the exception of the survey articles on broad topical categories (e.g., human geography, law, sociology, organizational behavior, psychology), which are much longer. Under the category of sociology alone there are approximately 300 entries under such broad themes as aging, community, criminology, family, gender, sociological thought, race/ethnicity, stratification, religion, theory, and more. There are numerous, page-long entries on more specific topics in each of these areas. For the most part, the essays are succinct overviews of key writing in that field, though they are not written for beginners and do require some background in the subject. Access to all of the entries is facilitated by an alphabetical list of entries, a thematic list, and a very detailed general index. In addition, there is a comprehensive booklist index. Though the essays do not substitute for dictionary or encyclopedia entries, the handbook is very good at accomplishing its stated mission.

67. Parker, Philip M. **Linguistic Cultures of the World: A Statistical Reference.** Westport, CT: Greenwood Press, 1997. 435 p. index. (Cross-Cultural Statistical Encyclopedia of the World, vol. 2). $104.95. LC 96-36681. ISBN 0-313-29769-X.

This book is aimed at economic planners, international marketers, and others who know that "[u]derstanding non-political borders is especially important for products and industries which are 'culture bound,' or those which require local adaptation" (p. 1). This particular volume in the Cross-Cultural Statistical Encyclopedia of the World series looks at these "non-political borders" from the angle of language. Two introductory chapters provide summary statistical information about the linguistic groups and national entities represented in the book, as well as notes on sources and methodology and a guide to looking comparatively at linguistic groups. The remaining chapters in the book cover the following general topics: economics, demography and sociology, cultural resources, mineral resources, land resources, marine resources, and climatic resources. Each chapter is prefaced with a summary set of indicators for all linguistic groups so that one will be able to compare, say, the amount of coastline enjoyed by Mandarin Chinese speakers versus the average. Four hundred and sixty linguistic groups are represented in the tables, and statistics are provided for 329 variables for each of these groups. A bibliography is included, and additional access to the entries is provided by indexes of countries, linguistics groups, and topics. Although many of the variables covered in this book have more in common with geography than sociology, sociologists will find the chapters on demography and culture particularly useful.

68. Parker, Philip M. **National Cultures of the World: A Statistical Reference.** Westport, CT: Greenwood Press, 1997. 249 p. index. (Cross-Cultural Statistical Encyclopedia of the World, vol. 4). $84.95. ISBN 0-313-29770-3.

This is the final volume in the series Cross-Cultural Statistical Encyclopedia of the World. This work seeks to present a wide variety of statistical information that will be useful to businesses, international marketers, and others from the perspective of national cultures—cultures that are "defined by national or territorial boundaries" (p. 11). Two introductory chapters explain the methodology and sources used in the book, as well as provide a guide for making comparisons between national cultures. The remaining chapters cover the general topics of economics, demography and sociology, cultural resources, mineral resources, land resources, marine resources, and climatic resources. Each chapter is prefaced by a set of summary statistics so that, for example, the infant mortality of any national culture may be compared against the mean. Included are a bibliography and indexes by country and subject.

69. Plake, Barbara S., and James C. Impara, eds. **The Fifteenth Mental Measurements Yearbook.** Lincoln, NE: Buros Institute of Mental Measurements, University of Nebraska-Lincoln; distr., University of Nebraska Press, 2003. 1143 p. index. $195.00. ISBN 0-910674-57-4.

The *Mental Measurements Yearbook* provides descriptive information, reference and reviews of English-language tests that are available for purchase. This latest edition includes tests that are new or revised since the last edition. Along with the earlier editions, this title constitutes a major source of reviews of tests and research instruments in education, psychology, and the social and behavioral sciences. Many subjects are covered, including achievement, behavior assessment, developmental tests, education, intelligence, personality, vocations, and more. Tests are grouped according to these categories.

Citations for particular tests include the appropriate grade or age level of the subjects, scores, administration, author, publisher, price, and other details.

They are often accompanied by relevant references and test reviews; if not, one is usually directed to a review in an earlier edition. Test title, name, acronym, classified subject, score, and publisher indexes are also provided. Also available as The Mental Measurements Yearbook Database (MMYD), a database comprised of the ninth through the fifteenth *Mental Measurements* yearbooks. From Ovid/SilverPlatter, please see: http://www.ovid.com/site/index.jsp.

70. Spitzer, Robert L., and Miriam Gibbon, eds. ***DSM-IV-TR Casebook: A Learning Companion to the Diagnostic and Statistical Manual of Mental Disorders.*** 4th ed. Washington, DC: American Psychiatric Publishing, 2001. 624 p. index. $53.95. ISBN 1-58562-059-9.

   See entry for *Diagnotistic and Statistical Manual of Mental Disorder, DSM-IV* (above).

71. **Subject Guide to Books in Print.** New York: Bowker, 1957– . 5v. annual. $525/set (2003–2004 ed.). ISSN 0000-0159.

   These are the companion volumes to *Books in Print* (see the entry above), providing subject access to *BIP* using Library of Congress subject headings. Information included in the entries is the same as that included in *Books in Print* (i.e., author, title, publisher, ISBN, price, pages, date of publication, edition). The last volume also contains a key to publishers' and distributors' abbreviations, as well as a list of Library of Congress subject headings that are used throughout these volumes.

72. **Thesaurus of ERIC Descriptors.** 14th ed. Phoenix, AZ: Oryx Press, 2001. 731 p. $72.95. ISBN 1-57356-330-7.

   This thesaurus is essential for proper subject searching of articles and documents in ERIC's printed indexes, *Current Index to Journals in Education and Resources in Education*, as well as its online and CD-ROM database version, ERIC. The thesaurus is also available in electronic format in most of the electronic versions of the database. ERIC uses its own controlled vocabulary of subject headings to classify every article or document in its printed and electronic databases. Generally speaking, one can retrieve more focused references by using ERIC's subject headings in a search. This thesaurus not only lists the subject headings alphabetically, but also indicates broader terms, related terms, and narrower terms, all of which are useful for expanding or narrowing searches.

   Appended are a rotated display of descriptors (i.e., terms listed in context), a two-way hierarchical display listing all broader and narrower terms related to each subject heading, and a descriptor group display (i.e., terms listed under broad subject categories). There is excellent and thorough explanatory material in the front of the thesaurus.

73. Weiner, Irving, ed. **Handbook of Psychology.** Hoboken, NJ: John Wiley & Sons, 2003. 12v. index. $995/set. ISBN 0-471-66675-0.

   The fifth volume of this set is devoted to the topic of personality and social psychology. The volume is broken down into three major sections: context, with essays discussing evolution and cultural perspectives; personality, which features descriptive essays on such topics as the biological basis of personality, interpersonal theory of personality, and the structures of personality traits; and, finally, social psychology, which covers social cognition, attitudes in social behavior, the social self, and aggression, violence, evil, and peace, among other essay descriptions. Each lengthy entry includes full author information, lists of descriptive terms, and cross-references to further enhance research, and an extensive list of references. The set provides illustrations, charts, tables, and graphs to further illustrate the text. Other volumes of this set that may be of interest to sociology researchers include, developmental psychology (volume 6), educational psychology (volume 7), and industrial and organizational psychology (volume 12).

Dictionaries and Encyclopedias

74. Barfield, Thomas, ed. **The Dictionary of Anthropology.** Malden, MA: Blackwell, 1997. 626 p. $94.95. LC 96-37337. ISBN 1-55786-282-6.

Intending to provide an "intelligent entry-point into the world of anthropology" (p. viii), this dictionary consists of more than 500 signed entries, which range from explanations of anthropological concepts to descriptions of anthropological subfields and the work of important anthropologists, such as Malinowski and Geertz. Entries typically include in-text citations to significant works, and these are included in the appended bibliography. Some of the concepts and methodologies covered are common to the other social sciences (e.g., power, phenomenology, work); however, these are explicated in anthropological terms. Other concepts are more traditionally assigned to anthropology, including descent, fictive kinship, and so on. Many of the entries contain cross-references. This is a very useful work for sociologists wishing to draw upon the insights of anthropologists in their work.

75. Barker, Robert L. **The Social Work Dictionary.** 5th ed. Washington, DC: NASW Press, 2003. 493 p. $49.99. ISBN 0-87101-355-X.

The field of social work is much broader in its areas of concern than the non–social worker may suspect, covering such subjects as family therapy, counseling and group work, cognitive and moral development, educational equity, social theory, criminal justice, health care, and more. This breadth of responsibility necessitates being familiar with terminology from many subjects and disciplines. Theories, theorists, key concepts, organizations, court cases, and various pieces of legislation may need to be understood for one to practice most effectively. All of these kinds of terms are included in this dictionary, which is intended both for social workers and related human service professionals, including sociologists.

Definitions range in length from a sentence to a long paragraph; italicized words in definitions are defined elsewhere in the dictionary. Cross-references direct the user from unused words, phrases, or acronyms to the preferred terms.

Supplementary information includes a list of acronyms frequently used by social workers and a chronology of milestones in the history of social work and social welfare.

This source has been regularly updated and expanded; the fifth edition includes more than 1,000 new entries and updates of over 2,000 definitions, as well as the URLs for hundreds of organizations. The definitions themselves are well written and cover a broad range of topics, making this a valuable complement to sociology and social science collections.

76. Bealey, Frank. **The Blackwell Dictionary of Political Science: A User's Guide to Its Terms.** Malden, MA: Blackwell, 1999. 384 p. index. $69.95. LC 98-33143. ISBN 0-631-20694-9.

The companion volume to the *Blackwell Dictionary of Sociology*, the *Dictionary of Political Science* provides concise definitions for roughly 1,000 terms used in political science. Terms covered range from theoretical concepts such as "alienation" to more prosaic ones such as "pocket veto." There are numerous cross-references within each entry, and brief bibliographies accompany many of the entries. The book also includes a set of biographical entries on important contributors to political science. Additional access to the entries is provided by a topical index.

77. Bolaffi, Guido, Raffaele Bracalenti, Peter Braham, and Sandro Gindro, eds. **Dictionary of Race, Ethnicity, and Culture.** Thousand Oaks, CA: Sage, 2003. 355 p. index. $89.95. ISBN 0-7619-6899-7.

This work contains 200 signed entries that focus on the variety of terms associated with the concepts of race, ethnicity, and culture, with particular reference to those terms that are ambiguous or politically sensitive. Many of the entries strive to provide multiple meanings to the more indefinite concepts, such as "multiculturalism" or "ethnicity," especially where meanings change across different national contexts. Each entry attempts to provide some insight into the origins of a particular concept. Cross-references are scattered throughout, and each entry contains a short bibliography. Additional access is provided through both a subject and personal name index. Given its international scope, this book should prove very useful for sociologists of ethnicity and race who wish to make use of the international, particularly European, literature on these topics.

78. Calhoun, Craig, ed. **Dictionary of the Social Sciences.** New York: Oxford University Press, 2002. 563 p. $75.00. ISBN 0-19-512371-9.

Covering many of the disciplines that comprise the social, human, and behavioral sciences, this encyclopedia provides well-written definitions of a few thousand terms and important individuals. The definitions range from a paragraph to a page, and, wherever appropriate, allude to the contested nature of a concept and its varying usages or interpretations. Within the definitions themselves, terms found elsewhere in the dictionary are noted in capital letters. *See* references also direct the reader from unused to preferred terms. Major sociological terms are found throughout, as are important theorists like Max Weber, Pierre Bourdieu, Karl Marx, Émile Durkheim, Jurgen Habermas, and many more. Given the interdisciplinary nature of much sociological writing, the breadth of coverage of this dictionary is a distinct asset. For more detailed coverage of terms within the specific disciplines (including sociology), the editor recommends those more specialized dictionaries. While clearly written, the dictionary is nonetheless best suited for readers with some background. Nonetheless, this is handy quick reference for any number of terms that may show up in one's reading. The appended bibliography is solid in its coverage of classic works.

79. Corsini, Raymond J. **Dictionary of Psychology.** Philadelphia: Brunner/Mazel 1999. 1156 p. $135.00. ISBN 1-58391-028-X.

This clear and concise dictionary contains over 30,000 short entries (averaging 31 words), and its interdisciplinary focus makes it a relevant tool for those researching social psychology and related topics. The dictionary makes use of *see* references for terms, and cross-references to related terms. If a term or phrase can be attributed to a person, then their name is included in the definition, and the dictionary features more than 125 illustrations to enhance definitions. There are also numerous appendices including those defining prefixes, suffixes, and affixes; systems of treatment; learning theory symbols, and Rorschach descriptors.

80. Craighead, W. Edward, and Charles B. Nemeroff eds., **The Corsini Encyclopedia of Psychology and Behavioral Science.** 3d ed. New York: John Wiley & Sons, 2001. 4v. $800/set. indexed. ISBN 0-471-23949-6.

While this encyclopedia is aimed at informing students and researchers in psychology and the behavioral sciences, it may also prove valuable to sociologists, particularly those with interests related to social psychology. Entries range from a few paragraphs to a few pages and are written by scholars with expertise in the area on which they are writing. Essays are accompanied by references to suggested readings and cross-references. The first three volumes include entries arranged alphabetically by subject, while the fourth volume includes biographies, a cumulative bibliography, name and subject indexes, an appended APA code of conduct and ethical principles, and guidelines for written contracts. This is also available as an electronic book via NetLibrary (http://www. netlibrary.com/).

81. Davies, Martin, ed. **The Blackwell Encyclopaedia of Social Work.** Oxford, United Kingdom; Malden, MA: Blackwell, 2000. index. $84.95. ISBN: 0-631-21450-X.

This concise, single-volume resource provides information on 400 topics relevant to contemporary social work practice. Over 400 signed entries are arranged alphabetically, and article contributors consist of some 250 experts (United Kingdom) in the field of social work. This source features three distinct levels of entries: term definitions of 100 words or less; glossary terms of 200 words that provide brief explanations of key concepts and "further reading" suggestions; and finally, major entries of 1,000 words or more that include more extensive "further reading" lists. Also included is a lexicon that provides broad subject headings with relevant entries; a separate list of contributors that includes the authors' affiliations; and a listing of references that have been mentioned by the authors in their articles. The contributors are all from the United Kingdom; however, the focus of this work is on current issues and topics encountered in contemporary social work practice. UK-specific legal and policy issues have meticulously been avoided making this guide a useful resource for any researcher.

82. Encyclopedia of Social Work. 19th ed., suppl. Washington, DC: NASW Press, 2003. index. $42.99. ISBN 0-87101-353-3.

As a supplement to the three-volume nineteenth edition of the *Encyclopedia of Social Work* (1995) this source includes expanded coverage of a number of key areas in social work such as education, mental illness, and social welfare. In addition, there are seventeen new entries on such current topics as hate crimes; conservatism and social welfare; and multiculturalism and cultural diversity. The signed entries are arranged in alphabetical order, each article is written by an expert in the field, and the author's affiliation and contact information is provided. Articles are accompanied by bibliographic references, suggestions for further reading, cross-references to related subjects, and important keywords. There are also three appendices for the *NASW Code of Ethics*; reader's guides (including new entries for the supplement), which provide the headings for major topics as well as a listing of all of the encyclopedia articles related to that subject; and a list of acronyms. Together with the 2003 supplement, the nineteenth edition of the *Encyclopedia of Social Work* and the *1997 Supplement* present comprehensive and accessible information on the profession of social work.

83. Guthrie, James W., ed. **Encyclopedia of Education.** 2d ed. New York: Macmillan Reference USA/Gale Group, 2003. 8v. index. $850/set. ISBN 0-02-865594-X.

After over thirty years since the first edition (1971), we now have a completely new and updated edition of the classic *Encyclopedia of Education.* Included in this eight-volume set are 857 articles on key educational concepts, theories, people, institutions, and organizations, with entries ranging from 500 to 5,000 words in length. The signed essays are accompanied by an extensive number of *see also* references, as well as a bibliography, and, often, a relevant Internet Web site and address. The essays fall within a very wide range of subject areas in education, including the foundations of education (e.g., history, philosophy, sociology, comparative education), educational psychology, curriculum and instruction, higher education, educational technology, educational policy, and teacher preparation, among others. There are an extensive number of entries on important educational associations, such as the American Association of School Administrators, the American Association of University Professors, the International Reading Association, the National Council of Teachers of Mathematics, and more. Similarly, there are 121 biographical entries on such historically important individuals as John Dewey, Jane Addams, Aristotle, St. Augustine, Alfred Binet, W.E.B. Du Bois, Paulo Freire, Maria Montessori,

Lawrence Kohlberg, Horace Mann, Jeanne Chall, Carter Woodson, Jean Piaget, and Mary Bethune. The last volume includes primary source documents (covering court cases, legislation, and international agreements), a thematic outline of the encyclopedia's entries, a list of widely used standardized tests (with addresses, phone numbers, and Web site addresses for the publishers), a list of state departments of education (with Web site addresses), a list of some education Web sites, and a bibliography of classic works in education. Finally, there is a substantial combined index to names, subjects, and titles. There should be much here of interest to students of educational sociology.

84. Kazdin, Alan, ed. **Encyclopedia of Psychology.** New York: Oxford University Press, 2000. 8v. $750/set. indexed. ISBN 1-55798-187-6.

Oxford University Press and the American Psychological Association have untied to produce and publish this substantial encyclopedia. Features of particular interest to sociology researchers include the in-depth coverage of the topic of social psychology, which is further divided into subtopics such as applied social psychology, gender roles, industrial psychology, and social roles. All of the alphabetically arranged entries are signed by the authors, the more extensive entries include bibliographies. Furthermore, aspects of larger topics are grouped together as composite entries, with several articles under one heading. Articles are cross-referenced so as to guide researchers from one article to related entries elsewhere in the text. Volumes 1 through 7, and part of volume 8, present the entries arranged alphabetically by subject, the remainder of volume 8 includes the directory of contributors, a synoptic outline of contents, and the cumulative index for the set.

85. Kuper, Adam, and Jessica Kuper, eds. **The Social Science Encyclopedia.** 2d ed. London: Routledge, 1999. 923 p. ISBN 0-415-20749-0.

This is a reprint of the 1996 second edition. Approximately 600 social scientific terms, fields, theories, and theorists receive fairly sophisticated descriptions in this encyclopedia. The signed entries, written by over 500 contributing experts, cover not only topics in the various social sciences, but also related topics in such disciplines as biology, business, media, and medicine. Major sociological fields and topics are treated. Sociological theorists are covered very selectively, with entries on major figures like Marx, Durkheim, and Weber.

Entries range in length from a few paragraphs to a few pages. Bibliographic references and suggested readings are appended to most articles, as are *see also* references to related terms. While the entries are generally well written, they are not for beginners, making this an excellent one-volume encyclopedia for the more advanced student or scholar. This edition is a major revision and update of the first edition, with half of the entries being "new or . . . completely rewritten" (p. vii). Consequently, many recent and important topics are included, such as postmodernism and cultural studies, among others.

86. Osborne, Richard. **Megawords: 200 Terms You Really Need to Know.** London: Thousand Oaks, CA: Sage, 2002. 258 p. $24.95 (pbk.). ISBN 0-7619-7474-1.

Osborne attempts to provide not only definitions of key terms in the social sciences and humanities, but also a context for why such words are important in intellectual and scholarly debates. Both the terms selected and their definitions reflect the somewhat critical orientation of the author. The writing is provocative and fairly conversational, helping the entries read more like essays than dictionary definitions. For many of the terms, Osborne contrasts them with competing terms, all of the while demonstrating that language is not neutral and that it can shape our understanding of the world. In short, this work is as much about the politics and social histories of terms as about their definitions. As such, it is thought provoking and useful, albeit for more advanced students. What one will not find here are definitions of many more common terms used in the social sciences and humanities. For that, other dictionaries would be more suitable.

87. Outhwaite, William, ed. **The Blackwell Dictionary of Modern Social Thought.** 2d ed. Malden, MA: Blackwell, 2003. 839 p. $124.95. ISBN 0-631-22164-6.

While many of the entries in this second edition have been revised in either their content or their recommended readings, this dictionary remains remarkably the same in its coverage and focus. The entries, which range across all of the social science disciplines, were written by experts from around the world and focus primarily on concepts, theories or schools of thought, and organizations and institutions. Overall, the essays are fairly lengthy for a dictionary, typically running to two, double-column pages. Concepts that are mentioned in the entries, and that are defined elsewhere in the dictionary, are capitalized. There are also *see* and *see also* references to direct the user to preferred and related subjects. Each entry is accompanied by a short, though consistently excellent, suggested reading list, with a substantial bibliography appended as well. Throughout, major sociological and sociology-related terms are included. As with the first edition, there are no biographical entries on important figures; the biographical appendix from the earlier edition has been deleted. This dictionary is not for beginning sociology students. However, it is well written and should be valuable for upper-level undergraduates, graduate students, and researchers exploring new subject areas.

88. Rohmann, Chris. **A World of Ideas: A Dictionary of Important Theories, Concepts, Beliefs, and Thinkers.** New York: Ballantine Books, 1999. 476 p. index. $24.95. ISBN 0-345-39059-8.

Rohmann defines "ideas" as "theories, philosophies, beliefs, ideologies, and the thinkers who have articulated them" (p. ix). This dictionary identifies and defines 444 such big ideas, with 111 of these being biographies focusing on the major ideas of important thinkers. Entries are drawn from the fields of "philosophy, psychology, politics, history, economics, sociology, religion, science, and the arts" (p. x). There is a clear theoretical orientation to the terms included here, and as Rohmann correctly points out, many of these terms constitute the "currency" of much of the reading, writing, and thinking in the social sciences. The entries themselves can range from a few paragraphs to a few pages, and they do have an essay-like quality to them. Within entries, terms found elsewhere in the dictionary appear in all capital letters. At the end of entries, there are often *see also* references to other terms. *See* references are used to direct users from unused to preferred terms. Occasionally, boxes are used within entries to highlight and define important subconcepts, people or events. At the end, there is a modest list of titles for further reading, as well as an index of key terms and proper names.

89. Sills, David L., and Robert K. Merton, eds. **Social Science Quotations: Who Said What, When, and Where.** New Brunswick, NJ: Transaction, 2000. 437 p. $39.95 (pbk.). ISBN 0-7658-0720-3.

This is a wonderful compilation of quotations from major figures in the history of the social sciences, including numerous sociologists from different theoretical perspectives and schools of thought. Over 250 pages of quotations are arranged alphabetically by the name of the social scientist. For each individual, there can be anywhere from one to over a dozen quotations taken from various sources. Each quotation is numbered and accompanied by the title of the source and the pages on which the quote is found. There is an appended bibliography of sources arranged alphabetically by author. In addition, there is a subject index that refers to the author of the quote and the number of the quote in that individual's series of quotes. There is a substantial list of advisers who submitted candidate quotes to be included, thus ensuring a fairly diverse collection of quotes. Any reader should find some pleasant surprises, such as the inclusion of two quotes from Michael Young's *The Rise of the Meritocracy.* While one could always argue over which quotes from an author are the best, there is no denying that the quotes included here make for enjoyable and thought-provoking reading.

90. Young, T. R., and Bruce A. Arrigo. **The Dictionary of Critical Social Sciences.** Boulder, CO: Westview, 1999. 353 p. $85.00. ISBN 0-8133-6672-0.

The authors' intent is to create a dictionary that both includes critical social science terminology and challenges orthodox renderings of terms and theories. Approximately 1,000 concepts, theories, individuals, and other terms are covered, and a wide range of theoretical perspectives is represented. Throughout, a fundamental purpose of the dictionary is to describe social science terms in a way that contributes to "a critique of alienating social relations and to the creation of life-affirming social interactions" (p. xi). Because many cutting-edge and conceptually difficult theories (e.g., postmodernism) and concepts are covered, the dictionary is not entirely for beginners. Many of the definitions of more theoretically advanced concepts (e.g., accenting the sign) are actually well done, but they nonetheless presume some knowledge, background, or interest. However, definitions of more mainstream social science concepts (e.g., structural functionalism, intergenerational mobility) are quite straightforward while still including alternative viewpoints and remaining true to the dictionary's editorial intent. Overall, this would be a useful work for more advanced students in the various social science disciplines.

Data and Statistics

Handbooks and Yearbooks

91. Becker, Patricia C., ed. **A Statistical Portrait of the United States: Social Conditions and Trends.** 2d ed. Lanham, MD: Bernan, 2002. 322 p. index. $147.00. ISBN 0-89059-584-4.

This work is comprehensive in scope. It covers demographic topics such as population characteristics and households and families, as well as more general socioeconomic topics like labor force and job characteristics, voting, and health. A narrative chapter containing charts, graphs and tables is devoted to each topical area. The chapters describe significant variables, such as age at marriage or propensity to marry, and then illustrate these variables with statistical data drawn from recent federal government statistical surveys. The appendix consists of detailed tables on the same topics covered in each of the narrative chapters. In many cases, these tables include historical statistical data, and so can be used to plot trend lines. Additional access to both the detailed tables and narrative chapters is provided through an index.

92. **County and City Data Book.** Washington, DC: Department of Commerce, Economic Statistics Administration, Bureau of the Census; distr., Washington, DC, GPO, 1949– . irregular. ISSN 0082-9455.

Now in its thirteenth edition (2000), this data book continues to be a good source of basic statistics on states, counties, cities (25,000 or more population), and places (2,500 or more population). Data included cover such broad areas as population, health, social welfare programs, crime, housing, work, education, labor force, income, government, employment, business statistics, elections, and agriculture. The contents of the statistical tables and how they were compiled are explained in an introductory section of source notes and explanations. These data are drawn from both governmental agencies (e.g., Bureau of Census, Bureau of Labor Statistics, National Center for Health Statistics) and private agencies (e.g., American Hospital Association).

The appendices include source notes and explanations for the different data tables, descriptions of the geographic and metropolitan statistical areas, county maps by state, and table outlines. Although the data book does not go into great depth, it can be excellent for comparative data on fundamental subjects. The thirteenth edition is also available on CD-ROM and on the World Wide Web at http://www.census.gov/statab/www/ccdb.html.

93. **County and City Extra: Annual Metro, City, and County Data Book.** Lanham, MD: Bernan, 1992– . annual. ISSN 1059-9096.

This annual volume provides a wide variety of up-to-date statistics for states, counties, cities, and congressional districts in the United States. The statistics are drawn from both government and private sources. Topics covered at each of these geographic levels include population and household characteristics, vital statistics, health, crime, education, income and personal taxes, construction and housing, labor force and employment, agriculture, government administration, real estate, trade, and resource use. Several prefatory tables show the type of statistics available for respective geographic levels (e.g., statistics on export of goods is available at the state level, but not at the county, city, or congressional district level). A "Highlights" section includes maps on selected topics, and an "Area Rankings" section provides useful lists such as "Largest Metropolitan Areas by Population." Several appendices present information on geographic concepts and codes (e.g., MSA, CMSA), metropolitan statistical areas and components, maps, and source notes.

94. **Historical Statistics of the United States: Colonial times to 1970.** Washington, DC: Bureau of the Census; distr., Washington, DC: GPO, 1975. 2v. LC 75-38832. ISBN 0-318-11732-0.

These two volumes contain historical statistics arranged under twenty-four major topics, covering population, health, resources, business and economics, government, social statistics, and other areas. As in other census publications, there are introductory sections describing data collection criteria and data comparability for the various tables. How far back each table goes varies. Each volume has a time period index, a subject index, and a list of contributors.

95. **Places, Towns, and Townships.** Lanham, MD: Bernan, 1993– . irregular. ISSN 1073-0001.

Like *County and City Extra*, this volume provides statistical information on a wide variety of topics, but with a focus on three geographic levels: incorporated places and minor civil divisions (MCD) of 10,000 or more population; incorporated places of 2,500 or more population; and, incorporated places, MCDs, and unincorporated areas (census-designated places or CDPs). Topics covered include population, households, housing, employment, residential construction, local government finances, manufacturing, retail trade, and service industries. A set of prefatory tables shows what type of statistics is available for which geographic level (e.g., the number of manufacturing establishments for places of 10,000 or more and for places 2,500 or more, but not for any other geographic level). Appendices include information about the sources used and an overview of the geographic concepts.

96. **State and Metropolitan Area Data Book.** Washington, DC: U.S. Department of Commerce, Bureau of the Census; distr., Washington, DC: GPO, 1979– . irregular. ISSN 0276-6566.

This is an abstract of both governmental and private data drawn from a variety of agencies and associations. Though billed as representing "some of the most up-to-date facts available" (4th ed., p. ix), the most recent edition was published in 1998. The data included are selective and cover such areas as population, crimes, health, income, labor force, school enrollment, and vital statistics. These are some of the same categories covered by the *County and City Data Book*, though broken down by different geographical areas.

The statistics are presented for four different areas: metropolitan areas (Metropolitan Statistical Areas [MSAs], Consolidated Metropolitan Statistical Areas [CMSAs], and New England County Metropolitan Areas [NECMAs]); metropolitan areas and their component counties; central cities of Standard Metropolitan Statistical Areas (SMSAs) (broken down by central city and metropolitan area); and states. There is a section of source notes and explanations that describes all of the data tables. Four other appendices help to clarify some of the concepts and categories: geographic concepts and codes; an alphabetical listing of Primary Metropolitan Statistical Areas (PMSAs) with CMSAs; component counties of metropolitan areas by state; and central cities of metropolitan areas by state. There are also table outlines for all tables and a subject index for the data on states. The fifth edition is also available on CD-ROM and on the World Wide Web at http://www.census.gov/statab/www/smadb.html.

97. **Statistical Abstract of the United States.** Washington, DC: Bureau of the Census; distr., Washington, DC, GPO, 1878– . annual. LC 4-18089. ISSN 0081-4741.

Supplemented by the *State and Metropolitan Area Data Book* and the *County and City Data Book*, as well as several other ancillary publications, this is a compendium of selective data on a wide range of subjects. Topics covered include population, vital statistics, immigration, health, education, law enforcement, environment, and elections. There is also a section of comparative international statistics. Though the data included throughout the volume are selective, source notes can lead to the original documents and, possibly, more extensive data on the subject.

Data presented in many of the tables are retrospective. This feature, combined with the number of years the abstract has been published, lends itself to the charting of historical trends. The appendices include information on metropolitan statistical areas, tables with historical statistics, methodology and limitations, sources of data, tables deleted from the previous edition, and tables added. There is a thorough subject index. A CD-ROM version of the *Statistical Abstract* first became available in 1993; World Wide Web versions of the 1995 through 2002 editions are available at http://www.census.gov/statab/www/.

98. **Statistical Yearbook.** Lanham, MD: UNESCO Publishing and Bernan Press, 1963– . annual. ISSN 0082-7541.

Included here are comparative data, by country, in the areas of education, scientific manpower, research and development expenditures, culture and communication (e.g., number of book titles published, radio and television receiver per 1,000 inhabitants, daily newspapers), printed materials (e.g., libraries, book production data), film and cinema, broadcasting, and international trade in printed matter. In all, data from over 200 countries are reflected in the tables. Due to variations in countries' record keeping, there are some gaps. Table headings and introductory sections are provided in English, Spanish, and French. There are appendices covering member states, school years, exchange rates, UNESCO statistical publications, and introductory texts in Russian and Arabic.

Sociologists interested in sociology of education or comparative development issues may find this particularly relevant. Some of the statistical tables are updated on the UNESCO Web site at http://www.unesco.org.

Dictionaries and Encyclopedias

99. Anderson, Margo J., ed. **Encyclopedia of the U.S. Census.** Washington, DC: Congressional Quarterly, 2000. 424 p. index. $125.00. ISBN 1-56802-428-2.

This is a useful work for any social scientist intending to make use of the United States decennial census. The 120 signed entries seek to "identify the principal techniques, terms, processes, issues, and concepts of census taking" (p. ix). Topics covered include accuracy and coverage evaluation, age questions in the census, the American Community Survey, archival access to census data, census tracts, sampling in the census, metropolitan areas, data products, the economic census, and many others. Each entry is several pages in length and includes *see also* references and a short bibliography. The appendix includes statistics and information on congressional apportionment, census forms, and census standards. Additional access to the entries is provided through an index.

Web Sites and Research Centers

100. **American Sociological Association, Available Data Resources.** Available: http://www.asanet.org/student/data.html (Accessed: January 15, 2004).

This focused set of links to major social science data sets includes notes on availability and scope. Data sets covered include the General Social Survey, British Household Panel Survey, American Religion Data Archive, and American FactFinder. Descriptions of commercial data vendors such as Public Data Queries, Inc., and the Sociometrics Corporation are also provided.

101. **Australian Social Science Data Archive (ASSDA).** Available: http://assda. anu.edu.au/ (Accessed: May 5, 2004).

ASSDA is an agent for the Australian Consortium for Political and Social Research, Inc., and is the Australian counterpart to the Inter-University Consortium for Political and Social Research. ASSDA is housed at the Australian National University and provides access to more than 1,000 datasets that have been deposited by government agencies, marketing companies, universities, and other organizations. The online Data Catalogue is divided into several sections: "Australian Studies," "Overseas Studies," "Opinion Polls," and "Historical Census Data." Each dataset description includes information about the principal investigator(s), an abstract, subject terms, the universe sampled, sampling procedure, method of data collection, dimensions of the data set, accessibility, and references to related studies. Both members and nonmembers of the Australian Consortium for Social and Political Research Incorporated (ACSPRI) access the datasets after completing both a data order form and an "undertaking form"; download costs are higher for non–ACSPRI members. Online documentation of many of the major datasets is provided in the "Publications" section of the Web site. The site also features an online analysis tool that allows users to work directly with major datasets such as the Australian Election Study and the National Social Science Survey. Included are Australian Population Census data from 1966, 1971, 1976, 1981, 1986, and 1991. The archive also includes datasets from other countries in the Asia Pacific region: New Zealand, Indonesia, Papua New Guinea, and Cambodia. Also included are overseas datasets acquired from numerous sources such as the National Center for Social Research in Britain; the Inter-University Consortium for Political and Social Research (ICPSR) (see entry below), and the Roper Center for Public Opinion Research (see entry below) both in the United States.

102. Cornell Institute for Social and Economic Research, Internet Data Sources for Social Scientists. Available: http://www.ciser.cornell.edu/info/ datasource.shtml (Accessed: January 15, 2004).

Sociologists looking for an extensive listing of datasets and data providers will find this Cornell University site useful. Web sites are organized into several categories, including direct access to selected datasets available on the Internet, data distributors and producers, data libraries and archives, social science research institutes, population centers, online reference tools, professional organizations, and state and local government information. The listing of Web sites is also searchable by keyword.

103. Council for European Social Science Data Archives (CESSDA). Available: http://www.nsd.uib.no/cessda/ (Accessed: April 23, 2004).

A consortium of data archives in Europe, CESSDA promotes the acquiring, archiving, distributing, and searching of social science datasets. Among the features on its Web site is an integrated data catalog that can search for relevant datasets in several of its members' data archives, including France, Denmark, the United Kingdom, Norway, Sweden, Israel, the Netherlands, Hungary, Germany, and the United States. It also provides links to the Web sites for data archives in Europe, North America, Australia, New Zealand, Israel, South Africa, and Uruguay. Other goals include support of the compilation of comparative international datasets and the support of similar new organizational development. The Web site provides links to data archives from around the world, with a focus on Europe, including Italy, Spain, and Romania, among others.

104. Economic and Social Data Service (ESDS). Available: http://www.esds. ac.uk/ (Accessed: April 28, 2004).

The ESDS was established in January 2003 to collect and disseminate datasets from throughout the United Kingdom. It was formed in partnership with several other organizations, including the UK Data Archive (UKDA) at the University of Essex, the Institute for Social and Economic Research (ISER), Manchester Information and Associated Services (MIMAS), and the Cathie Marsh Centre for Census and Survey Research (CCSR). Researchers can search for datasets by using the UK Data Archive's online catalog or by using the Qualidata catalog for qualitative datasets. Datasets are available in a range of formats— SPSS, SAS, ASCII tab-delimited, and STATA. Registered users may download most datasets, as well as use an online statistical analysis tool. The data found via this site is both qualitative and quantitative and covers a variety of social science disciplines. This service is funded by both the Economic and Social Research Council (ESRC) and the Joint Information Systems Committee (JISC).

105. **FedStats.** Available: http://www.fedstats.gov/ (Accessed: January 15, 2004).

FedStats serves as a clearinghouse to statistical products created by federal agencies and departments. The Web site provides access to statistical data through a geographic feature, an agency listing, a topical listing, and a listing of popular statistical products. This is a useful resource for social scientists looking for basic government statistics.

106. **General Social Survey Data and Information Retrieval System (GSS-DIRS).** Available: http://www.icpsr.umich.edu/gss/ (Accessed: May 7th, 2004).

Researchers interested in the *General Social Survey* and its cumulative dataset will find this Web site useful. It has an introduction that includes a site map, a section about GSSDirs, a GSS news section, and credits. The "Codebook Indexes" include a collections index, as well as main codebook pages. "GSS Publications" includes questionnaires, an appendix, reports, and an updated and searchable bibliography of works citing the *General Social Survey*, an online and more current version of the print bibliography.

107. **Inter-university Consortium for Political and Social Research (ICPSR).** Available: http://www.icpsr.umich.edu/ (Accessed: April 20, 2004).

The ICPSR is a consortium of over 500 U.S. and Canadian colleges and universities, as well as a few hundred more institutions from other parts of the world. The consortium collects and distributes, to members, datasets of research on a variety of topics primarily in the social and behavioral sciences. Many universities own some of these datasets and make them available to campus researchers; datasets not owned can be ordered from ICPSR by the campus Official Representative (OR) or directly by users. The list of available datasets and services can be found on the Web site. Codebooks for most datasets are available for free downloading by members and nonmembers alike. Dataset descriptions include information on principal investigator(s), abstracts, sampling universe and method, and file descriptions. The Web site also provides access to several special topic archives, such as the General Social Survey and the International Archive of Education Data. Online statistical analysis is available for roughly 150 studies. ICPSR also conducts summer workshops in advanced research methods and statistical techniques.

108. **National Opinion Research Center (NORC).** Available: http://www. norc.uchicago.edu (Accessed: May 4, 2004).

Affiliated with the University of Chicago, NORC specializes in survey research and conducts some of the most prominent studies in the social sciences, education, and health services. This site provides a history and overview of NORC, a description of research departments, academic centers, research capabilities, and an overview of the General Social Survey (which it conducts), a description of NORC's publications, and educational and employment opportunities. There are also descriptions of key studies in its various areas of research, as well as descriptions of recent projects.

109. New Zealand Social Research Data Archives (NZSRDA). Available: http://www.massey.ac.nz/~nzsrda/nzsrda/archive.htm (Accessed: April 19, 2004).

Started in 1992, this archive is a collection of machine-readable datasets in the social sciences. NZSRDA currently has thirty-three social sciences datasets on such topics as national identity, religion, and social inequality; all datasets are thoroughly described. This site includes information on depositing and acquiring data, as well NZSRDA and international contact addresses.

110. The Odum Institute Data Archive. Available: http://www.irss.unc.edu/data_archive/home.asp (Accessed: January 15, 2004).

The Odum Institute Data Archive, located at the University of North Carolina, is home to the Louis Harris public opinion data, as well as collections of significant datasets from the U.S. Census Bureau, North Carolina, National Network of State Polls, among others. The Institute maintains its own data retrieval system, along with a public opinion poll question database; Web access is provided to both of these.

111. QUALIDATA. Available: http://www.essex.ac.uk/qualidata/ (Accessed: April 21, 2004).

This dataset service is part of the ESDS (see entry above) and led by the UK Data Archive (UKDA). This service focuses on locating, evaluating, cataloging, and finding a suitable archival home for qualitative data. The site includes recent news, guidelines for depositing qualitative data, as well as UKDA and ESDS online data catalogs. User support for working with the available datasets is also provided.

112. The Roper Center for Public Opinion Research. Available: http://www. ropercenter.uconn.edu/ (Accessed: January 15, 2004).

The Roper Center not only conducts polls on a variety of social and public policy issues, but also maintains a collection of some 12,500 machine-readable datasets of surveys conducted in the United States and over seventy foreign countries. Some questions go back as far as 1936. The center has its own retrieval system, iPOLL, for searching these datasets, and various subscription options are available. Survey results from academic, commercial and media survey organizations such as the Pew Research Center, the New York Times, the Gallup Organization, and many others are included. Registered access to JPOLL (Japanese Data Archive), free access to presidential approval ratings, and a selection of public opinion statistics on various topics, are also featured on the Web site. Featured sections of this site include: Polling 101, a tutorial on the basics of public opinion polling; Internet polling; Election 2004, highlighting primary results; and a section on exit poll data. The Roper Center survey and data analysis services are also reviewed, as is its bimonthly magazine, *The Public Perspective.* Roper Center membership information is also provided.

113. **Social Science Data Archives.** Available: http://www2.fmg.uva.nl/ sociosite/databases.html (Accessed: January 15, 2004).

This is a useful directory of data archive and national statistical agency Web sites organized by geographic region. The site is comprehensive in scope, ranging from commercial and university data archives in the United States to the national statistical agency of Cape Verde. Many of the links are briefly annotated.

114. **UK Data Archive.** Available: http://www.data-archive.ac.uk/ (Accessed: January 15, 2004).

The UK counterpart to the Inter-university for Political and Social Research, the UK Data Archive collects and distributes datasets on a wide variety of social science topics. The Web site features a catalog. Descriptions of datasets include an abstract, explanation of sampling methodology, and information on access. Registered and nonregistered users alike may access the online documentation; however, only registered users may download datasets. Fee schedules vary with affiliation. Registered users can also access selected datasets online using a Web-based statistical software program.

115. **University of California, San Diego, Data on the Net.** Available: http://odwin.ucsd.edu/idata (Accessed: January 15, 2004).

Data on the Net is a searchable collection of links to sources of statistical data on a variety of topics. Each link is annotated, providing an idea of the subjects covered by a particular statistical series or product. Annotated links to distributors/vendors of data and to data catalogs are also provided.

Directories

116. **Anthropology Resources on the Internet.** Available: http://www.an thropologie.net/ (Accessed: March 8, 2004).

Maintained by Bernard Clist, *Anthropology Resources on the Internet* is a directory site that focuses on anthropology and its various subfields, such as archaeology. The site also covers Web sites useful for area studies.

117. Bulmer, Martin, Wendy Sykes, and Jacqui Moorhouse, eds. **Directory of Social Research Organisations in the United Kingdom.** 2d ed. London: Mansell, 1998. 634 p. index. ISBN 0-7201-2371-2.

More than 1,000 British social research organizations and independent researchers are described in this directory. To be included, the organization or researcher had to either conduct or commission empirical social research. These organizations reflect a range of institutions and settings, including governmental research units, private research institutes, market research firms, higher education research centers, public companies, and more. The organizations are listed alphabetically in the main section of the directory. For each, there are a number of common categories of information: address, phone, fax, Web address, e-mail, head (chair or director), description, sector (type of organization), number of researchers, fields of research, commission research, recent projects, training opportunities, research services offered, main contact, and other contacts. In addition to the organization entries, there are entries for independent researchers, professional associations, and philanthropic organizations that also support or engage in social science research. The directory also provides some brief, introductory essays on the state of social research in Britain, on commissioning social research, on research ethics, and on the future of research training (with a supplementary section on training courses). There are multiple indexes for accessing the entries, including organization name or acronym, individual name, organization by geographic location, topics, subjects, methodological expertise, and methodological services.

118. **Encyclopedia of Associations, Vol. 1: National Organizations of the U.S.** Detroit, MI: Gale, 1961– . 3v. annual. $650.00 (2004 ed.). ISSN 0071-0202.

Included here are brief descriptions of approximately 22,000 national and international organizations and associations. Entries are organized by broad subject categories in the first two volumes, which are labeled volume 1, part 1 and volume 1, part 2. These include categories for educational, cultural, social welfare, health, public affairs, and other organizations. For effective searching, one needs to use the name and keyword index found in the third volume, which is labeled volume 1, part 3. Citations include the address, phone number, fax, Web address, director, membership size, purpose of the organization, publications, and annual conventions, among other details. Other volumes in the series include *Encyclopedia of Associations: International Organizations* (ISSN 1041-0023) and *Encyclopedia of Associations: Regional, State, and Local Organizations* (ISSN 0894-2846). This is an invaluable guide for identifying professional sociological and sociology-related organizations.

119. **Politics Gateway.** Available: http://www.psa.ac.uk/www/default.htm (Accessed: March 8, 2004).

This directory of Web sites is maintained by the Political Studies Association. The sites are organized by broad topic areas—constitutions, data archives, elections, gender and politics, journals, libraries and archives, mass media, politics departments, political science associations, and political resources. Additional access to the Web sites is provided geographically through a click-on world map and through an internal search engine. Coverage is international. Many of the sites are accompanied by brief notes on institutional affiliations and/or content. This is a useful and well-organized directory that should appeal to political sociologists.

120. **Research Centers Directory.** Detroit, MI: Gale, 1960– . 2v. annual. $690.00 (2004 ed.). ISSN 0800-1518.

Over 13,000 research centers are listed in each directory, including "centers, laboratories, institutes . . . research support facilities, technology transfer centers, think tanks . . . and more" (28th ed., 2002, p. viii). The entries are organized under seventeen broad subject categories, where they are then arranged alphabetically by the center's name. Of particular interest to sociologists might be the categories for medical and health sciences (medical sociology), government and public affairs (policy studies), labor and industrial relations (industrial sociology, sociology of work), behavioral and social sciences (gerontology, marriage and the family, ethnic studies, conflict, and more), education (sociology of education), and humanities and religion (sociology of religion). For each research center the information includes such items as address, phone number, contact e-mail address, Web site address, date founded, director, staff, source of support, research activities and fields, and publications and services. There are subject, geographic, and personal name indexes. Additionally, a master index lists centers by name, keyword in the name, and college/university affiliation. This directory is supplemented by New Research Centers (1965–). An expanded version of this directory is available through the Dialog database service (File 115, *Research Centers and Services Directory*); it also includes government centers, international centers, and research services.

121. **Resources for Economists on the Internet (RFE).** Available: http://rfe.org/ (Accessed: March 8, 2004).

Maintained for the American Economic Association by Dr. William Goffe, a faculty member at the State University of New York-Oswego, *RFE* is a directory of more than 1,000 Web sites of interest to economists and other social scientists. The sites are organized into several broad categories, including dictionaries and glossaries and encyclopedias; forecasting and consulting; scholarly communication; software and so on. An abridged table of contents provides subheadings of these topics; a complete listing of Web sites under each heading and subheading is also available. Each site is briefly annotated. The directory includes cross-references and is searchable by keyword.

122. **WebEc: World Wide Web Resources in Economics.** Available: http://www.helsinki.fi/WebEc/ (Accessed: March 8, 2004).

WebEC is maintained by Mr. Lauri Saarinen, a research fellow at the Center for Innovative Education, Helsinki School of Economics. The site is essentially a directory of Web sites geared towards academic economists, although several of the subject categories will also appeal to sociologists including labor and demographics; industrial organization; mathematical and quantitative methods; and development, technological change and growth. Each main category is further subdivided, and the links under each of these subdivisions are annotated. The site is searchable and also features a listing of online journals.

123. **The World of Learning.** London: Europa Publications, 1947– . annual. $620.00 (2004 ed.). ISSN 0084-2117.

Now in its fifty-fourth edition (2004), this is an excellent international directory of educational and cultural institutions, organizations, and centers. It is arranged alphabetically by country. For each country, there are entries for its various academies, learned societies, libraries, museums and art galleries, universities, colleges, and research institutes. The address, phone number, founding date, membership, director's name, and publications are listed for many of the institutions. Some entries are descriptively annotated. Many college and university entries, both for the United States and elsewhere, include faculty members listed by their departmental/faculty affiliation. An introductory section lists some international organizations and associations, with accompanying addresses, phone numbers, functions, and contact names. There is a thorough index to the cited institutions. This source should help those trying to locate international sociology and sociology-related departments, colleagues, associations, or research centers.

Biographies

124. **National Faculty Directory.** 34th ed. Detroit, MI: Gale, 2003. 3v. $685.00. ISBN 0-7876-6322-0.

This is a straightforward alphabetical list of approximately 780,000 teaching faculty members at 3,600 American and 240 Canadian institutions of higher education, including junior colleges, colleges, and universities. Faculty with non–teaching responsibilities, or librarians with faculty rank, are not included. For faculty members who are included, name, departmental affiliation, university, institutional address, and phone number are provided. There is no phone number, nor is the individual's academic rank given. An introductory "Roster of Colleges and Universities" lists institutions alphabetically within each state and provides an address and phone number. While journal articles or books often mention the institutional affiliation of authors, they may not be current. This work can be valuable in attempting to track down the current affiliation of faculty in North American higher educational institutions.

Sociology

Chapter

2

Guides

125. **ASA Resources for Students.** Available: http://www.asanet.org/student/student.html (Accessed: March 18, 2004).

This is an American Sociological Association Web page for undergraduate and graduate students. It includes online newsletters and discussion groups; employment and career bulletins and resources; examples from the ASA style guide (in *The Student Sociologist* newsletter); funding opportunities; online copies of *Footnotes*, the ASA's newsletter; and more. Overall, the site is a useful guide to a broad range of career development information relating to employment, further education, and development of scholarly skills.

126. **ASA Style Guide.** 2d ed. Washington, DC: American Sociological Association, 1997. 39 p. $10.00. ISBN 0-912764-29-5.

Though published in 1997, the second edition of this style guide remains the current recommended one for the American Sociological Association and its journals. Included here are sections addressing matters of style (e.g., clarity, verbs, wordy phrases), mechanics of style (e.g., punctuation, capitalization, spelling, dates, numbers), manuscript preparation (e.g., page format, footnotes or endnotes, references, tables), submitting your manuscript, interpreting copy editor's notations, and reference list formats. There is also an appended list of acceptable computer file formats that are acceptable for some ASA journals, though surely this list is now out of date. This second edition also includes a few reference examples for citing electronic sources; these are somewhat minimal given the current electronic environment. Despite being dated technologically, the style guide has some excellent and fairly concise recommendations for good writing and manuscript preparation.

127. Giarusso, Roseann, et al. **A Guide to Writing Sociology Papers.** 5th ed. New York: Worth Publishers, 2001. 189 p. index. $20.50. ISBN 1-57259-951-0.

Becoming a polished academic writer requires clear instruction and detailed feedback, accompanied by plenty of practice. This guide, now in its fifth edition, can help with the first two items. It provides excellent instruction about the writing process, particularly as applied to the field of sociology. In this new edition, the first four chapters talk about getting started on a paper, the writing process, acknowledging sources, and polishing your paper. These are general features of good writing in any discipline. However, where appropriate, the book includes examples and explanations from sociology. This is particularly evident in the discussion of selecting a topic and framing a question. The four chapters comprising the second part of the book address various types of sociology writing assignments: the textual analysis paper, the general research paper based on library or Internet data, the ethnographic field research paper, and the quantitative research paper. In each chapter, there is valuable information on identifying the task or forming a question, gathering information and collecting data, organizing the information, and writing the paper. The chapter on the research paper using library or Internet data discusses the use of specific resources for sociological research, including database and Internet search engine (e.g., Google) search techniques. Each chapter in part 2, except for the one on library/Internet research, also includes a sample student paper with accompanying annotations and feedback indicating its strengths and weaknesses. A final chapter contains a checklist for evaluating papers before they are submitted. There is also a subject index.

128. Johnson, William A., Jr., Richard P. Rettig, Gregory M. Scott, and Stephen M. Garrison. **The Sociology Student Writer's Manual.** 4th ed. Upper Saddle River, NJ: Pearson Education, 2004. 254 p. index. $32.00. ISBN 0-13-111388-7.

This manual provides useful direction to sociology students on how to write and do research in sociology. It is broken into a number of parts, some with general advice on writing, some with advice and information on sociology and its types of assignments, and some merging both concerns. Part 1, "A Handbook of Style for Sociology," provides an overview of the purposes and processes of writing, writing rules and punctuation, formatting of papers, and the citation of sources. This is information that could apply to writing in any discipline. The chapters in part 2, "Conducting Research in Sociology," focus on the research process, including understanding assignments and focusing topics, using the library and the Internet, and the fundamentals of doing quantitative research. Part 3, "How to Write Different Types of Sociology Papers," provides examples of various kinds of sociological research and writing projects or assignments, along with suggestions on how to dissect topics and organize one's research and writing. These project types include social issue papers (i.e., issue reaction, social issue analysis); critical evaluations of sociological literature (i.e., book reviews, article critiques, literature reviews, annotated bibliographies); quantitative research (i.e., research design, survey-based papers); and qualitative research (e.g., case studies). At the end, there is a list of references, a glossary of terms, and a combined name/title/subject index. Though this could be a stand-alone reference book, it would probably be best used as a supplementary text in a sociology course where its insights and methods could be systematically explored with an instructor.

129. Lambert, Stephen. **Great Jobs for Sociology Majors.** 2d ed. Chicago: VGM Career Books, 2003. 252 p. index. $14.95. ISBN 0-07-140301-9.

Now in its second edition, this work is a career guide for sociology students. The introduction provides an impressionistic and somewhat uneven overview of the field of sociology and its specializations. The body of the work is divided into two sections: the job search, and career paths. The "job search" section is very practical, though not related exclusively to sociology. There are specific chapters on self-assessment, cover letters and resumes, interviewing, networking, considering offers, choosing graduate schools, and more. The information is detailed, reflecting the author's experience in career development and counseling. The second major section of the book, "career paths," is comprised of descriptions of five possible career paths that a sociology major might pursue: teaching with an advanced degree; human services; human resources management; public employment; and social research and data analysis. Overall, the book is strongest when it gets into the technique of conducting a job or graduate school search.

Bibliographies

130. **General Social Survey Bibliography (GSS).** Available: http://webapp.icpsr.umich.edu/GSS/ (Accessed: April 9, 2004).

This is the online version of the *Annotated Bibliography of Papers Using the General Social Surveys*, formerly published by the National Opinion Research Center (NORC). The *General Social Survey (GSS)* is an ongoing research program and dataset that collects demographic, behavioral, and attitudinal data that span the social sciences. Data can touch on important sociological topics, such as race relations, job satisfaction, political participation, or group membership, not to mention a host of demographic variables. These data are used extensively in social science research, which is identified in this bibliography. Books, journal articles, conference papers, reports, theses, and dissertations using *GSS* data are cited here alphabetically by author. Each entry includes not only a full reference and an abstract of findings, but also an indication of the *GSS* years used and other datasets employed in the research. Each citation lists and provides links to the *GSS* mnemonics (variables) used. College or universities that are members of the Inter-university Consortium for Political and Social Research (ICPSR) will have access to the *GSS* dataset, while the bibliography itself is publicly accessible on the ICPSR Web site.

131. **International Bibliography of Sociology.** Vol. 1– . London: Routledge, 1952– . annual. index. (International Bibliography of the Social Sciences). ISSN 0085-2066.

This is part of a series of annual volumes called the International Bibliography of the Social Sciences. Other volumes cover economics, political science, and social and cultural anthropology. More than 6,000 articles and books are cited in the current sociology volumes, representing items published in over sixty countries and in more than seventy languages. There is an extensive classification scheme for the arrangement of entries. This includes eleven major subject headings: general studies; theory and methodology; individuals, groups, and organizations; culture; social structure; population, family, gender, ethnic group; environment, community, rural, urban; economic life; labor; politics, state, international relations; and social problems, social services, social work. Each of these subject sections has many more subheadings. All headings are in English and French. There is both an author index and English and French versions of an extensive subject index. Also included are lists of periodicals consulted (more than 2,500) and their abbreviations, which are used in article citations. The international coverage of this bibliography is a major strength. Also, the turnaround time for publication of the annual bibliographies is less than a year after the publication year of the cited sources; this is good for a source that is wide-ranging and international. The *International Bibliography of Sociology* is available online and on CD-ROM as part of the International Bibliography of the Social Sciences (see http://www.lse.ac.uk/collections/IBSS/Default.htm for details).

Indexes, Abstracts, and Databases

132. Combined Retrospective Index Set to Journals in Sociology, 1895–1975. Annadel N. Wile, ed. Washington, DC: Carrollton Press, 1978. 6v. LC 77-70347. ISBN 0-8408-0194-7.

Part of the Combined Retrospective Index Series (CRIS), these volumes provide subject and author access to sociological articles in journals in an eighty-year period. Over one hundred sociology journals are indexed. The first five volumes are the subject indexes, with each one covering different major headings (e.g., culture, family, group interactions). There are a modest number of subheadings as well. Citations are then filed in alphabetical order by the keyword in the title. This is followed by a short title, author, journal number, year, volume, and page. Journal titles corresponding to the numbers are found inside the front and back covers. The author index is arranged alphabetically, accompanied by citations identical to those in the subject index. Overall, this may provide valuable historical coverage to the sociological journal literature.

133. Lantz, Judith C., comp. **Cumulative Index of Sociology Journals, 1971–1985.** Washington, DC: American Sociological Association, 1987. 763 p. index.

This source allows the user to search the contents of ten major sociology journals. The journals covered include *American Journal of Sociology*, the *American Sociological Review*, *The American Sociologist*, *Contemporary Sociology*, the *Journal of Health and Social Behavior*, *Social Forces*, *Social Psychology Quarterly* (a.k.a. *Sociometry*), *Sociological Methodology*, *Sociological*

Theory and *Sociology of Education*. All but two of these titles, the *American Journal of Sociology* and *Social Forces*, are American Sociological Association journals. There are both author and subject indexes; in each, article references include the abbreviated journal title, the month, the publication year, and the pages of the article. While this index does help in identifying some older articles in key journals, the entries may not be sufficiently detailed for interlibrary loan requests (titles are omitted, as are volume numbers).

134. **Sociology: A Sage Full-Text Collection.** [electronic resource]. Thousand Oaks, CA. Available: http://www.sagefulltext.com/ (Accessed: April 12, 2004).

This growing collection of full-text journals in sociology currently includes thirty titles ranging from *Current Sociology* to *Journal of Sport and Social Issues* to *Work and Occupations*. Most of the titles are Sage publications, but others from participating societies are also included. Extensive full-text backfiles are provided for each journal title, although the coverage for some, such as the *American Behavioral Scientist*, is not as comprehensive as that provided by the JSTOR collection. On the other hand, the *Full-Text Collection* provides good access to recently published articles. Each record within the database includes a full citation, abstract, and list of references cited. The citations, abstracts, and full-text articles are all searchable. The *Full-Text Collection* is available from Sage and from other vendors, such as CSA.

135. **Sociological Abstracts.** [electronic resource]. Bethesda, MD: CSA. Available: http://www.csa.com/ (Accessed: April 12, 2004).

CSA's Sociological Abstracts database comprises the Sociofile database which was formerly available on CD-ROM and Sociological Abstracts. It differs slightly from the print edition of Sociological Abstracts in that its dates of coverage run from 1963 to the present, rather than from 1953 to present. Sociological Abstracts is one of the most important guides to the broad range of literature in sociology and its subdisciplines, including history and theory, social psychology, urban sociology, social differentiation, family and socialization, and mass phenomena, among others. It not only abstracts journal articles, books and conference papers, but also indexes book reviews. Sources from all over the world are cited, including some in foreign languages (though abstracts are in English). Abstracts are generally available only for items included since 1974. Each record within the database includes a listing of class descriptors and minor descriptors that correspond to classifications in the print edition. The database is available through CSA, as well as through other vendors.

136. **Sociological Collection.** [electronic resource]. Ipswich, MA: EBSCO. Available: http://www.epnet.com/academic/sociologicalcoll.asp (Accessed: April 12, 2004).

Sociological Collection is a subset of the EBSCO universe of indexed and full-text journals. It includes about 580 scholarly or peer-reviewed journals and over 600 full-text titles. Its advanced search option allows the user to search in up to three search windows, specifying in which field the term should be searched (e.g., author, default field/keyword, subject, title, journal name, text, geographic name, etc.). There are limits available for full-text and peer-reviewed journal articles, as well as for publication name, dates, article type, image type (pdf vs. HTML full text), and more. The retrieved citations, abstracts, and full-text can be marked for printing or e-mailing. The database is updated monthly.

Handbooks and Yearbooks

137. **Annual Review of Sociology.** Vol. 1– . Palo Alto, CA: Annual Reviews, 1975– . annual. $192.00. ISSN 0360-0572.

Each volume contains twenty or more articles organized under broad subject categories, with a number of articles under each category. These categories include theory and methods, social processes, institutions and culture, formal organizations, differentiation and stratification, demography, political and economic sociology, individual and society, and more. Of late, issues have also included a prefatory section that can include, among other things, memoirs by or biographical essays on distinguished sociologists (e.g., Peter Blau, Seymour Martin Lipset, and Judith Blake), or articles on compelling topics (e.g., rational choice theory, by Raymond Boudon). There is a subject index, as well as cumulative indexes of authors and titles. These sources are now available to subscribers online (http://arjournals.annualreviews.org/loi/soc) with full text from 1975 to the present from Annual Reviews, Inc. JSTOR also provides full-text coverage with a rolling blackout period of five years.

138. Bach, Rebecca, comp. and ed. **Managing Hostility in the Classroom: A Book of Resources for Teaching.** Washington, DC: American Sociological Association, 2002. 109 p. (ASA Resource Materials for Teaching).

As the author points out, sociology can be a disruptive and potentially upsetting perspective for students who are new to it. Many of sociology's topics are quite familiar to our students at some level, yet the discipline examines them in what are often totally new ways. Cherished beliefs and assumptions are often held up to critical scrutiny. Topics often taken for granted or considered somewhat taboo are studied and dissected from numerous angles. Consequently, sociology instructors often have to learn to manage hostility in their classrooms. Discussions of race, inequality, religion, and sex roles, to name a few, are potentially touchy subjects. The twenty essays in this volume address this issue and, in the sociological tradition, critically reflect on it. They do so in two ways. The initial ten essays talk about general issues of hostility in the classroom. They discuss not only the origins of this hostility, but also some pedagogical responses to manage it. The last ten essays focus on more specific techniques for dealing with classroom hostility. These can include not only decreasing hostility and resistance, but also turning such circumstances into "teachable moments." There is even an article discussing how to train graduate student instructors to deal with hostility in the classroom. These essays should be valuable for instructors in a variety of fields, not just sociology.

139. Deutschmann, Linda B., comp. and ed. **Syllabi and Instructional Materials for Teaching Comparative and Historical Sociology.** 4th ed. Washington, DC: American Sociological Association, 2001. 167 p. (ASA Resource Materials for Teaching).

As the editor points out in the introduction, virtually all sociology can or should be comparative and historical in some fashion. The seventeen syllabi included here span undergraduate and graduate-level courses in a wide variety of specializations. While some of the initial syllabi focus on comparative and historical research methods, subsequent ones focus on subject areas such as social change, inequality, world systems, environmental sociology, globalization, gender, social identities, inequality, democratization, and crime and justice, to name a few. All of these more subject-specific courses utilize comparative and historical analysis as part of their approach. In addition to these syllabi, there are appended materials for historical-comparative home pages, syllabi on the Net, online presentations (i.e., three PowerPoints), and suppliers of film and video resources.

140. **Sociology Basics.** Carl L. Bankston III, ed. 2v. Pasadena, CA: Salem Press, 2000. (Magill's Choice). $104.00. ISBN 0-89356-205-X.

These two volumes are comprised of selected essays or articles distilled from the previously released *Survey of Social Science: Sociology Series*, published in 1994. The entries are more detailed than an encyclopedia entry and are presented well for readers new to the topics. Each entry includes a list of key terms and their brief definitions, followed by an overview of the topic, its applications, and the context of the topic. The end of the entry includes a bibliography and some cross-references to related entries found elsewhere in the volumes. Appended is a glossary of key terms, as well as an alphabetical index of topics, a categorical index, and a subject index. This title is also available online through netLibrary.

Dictionaries and Encyclopedias

141. Abercrombie, Nicholas, Stephen Hill, and Bryan S. Turner. **The Penguin Dictionary of Sociology.** 4th ed. London: Penguin, 2000. 449 p. $15.00. ISBN 0-14-051380-9.

This latest edition continues to provide a balance between traditional sociological terms or concepts and more contemporary terms. Since the third edition, the authors have added numerous terms falling within eight broad topical categories: gender and feminist issues; popular culture, media and information technology; globalization; ubiquitous social change; race, ethnicity, and religious divisions; sociobiology; space and time; and the individual subject. The definitions are clearly written and relatively jargon free, though some of the more theoretically sophisticated entries (e.g., Foucault) presume more knowledge and would be challenging for a beginning sociology student. The definitions refer the reader to terms defined elsewhere in the dictionary. There are also *see* references to related concepts, as well as references to further reading cited in the appended bibliography. Another nice feature is the inclusion of biographies on key theorists. To its credit, the dictionary defines key terms from a variety of theoretical perspectives, including radical ones. The authors note a growing convergence between European and American traditions in sociology, and both differences and similarities are reflected in the dictionary's entries. The appended bibliography is retrospective and has been modestly updated since the previous edition. Overall, this dictionary provides excellent definitions of both traditional and contemporary sociological concepts and theorists.

142. Bardis, Panos D. **Dictionary of Quotations in Sociology.** Westport, CT: Greenwood Press, 1985. 356 p. index. $69.50. ISBN 0-313-23778-6.

Bardis has pulled together a historical assortment of quotes from sociologists, social philosophers, and others on some of the major concepts in sociology. For each concept or term, quotes are listed chronologically from the earliest source to the most recent. The sources of the quotes, which range from a few sentences to a long paragraph, are cited with an author, title, and publication year. A selected bibliography is also provided, as are subject and name indexes. These indexes are valuable in fully utilizing the volume. The subject index permits searching more specific topics than are found in the broad subject categories. The name index allows one to assemble a variety of quotes by a specific individual across a range of topics. The comparative nature of the quotes, both historically and culturally, makes for interesting reading. These could provide a useful key to further reading.

143. Booth, Barbara. **Thesaurus of Sociological Indexing Terms.** 5th ed. Bethesda, MD: Cambridge Scientific Abstracts, 1999. 351 p. ISBN 0-930710-15-0.

This lists all of the official subject terms used to classify entries in the print or electronic versions of the Sociological Abstracts database, as well as *Social Planning/Policy & Development Abstracts*. Sociological concepts, geographic place names, and some personal names are included. The main section of the thesaurus is an alphabetical list of subject headings (descriptors). These terms are typically accompanied by a list of broader, narrower, and related terms, all of which are headings that can be found elsewhere in the thesaurus. These other terms are often useful in broadening or focusing one's search. Entries for terms may also include a "scope note" (SN), which defines the term, and a "historical note" (HN), which may indicate when a term was added or what term(s) it superseded. An entry may also include a list of "used for" (UF) terms to which it is preferable. Throughout the thesaurus, these unused terms are listed with a "use" cross-reference to the preferred term. A "Rotated Descriptor Display" is appended that lists all keywords, including words in phrases, in alphabetical order and in the context of their keyword phrase. A final section lists six broad concepts and, in alphabetical order, all of the subject terms that relate to them.

This thesaurus is invaluable for thorough subject searching in Sociological Abstracts in its various print and electronic formats.

144. Boudon, Raymond, and Francois Bourricaud. **A Critical Dictionary of Sociology.** Chicago: University of Chicago Press, 1989. 438 p. index. $60.00. ISBN 0-226-06728-9.

Rather than providing conventional definitions on a fairly comprehensive set of terms, the authors have written more personal essays on seventy-three sociological concepts, theories, and theorists. Furthermore, the terms discussed are not narrowly sociological, but instead reflect the more cosmopolitan approach of these two French sociologists. Consequently, the essays are probing and thought-provoking features that help explain the term "critical" in the title. The authors point out that their focus is on the more enduring questions in sociology, rather than on a discrete number of terms with fixed meanings. Despite these idiosyncrasies, there are many expected terms here, such as "alienation," "anomie," "functionalism," "structuralism," "ideologies," "capitalism," "authority," "bureaucracy," "suicide," and "rationality." Similarly, some major sociologists are covered, including Auguste Comte, Karl Marx, Émile Durkheim, Herbert Spencer, and Max Weber. One also finds entries on Jean Jacques Rousseau, Niccolo Machiavelli, and Joseph Schumpeter, which are more surprising in such a selective list. Throughout, the essays are well written and presume a certain amount of knowledge; a beginning student may be better off with one of the more conventional dictionaries, at least initially. Entries have cross-references to related terms, as well as bibliographies of recommended readings. There is also a thematic (subject/name) index.

145. **Encyclopedia of Sociology.** Edgar F. Borgatta, and Rhonda J. V. Montgomery, eds. 2d ed. New York: Macmillan Reference USA, 2000. 5v. $525.00. ISBN 0-02-864853-6 (set).

This five-volume set includes two- to nine-page entries on approximately 400 key subject areas in the field of sociology. The second edition has sixty-six new article entries and substantial revisions of many previous articles. These new and revised entries pay more attention to the practical implications of the research on a topic and to the suggestions for further research. In this edition, brief or narrowly treated topics have sometimes been combined, bundled into broader subjects, or dropped altogether. Major sociological topics, theories, research methods, schools of thought, and subdisciplines are represented. Experts wrote the essays on the various subjects and they provide an excellent introduction to and overview of their topics. Each entry is accompanied by a substantial and up-to-date list of references for further reading. There is also liberal use of *see* and *see also* references to direct the user to preferred or related subject categories. Though there are no biographical entries for theorists, their ideas are often discussed at length within the relevant topics. More specific access to the terms, theories, and theorists within the entries is provided by a detailed subject index. These essays provide valuable and relatively current overviews of fundamental topics in the field. There is an introductory alphabetical list of the encyclopedia's articles, accompanied by the author's name, as well as an alphabetical list of authors, including their institutional address and the entries they wrote. A list of the second edition's new entries would have been useful.

146. **Encyclopedic Dictionary of Sociology.** Richard Lachmann, ed. 4th ed. Guilford, CT: Dushkin, 1991. 321 p. $12.95. ISBN 0-87967-886-0.

Included here are "more than 1,350 entries, each prepared by one of 120 authorities . . . Rather than provide exhaustive information on particular topics, the goal of this encyclopedia is to answer specific questions on the interrelationship among sociological concepts . . . Entries are arranged alphabetically, with some containing cross-references to either connect interrelated items or to deepen comprehension of the subject" (Oleg Zinan, *American Reference Books Annual*, 1993, pp. 355–356).

147. **International Encyclopedia of Sociology.** Frank N. Magill, ed. London; Chicago: Fitzroy Dearborn, 1995. 2v. $275.00. ISBN 1-884964-54-0.

Written for general readers or nonspecialists, this encyclopedia provides very readable, four-page entries on 338 topics, ranging from traditional sociological subjects (e.g., anomie and deviance) to more contemporary issues (e.g., free speech in the schools; comparable worth). Some of the topics may seem too popular at first glance, but they reinforce the idea that the field of sociology has something to say about the hottest of popular topics. The entries begin with a categorization of the topic according to the type of sociology it relates to (e.g., social institutions; sex and gender) and its broader field of study (e.g., education; family). There is then a paragraph-long elaboration of the topic and definitions of principal terms used in its discussion. Each article includes an overview of the topic, a discussion of how it manifests itself in real settings (i.e., applications), and finally an explanation of the topic's place in the discipline of sociology. There are brief, annotated bibliographies with each article, as well as cross-references to related topics found elsewhere in the encyclopedia. The signed articles are written by experts in the various fields, and their names and affiliations are listed alphabetically at the beginning of the encyclopedia. There is also a list of various topics under the broader sociological categories (i.e., types of sociology) to which they relate. Appended is a glossary of 450 terms with definitions, a select bibliography arranged under broad subject categories (e.g., sociological theory; race and ethnicity), and a combined name/subject index. As advertised, this encyclopedia would be excellent for general readers and undergraduate students.

148. Jary, David, and Julia Jary. **The HarperCollins Dictionary of Sociology.** New York: HarperCollins, 1991. 601 p. LC 91-55446. ISBN 0-06-271543-7.

Intended primarily as a study aid, this dictionary has a broad scope, including not only key sociological terms and theorists, but also terms from the other social sciences that "have achieved wide use within sociology" (p. iii). For quick reference, all of the entries begin with a brief definition. Most of these definitions are followed by longer descriptions ranging from a paragraph to three or four pages. Methodological and statistical terms are included as well. In all of the definitions, terms defined elsewhere in the dictionary are indicated in capital letters. Key sociological works are cited within the definitions and listed in the appended bibliography. The initial, brief definitions are indeed convenient. However, the lengthier descriptions of many terms are also well done, giving this dictionary a well-rounded appeal to a variety of users.

149. Johnson, Allan G. **The Blackwell Dictionary of Sociology: A User's Guide to Sociological Language.** 2d ed. Malden, MA: Blackwell, 2000. 413 p. index. $49.95. LC 99-049053. ISBN 0-631-21681-2.

Sociological language provides a lens through which aspiring sociologists may view the world. As the author points out, this is both liberating, in that it lets us see new aspects of reality, and constraining, in that definitions may imply a consensus or closure that does not exist. This dictionary provides well-written and concise definitions of fundamental concepts in sociology. The author's intent here was to render sociological terms more understandable, and to avoid overly sophisticated treatments of fewer terms. There is a reasonable mix of traditional and contemporary terms, and important concepts from related fields, such as philosophy, are also included. The definitions range from a paragraph to a page and are notable for their clarity and avoidance of jargon, even for theoretically difficult concepts. All definitions are accompanied by a few references for further reading, as well as *see also* references to related terms. The dictionary also makes extensive use of *see* references to direct the user to the correct term. Throughout the dictionary, terms defined elsewhere are indicated by capital letters. A final section includes brief biographical sketches of major sociological figures, along with a short list of their important works. The subject index is a helpful addition, given that important concepts not elsewhere defined can be buried within the entries.

150. Lawson, Tony, and Joan Garrod. **Dictionary of Sociology.** London; Chicago: Fitzroy Dearborn, 2001. 273 p. $45.00. ISBN 1-57958-291-5.

There are approximately 1,400 briefly defined terms included in this dictionary. Definitions range from a sentence to a paragraph and include not only italicized terms defined elsewhere, but also *see* references to related definitions. There are short biographies on select, major sociologists, though very few of them. The definitions are simply and straightforwardly written, even some of the more technical ones. The terms included reflect a variety of theoretical perspectives and methodological techniques. Given the nature of the prose, this is probably best suited for undergraduate sociology students. Though British in origin, the dictionary is virtually free of proper names of country-specific organizations or agencies, making it valuable in a range of English-speaking countries.

151. Marshall, Gordon, ed. **A Dictionary of Sociology.** 2d ed. New York: Oxford University Press, 1998. 712 p. $16.95. ISBN 0-19-280081-7.

Included here are more than 2,500 entries on terms from sociology and related disciplines, with 150 new terms added since the first edition. The best definitions are quite conversational in tone and range anywhere from a paragraph to a few pages in length. The essay format of some of the longer definitions helps the readability and clarity of the definitions. References to relevant readings are integrated into the definitions themselves. Terms that are used in the definitions, and that are also defined elsewhere, are indicated with an asterisk. At the end of most definitions there is a list of *see also* references to related terms defined elsewhere in the dictionary. Throughout the dictionary, there are liberal cross-references from unused to used terms. Biographies are included, though only on deceased sociologists. Good writing and the inclusion of many recent important theoretical and social developments make this dictionary particularly valuable, though it is nonetheless fairly sophisticated in its treatment of many sociological concepts and therefore suitable for more advanced sociology students.

152. Palmisano, Joseph M., ed. **World of Sociology.** Detroit, MI: Gale, 2001. 2v. $150.00. ISBN 0-7876-4965-1.

Intended for students and general readers, this dictionary/encyclopedia attempts to provide readable definitions of important terms in sociology. Included among the terms are basic concepts, theories, organizations, and people. In all, there are approximately 1,000 entries, with the definitions ranging in length from a paragraph to a few pages. Within definitions, terms defined elsewhere are indicated in bold print. In addition, there are *see also* references to related terms at the end of some entries. Besides the definitions, there is also a historical chronology of important social science–related events from 1640 to 2000. A nationality index tracks biographical entries by nationality, while a general index covers the entire work and includes subjects, organization names, and people. This is a useful and fairly approachable guide to key concepts in sociology. With multiple contributors, it is not surprising that the definitions vary somewhat in their simplicity and clarity. Many of these concepts cannot be oversimplified without doing them an injustice. Given such inherent constraints, this dictionary is well done and appropriate for public and academic libraries.

153. Thompson, Kenneth. **Key Quotations in Sociology.** London: Routledge, 1996. 207 p. index. $15.95. ISBN 0-415-05761-2.

Students looking for quotes to use in papers, or faculty using quotes for their teaching and writing, are the intended audience for this compilation. The quotations are arranged into two sections: by subject and by theorist. The subject section includes major sociological concepts, usually with multiple quotations taken from a variety of sociological works. The source of each quote is fully cited. The section on sociological theorists is arranged alphabetically by theorist, with subsections for some specific topics. Within these subtopics, there may be a number of quotes. Durkheim, for example, has subsections for sociological method, the division of labor, religion, politics, and moral education, each with multiple quotations. Both current and historical theorists are included, ranging from Auguste Comte to Pierre Bourdieu and Anthony Giddens. Throughout the book, there are cross-references to related terms or relevant theorists. The number and variety of quotations on particular topics gives this book the feel of a dictionary or one-volume encyclopedia. In many cases, a reader could get a good grasp of a concept by reading the various quotes, as exemplified by the entries on "ideology." Name and subject indexes are included, with references to the page and the specific, numbered quote on that page.

Journals

154. **Administrative Science Quarterly.** Vol. 1– , No. 1– . Ithaca, NY: Johnson Graduate School of Management, Cornell University, 1956– . quarterly. $190/yr. (institutions). ISSN 0001-8392. Available: http://www.johnson.cornell. edu/publications/asq/ (Accessed: December 20, 2004).

Specialists in the sociology of organizations consider this a fundamentally important journal. Issues include both empirical and theoretical articles, as well as book reviews and, occasionally, a review symposium. Indexed in: *Social Sciences Index, Sociological Abstracts, Social Sciences Citation Index.*

155. **American Journal of Community Psychology.** Vol. 1– , No. 1– . New York: Plenum Press, 1973– . bimonthly. $880/yr. (institutions). ISSN 0091-0562. Available: http://www.kluweronline.com/issn/0091-0562 (Accessed: December 20, 2004).

Sociologists in the areas of medical sociology, mental health service organizations, community and social support services, and family caregiving should find this useful. Approximately six articles per issue have primarily an applied focus. The journal is published in association with the Society for Community Research and Action (the Division of Community Psychology of the American Psychological Association). Indexed in: *Current Contents/Social and Behavioral Sciences, Social Work Abstracts, Social Sciences Citation Index, Psychological Abstracts, Sociological Abstracts.*

156. **American Journal of Sociology.** Vol. 1– , No. 1– . Chicago: University of Chicago Press, 1895– . bimonthly. $325/yr. (institutions). ISSN 0002-9602. Available: http://www.journals.uchicago.edu/AJS/home.html (Accessed: December 20, 2004).

Each issue includes as many as ten research articles, review essays, and two- to three-dozen book reviews. The research articles cover a wide range of topics and methodologies. Indexed in: *Sociological Abstracts, Social Science Citation Index, Sociological Collection, Social Sciences Index,* and *Social Work Abstracts.*

157. **American Sociological Review.** Vol. 1– , No. 1– . Washington, DC: American Sociological Association, 1936– . bimonthly. $180/yr. (institutions). ISSN 0003-1224. Available: http://www.asanet.org/journals/asr/ (Accessed: December 20, 2004).

Issues of this American Sociological Association (ASA) journal include approximately a dozen articles. While most of the articles use quantitative methodologies, some use other techniques (e.g., historical, ethnographic) or focus on theoretical issues. Topics covered span the subject specializations within sociology. Indexed in: *Social Sciences Index, Social Work Abstracts, Sociological Abstracts, Social Science Citation Index, Current Contents/Social and Behavioral Sciences.*

158. **Berkeley Journal of Sociology.** Vol. 1– . Berkeley, CA: Sociology Department, University of California at Berkeley, 1955– . annual. $18.75/yr. (institutions). ISSN 0067-5830. Available: http://sociology.berkeley.edu/bjs (Accessed: December 20, 2004).

Issues may address a particular theme, or they may be on diverse topics. However, the editors "tend to favour works of a critical political persuasion." A recent theme issue addressed the sociology of work, while another addressed HIV, sexuality, and sexual orientation. Articles in other issues have been on such topics as race, class, and cultural resources in educational participation of black parents; immigration and destination choices; interpreting weight (i.e., "fatness and thinness as social problems"); nationalism and modernity; negotiating gender; and more. Indexed in: *Sociological Abstracts, Alternative Press Index.*

159. **British Journal of Sociology.** Vol. 1– , No. 1– . London: Routledge, 1950– . quarterly. $320/yr. (institutions). ISSN 0007-1315. Available: http://www.blackwellpublishing.com/journal.asp?ref=0007-1315&site=1 (Accessed: December 20, 2004).

Published on behalf of the London School of Economics, this journal publishes approximately five to ten articles and numerous reviews per issue. Subject coverage is broad, with recent articles on social networks, Norbert Elias, Raymond Williams and the sociology of culture, gender and work, intermarriage and secularization, Islam, and more. Though often quantitative, articles also engage in historical and theoretical analysis. Indexed in: *Sociological Collection, Sociological Abstracts, Social Sciences Index, Social Science Citation Index, Current Contents/Social and Behavioral Sciences.*

160. **British Journal of Sociology of Education.** Vol. 1– , No. 1– . Abingdon, Oxfordshire, England: Carfax, 1980– . quarterly. $1292/yr. (institutions). ISSN 0142-5692. Available: http://www.tandf.co.uk/journals/titles/01425692.asp (Accessed: December 20, 2004).

There are anywhere from six to nine articles per issue, spanning a range of topics and, to some extent, countries. Recent articles have addressed leaving school, Pierre Bourdieu on higher education, student and gender identities, class barriers to equality in higher education, the construction of masculinity, globalization and education, school choice, school restructuring, teacher attitudes and the reproduction of social inequality, Basil Bernstein's code theory, and much more. Review symposia and review essays are also included in some issues. Indexed in: *Sociological Abstracts, Sociology of Education Abstracts, Social Sciences Citation Index, British Education Index,* PsycINFO.

161. **Canadian Journal of Sociology Online.** Available: http://www.arts.ualberta.ca/cjscopy/ (Accessed: December 20, 2004).

The print version of the *Canadian Journal of Sociology* was founded in 1975. This electronic version offers tables of contents of issues, abstracts of articles, and samples of book reviews, as well as announcements regarding teaching positions, upcoming conferences, calls for journal submissions, an e-mail notification service, and more. The journal covers a wide range of topics, theoretical perspectives, and methodologies, with recent articles on such subjects as political sociology, domestic labor, and the social construction of social problems.

162. **Canadian Review of Sociology and Anthropology.** Vol. 1– , No. 1– . Montreal: Canadian Sociology and Anthropology Association, 1964– . quarterly. Can.$75/yr. (institutions). ISSN 0008-4948. Available: http://crsa.icaap. org/ (Accessed: December 20, 2004).

Published by the Canadian Sociology and Anthropology Association, this journal provides broad coverage of the field. Recent articles have focused on such topics as disability, college student life paths, youth labor markets, poverty in Canada, and parental (mother) coping with attention deficit disorder, among others. Articles may be in either English or French, though the abstracts are in both languages. Many of the articles focus on Canadian society. Issues also include book reviews, and fairly recent issues of the journal (with approximately a two-year lag) are available full-text online. A selective conference lecture series is also available full text, as are links to selective other associations and subject pages. Indexed in: *Sociological Abstracts, Social Sciences Index, Sociological Collection, Social Sciences Citation Index, Canadian Periodicals Index.*

163. **Contemporary Sociology: A Journal of Reviews.** Vol. 1– , No. 1– . Washington, DC: American Sociological Association, 1972– . bimonthly. $185/yr. (institutions). ISSN 0094-3061. Available: http://www.asanet.org/pubs/journsub.html (Accessed: December 20, 2004).

The reviews in this ASA journal are divided into two sections: featured essays (review essays), and reviews. The featured essays review new books at some length, and it is common for particular essays to review a number of new books on the same topic. These essays can run to three, double-column pages in length and may include references. The featured essays sometimes focus on a common theme. The second section contains the vast majority of the reviews, which are shorter than the review essays and are organized under broad subject categories for the major specializations in sociology (e.g., theory; methodology and research techniques; inequalities; ideology and cultural production; intimate relationships, family, and life course). Each issue also includes a list of publications received for review, as well as a section for commentary. Indexed in: *Social Sciences Index, Social Science Citation Index, Sociological Abstracts, Book Review Digest, Book Review Index.*

164. **Contexts: Understanding People in Their Social Worlds.** Vol. 1– , No. 1– . Berkeley, CA: University of California Press, 2002– . quarterly. $139/yr.

(institutions). ISSN 1536-5042. Available: http://www.ucpress.edu/journals/ctx/ (Accessed: December 20, 2004).

This is the award-winning new journal from the American Sociological Association. Its purpose is to address a broader readership on important and interesting sociological issues presented in a more accessible way than is done in a traditional research journal. Included are articles, research notes, reviews, letters, and opinions.

165. **Criminology: An Interdisciplinary Journal.** Vol. 1– , No. 1– . Columbus, OH: American Society of Criminology, 1963– . quarterly. $125/yr. (institutions). ISSN 0011-1384. Available: http://www.asc41.com/publications.html (Accessed: December 20, 2004).

Drawing on the social and behavioral sciences, law, criminal justice, and history, articles here focus primarily on empirical research into crime and deviant behavior. Issues typically include six or more articles and exchanges over particular articles. There are also occasional research notes, and a presidential address from the annual conference of the American Society of Criminology, the journal's sponsor. Indexed in: *Sociological Abstracts, Current Content/Social and Behavioral Sciences, Social Sciences Citation Index, Criminal Justice Abstracts, Sociological Collection.*

166. **Critical Sociology.** Vol. 15– , No. 1– . Boston: Brill Academic Publishers, 1988– . 3 issues/yr. $120/yr. (institutions). ISSN 0896-9205. Available: http://www.brill.nl/m_catalogue_sub6_id9386.htm (Accessed: December 20, 2004).

Formerly the *Insurgent Sociologist*, each issue of the journal publishes approximately six articles, as well as book reviews. The articles are written from what may be loosely considered a radical or critical sociological perspective, including Marxist, feminist, postmodernist, and other critical theoretical traditions. Indexed in: *Alternative Press Index, Sociological Abstracts, Academic Search Premier.*

167. **Current Research in Social Psychology.** Iowa City, IA: Center for the Study of Group Processes at the University of Iowa, 1995– . irregular. free. ISSN 1088-7423. Available: http://www.uiowa.edu/~grpproc/crisp/crisp.html (Accessed: December 20, 2004).

This is an electronic, peer-reviewed journal published out of the Center for the Study of Group Processes at the University of Iowa. Its full-text articles are freely available at its Web site. While its publication schedule is somewhat irregular, there are upwards of twenty issues published per volume, with each issue comprised of one article. The journal's editorial policy suggests it will publish articles from diverse theoretical, methodological, and analytical perspectives. Recent articles have addressed issues as ideological consistency in attitude inferences, individual and cultural gender roles, aversive bias towards gay men, and prejudice, among others.

168. **Current Sociology.** Vol. 1– , No. 1– . London: Sage, 1952– . bimonthly. $699.84/yr. (institutions). ISSN 0011-3921. Available: http://www.sagepub.com/journal.aspx?pid=77 (Accessed: December 20, 2004).

Published for the International Sociological Association, this peer-reviewed journal focuses on "shorter articles in all areas of sociology—theories, methods, concepts, substantive research, and national/regional developments of interest to sociologists internationally" (Web site). Particular themes addressed in recent issues include globalization, innovations in statistical analysis, occupational mobility, welfare regimes in advanced countries, Latin American sociology, and much more. It also now includes book review essays on thematically related recent books in the field. Indexed in: *Social Sciences Index, Sociological Abstracts.*

169. **Demography.** Vol. 1– , No. 1– . Silver Spring, MD: Population Association of America, 1964– . quarterly. $100/yr. ISSN 0070-3370. Available: http://www.popassoc.org/publications.html (Accessed: December 20, 2004).

Published by the Population Association of America, this journal includes articles drawn from the social sciences, geography, business, statistics, public health, biology, history, and epidemiology. Articles on theory, methods, or policy are welcome, as are comparative and historical works. Studies on developed and developing countries are also represented. Within issues, articles are grouped under such categories as migration, outcomes for children, labor force, population forecasting, fertility and contraception, mortality, and family and household. The journal is also available full-text online through Project Muse. Indexed in: *Social Sciences Index, Current Contents/Social and Behavioral Sciences, Social Sciences Citation Index.*

170. **Discourse: Studies in the Cultural Politics of Education.** Vol. 1– , No. 1– . Abingdon, Oxfordshire, England: Carfax, 1980– . 3 issues/yr. $535/yr. (institutions). ISSN 0159-6306. Available: http://www.tandf.co.uk/journals/titles/01596306.asp (Accessed: December 20, 2004).

Broadly critical and multidisciplinary in orientation, this journal nonetheless has a distinctly sociological and policy focus. Issues typically contain approximately eight articles, one or two essay reviews, and sometimes shorter book reviews. Throughout, issues of class, gender, race, educational inequality, and the creation of social identity are prominent. The journal is also international in scope. Indexed in: *Sociological Abstracts, Sociological Collection.*

171. **Electronic Journal of Sociology.** 1994– . 3 issues/yr. free. ISSN 1198-3655. Available: http://www.sociology.org (Accessed: December 20, 2004).

The *Electronic Journal of Sociology* is a refereed electronic journal available on the Internet in HTML, pdf, and ASCII formats. Begun in 1994, it publishes three to four issues per year with two to four articles per issue. Editorially, the journal is theoretically, methodologically, and topically diverse. Recent issues include articles on such subjects as male identity development, masculinity and crime, euthanasia, network analysis, Foucault and gerontology, and the Internet, to name but a few. The turnaround time for considering submissions is claimed to be much faster than for print journals. Online publication is touted as a partial response to the concentrated control of and increased price of traditional print journals.

172. **Gender & Society.** Vol. 1– , No. 1– . Thousand Oaks, CA: Sage, 1987– . bimonthly. $518.40/yr. (institutions). ISSN 0891-2432. Available: http://www. sagepub.com/journal.aspx?pid=50 (Accessed: December 20, 2004).

Published in association with the organization Sociologists for Women in Society, this journal is multidisciplinary in appeal and contains numerous articles and reviews dealing with such topics as race and class bias, media representation, sexual harassment, economic inequality, battered women, transgenderism, motherhood and child care, and much more. There are occasional theme issues devoted to a single topic. Indexed in: *Sociological Abstracts, Psychological Abstracts, Women Studies Abstracts, Social Sciences Index, Social Science Citation Index.*

173. **The Gerontologist.** Vol. 1– , No. 1– . Washington, DC: Gerontological Society of America, 1960– . bimonthly. $225/yr. (institutions). ISSN 0016-9013. Available: http://gerontologist.gerontologyjournals.org/ (Accessed: December 20, 2004).

Aging is dealt with in a variety of social and psychological contexts, including work, caregiving and social support, self-esteem, gay and lesbian elders, social engagement, end of life issues, gerontological practice, long-term care, demographic trends, policy, and more. Most issues contain more than a dozen articles grouped around a handful of themes; a symposium section usually has four or five articles on an issue. There are also book and audiovisual reviews. There are four special issues per year. Indexed in: *Social Sciences Index, Social Work Abstracts, Social Science Citation Index*, PsycINFO, *Abstracts in Social Gerontology, Current Contents/Social and Behavioral Sciences.*

174. **Human Organization.** Vol. 1– , No. 1– . Oklahoma City, OK: Society for Applied Anthropology, 1941– . quarterly. $75/yr. ISSN 0018-7259. Available: http://www.sfaa.net/ho/ (Accessed: December 20, 2004).

Though primarily an anthropology journal, this nonetheless publishes articles in social organization and the anthropology of urban life, both of which should interest sociologists. Articles are often international in scope. Recent articles have been on such topics as political ecology, sports, globalization and illegal drug diffusion, and sustainability, among others. As well, the ethnographic techniques should interest qualitative researchers. Indexed in: *Sociological Abstracts, Social Sciences Index*, PsycINFO, *Social Sciences Citation Index.*

175. **Humanity and Society.** Vol. 1– , No. 1– . Indianapolis, IN: Association for Humanist Sociology, 1977– . quarterly. $50/yr. ISSN 0160-5976. Available: http://www.humanistsoc.org/hs.html (Accessed: December 20, 2004).

The journal of the Association for Humanist Sociology, recent articles have covered a wide range of topics from diverse theoretical perspectives, touching on such subject areas as the family, inequality, sex roles, sociological theory, the sociology of knowledge, social change, crime and deviance, and much more. The common thread throughout is the journal's dedication to "contributing to a more human and egalitarian society" (Web site). Indexed in: *Sociological Abstracts, Criminal Justice Abstracts.*

176. **International Journal of the Sociology of Law.** Vol. 1– , No. 1– . London: Academic Press, 1972– . quarterly. $323/yr. ISSN 0194-6596. Available: http://www.elsevier.com/wps/find/journaldescription.cws_home/622848/description#description (Accessed: December 20, 2004).

Issues focus on the "social context and social implications of law, law enforcement, and legal processes" (Web page). Some of the themes covered include immigration law, informal systems of justice, sentencing and punishment, antidiscrimination law, and much more. Articles may focus on not only theoretical research, but also social policy and practice. They are often comparative in scope, and an occasional journal issue is devoted to a special topic. Indexed in: *Current Contents, Sociological Abstract, Criminal Justice Abstracts.*

177. **International Migration Review.** Vol. 1– , No. 1– . New York: Center for Migration Studies, 1966– . quarterly. $96/yr. (institutions). ISSN 0197-9183. Available: http://cmsny.org/imr-publication.htm (Accessed: December 22, 2004).

Each issue has a substantial number of articles and reviews. Articles are often comparative or multidisciplinary, and they address such issues as the labor market, transnational migration, neighborhood change, trade unions, the impact of immigration legislation (e.g., the Personal Responsibility and Work Reconciliation Act), national identity, and more. Indexed in: *Sociological Abstracts, Social Sciences Index, Social Sciences Citation Index, Current Contents/Social and Behavioral Sciences.*

178. **International Studies in Sociology of Education.** Vol. 1– . Wallingford, Oxfordshire: Triangle Books, 1991– . 3 issues/yr. $346/yr. ISSN 0962-0214. Available: http://www.triangle.co.uk/iss/index.htm (Accessed: December 22, 2004).

International in scope, each theme issue includes approximately six articles by often well-known contributors to the sociology of education. There is plenty of policy analysis here, as well as a focus on qualitative methodologies (case studies, historical analysis) and theory. Recent themes have addressed class, inequality, and social reproduction; globalization; class, race, gender and disability; and the state, teacher education, and policy development, among others. Within these themes, compelling topics are addressed, such as home schooling, teacher identities, school choice, inequality and Catholic schooling, citizenship education, geopolitical knowledge among teachers, and inequality in the knowledge economy. Book reviews are included as well. Indexed in: *Sociology of Education Abstracts, Multicultural Education Abstracts.*

179. **Journal of Health and Social Behavior.** Vol. 1– , No. 1– . Washington, DC: American Sociological Association, 1960– . quarterly. $155/yr. (institutions). ISSN 0022-1465. Available: http://www.asanet.org/pubs/journsub.html#JHSB (Accessed: December 22, 2004).

Formerly the *Journal of Health and Human Behavior*, this ASA journal covers a broad range of topics in medical sociology and the social contexts of health, illness, and medicine. Recent articles have focused on such topics as poverty and health trajectories, psychological distress among widows, twin research, contingent staffing in drug treatment organizations, contraceptive self-efficacy among teenagers, and stressful neighborhoods and depression. Indexed in: *Sociological Abstracts, Social Sciences Index,* PsycINFO, *Social Sciences Citation Index.*

180. **Journal of Marriage and the Family.** Vol. 1– , No. 1– . Minneapolis, MN: National Council on Family Relations, 1938– . quarterly. $190/yr. (institutions). ISSN 0022-2445. Available: http://www.ncfr.com/jmf/default.htm (Accessed: December 22, 2004).

Included here are upwards of twenty articles and numerous reviews per issue, with articles arranged under broad subject categories (e.g., parent and child relations, work and family, fathers and fatherhood, child and adolescent well-being, marriage and premarital relationships, cohabitation and marriage). Articles come from various disciplines and reflect a diversity of theoretical and methodological approaches. There are also comments on earlier articles, as well as an occasional symposium or group of articles on a particular theme. Indexed in: *Sociological Collection, Sociological Abstracts, Social Work Abstracts, Social Sciences Index, Social Sciences Citation Index,* PsycINFO.

181. **Journal of Social Policy.** Vol. 1– , No. 1– . Cambridge: Cambridge University Press, 1972– . quarterly. $320/yr. (institutions). ISSN 0047-2794. Available: http://uk.cambridge.org/journals/journal_catalogue.asp?mnemonic=jsp (Accessed: December 22, 2004).

Though primarily British in focus, this journal's international and comparative coverage should be of interest to policy sociologists. Included are theoretical and empirical research articles on a range of policy issues, such as youth unemployment, poverty, the labor market, the welfare state and welfare policy, disability, postmodern social policy, housing debt crises, researching living standards, feminism and child daycare, women and health in China, and work and care in the life course, among others. The social policy digest that summarizes recent policy developments in the United Kingdom has migrated from the print journal to online. There is also a large section of book reviews. This is the journal of the Social Policy Association. Indexed in: *Social Sciences Index, Sociological Abstracts, Social Sciences Citation Index.*

182. **Journal of Social Psychology.** Vol. 1– , No. 1– . Washington, DC: Heldref, 1930– . bimonthly. $181/yr. ISSN 0022-4545. Available: http://www.heldref.org/jsp/php (Accessed: December 22, 2004).

The emphasis here is on "experimental, empirical, and field studies of groups, cultural effects, cross-national problems, language, and ethnicity" (Web site). In addition to the approximately eight articles per issue, there is often a shorter article included in a section titled "Replications and Refinements." Indexed in: *Current Contents/Social and Behavioral Sciences, Social Sciences Citation Index,* PsycINFO, *Sociological Collection, Social Sciences Citation Index.*

183. **Journal of Sociology.** Vol. 1– , No. 1– . Thousand Oaks, CA: Sage, 1965– . quarterly. $361.92/yr. (institutions). ISSN 1440-7883. Available: http://www.sagepub.com/journal.aspx?pid=273 (Accessed: December 22, 2004).

Formerly the *Australian and New Zealand Journal of Sociology*, recent issues address areas such as class/inequality, social networks, gender roles, the family, and work, among others. This was formerly the journal of the Sociological Association of Australia and New Zealand, which has now split into The Australian Sociological Association, the current sponsor of the journal, and the Sociology Association of Aotearoa (New Zealand). Indexed in: *Social Science Citation Index, Psychological Abstracts*, PsycINFO, *Sociology of Education Abstracts, Current Contents/Social and Behavioral Sciences.*

184. **Journal of Sport and Social Issues.** Vol 1– , No. 1– . Thousand Oaks, CA: Sage, 1976– . quarterly. $382.08/yr. (institutions). ISSN 0193-7235. Available: http://www.sagepub.com/journal.aspx?pid=149 (Accessed: December 22, 2004).

The official journal of the Center for the Study of Sport in Society at Northeastern University, each issue includes a "Focus" section or symposium of research articles and commentary on a theme; a "Trends" section on breaking issues; and a "View" section of commentaries. Topics are quite diverse, with recent articles on the home advantage, tobacco sponsorship of sports, major league baseball reform, sport and politics, race, sports films, football (soccer) and labor migration, and more. Articles are frequently, though not exclusively qualitative in their methodology, and a variety of disciplines and theoretical perspectives are represented. Indexed in: *Alternative Press Index, Sociological Abstracts, Sport Discus, Social Science Citation Index.*

185. **Journals of Gerontology. Series B, Psychological Sciences and Social Sciences.** Vol. 50B– , No. 1– . Washington, DC: Gerontological Society of America, 1995– . bimonthly. $273/yr. (institutions). ISSN 1079-5014. Available: http://psychsoc.gerontologyjournals.org/ (Accessed: December 22, 2004).

Formally the *Journal of Gerontology*, this is now two journals focusing on gerontology published in one bound issue. One journal is for the psychological sciences and one is for the social sciences, with each journal taking up half of the issue and having its own title page, table of contents, and editorial statements. Approximately six to eight articles are included in each of these two journals. Throughout, articles use quantitative methodologies while focusing on a variety of topics, such as the effect of illness and religion on activity level, trends in cognitive ability among the elderly, suicide trends among the old and oldest old, support provision by disabled older adults, and place integration in assisted living facilities, among others. Indexed in: *Social Sciences Index, Abstracts in Social Gerontology, Social Sciences Citation Index,* PsycINFO, *Current Contents/Social and Behavioral Sciences.*

186. **Population Studies.** Vol. 1– , No. 1– . London: Routledge, 1947– . 3 issues/yr. $208/yr. ISSN 0032-4728. Available: http://www.tandf.co.uk/journals/titles/00324728.asp (Accessed: December 22, 2004).

Published on behalf of the Population Investigation Committee at the London School of Economics, this is an important source of research in demography and population. There are approximately seven or eight articles per issue focusing on "advances in methods of demographic analysis, conceptual and mathematical theories of demographic dynamics and behavior, and the use of these theories and methods to extend scientific knowledge and to inform policy and practice" (Web page). A substantial number of book reviews are included as well. Indexed in: *Social Science Citation Index, Sociological Abstracts, Current Contents/Social and Behavioral Sciences.*

187. **Public Opinion Quarterly.** Vol. 1– , No. 1– . Oxford, United Kingdom: Oxford University Press, 1937– . quarterly. $125/yr. (institutions). ISSN 0033-362X. Available: http://www.poq.oujournals.org/ (Accessed: December 22, 2004).

This is the journal of the American Association of Public Opinion Research and is a major source of research on survey research methods and techniques. Issues include research articles, articles on polls, review essays, and book reviews. Starting with volume 68, this will be published by Oxford University Press. Indexed in: *Social Sciences Index, Sociological Abstracts, Sociological Collection,* PsycINFO.

188. **Race & Class.** Vol. 16– , No. 2– . London: Sage, 1974– . quarterly. $287/yr. (institutions). ISSN 0306-3968. Available: http://www.sagepub.co.uk/journal.aspx?pid=75 (Accessed: December 22, 2004).

The journal's subtitle (*A Journal on Racism, Empire and Globalisation*) suggests its critical and international orientation. The Web site states that it is the "foremost English language journal on racism and imperialism in the world today" (Sage Web site). Issues can include half a dozen articles, a few commentaries, and some book reviews. Over and above the topics of race, racism, and the reproduction of class inequalities, issues of decolonialization, globalization, nationalism, and development are prominent. Indexed in: *Alternative Press Index, Sociological Abstracts, Social Sciences Citation Index.*

189. **Rural Sociology.** Vol. 1– , No. 1– . Columbia, MO: Rural Sociological Society, 1936– . quarterly. $125/yr. (institutions). ISSN 0036-0112. Available: http://www.ruralsociology.org/pubs/RuralSociology (Accessed: December 22, 2004).

While falling within the purview of rural sociology, articles still cover a range of subtopics. These can include such subjects as social capital in rural community improvement, economic development, countywide support for environmental protection, suburbanization and rural communities, globalization, rural-urban contrasts, and more. There are approximately six articles per issue, and a comparable number of book reviews are also included. Indexed in: *Sociological Collection, Social Sciences Index, Social Sciences Citation Index, Sociological Abstracts.*

190. **Social Forces.** Vol. 1– , No. 1– . Chapel Hill, NC: University of North Carolina Press, 1922– . quarterly. $92/yr. (institutions). ISSN 0037-7732. Available: http://socialforces.unc.edu/ (Accessed: December 22, 2004).

Associated with the Southern Sociological Society, *Social Forces* publishes approximately a dozen articles and some two dozen reviews per issue. The topics covered span the subject specializations in sociology, including work, social groups and movements, gender, family, crime, social inequality, social mobility, social support/networks, and more. Articles employ both quantitative and qualitative/historical methodologies. Indexed in *Sociological Abstracts, Social Sciences Index, Social Sciences Citation Index, Sociological Collection.*

191. **Social Identities.** Vol. 1– , No. 1– . Basingstoke, United Kingdom: Carfax, 1995– . 6 issues/yr. $748/yr. (institutions). ISSN 1350-4630. Available: http://www.tandf.co.uk/journals/carfax/13504630.asp (Accessed: December 22, 2004).

As stated by the editors in the first issue, the journal's intent is "to serve as a forum for contesting ideas and debates pertaining to the formations of, and transformations in, socially significant identities such as race, nation, ethnicity, gender and class, their attendant forms of material exclusion and power, as well as the political and cultural possibilities these identifications open up" (vol. 1, no. 1, p. 3). The journal is international and multidisciplinary, and sociological concerns, broadly construed, are clearly central. Issues include six or more articles and an occasional book review. Indexed in: *Sociological Abstracts, Sociological Collection,* PsycINFO.

192. **Social Indicators Research.** Vol. 1– , No. 1– . Dordrecht, Netherlands: Kluwer, 1974– . 9 issues/yr. $1350/yr. ISSN 0303-8300. Available: http://www.kluweronline.com/issn/0303-8300 (Accessed: December 22, 2004).

Approximately six articles per issue focus on quality-of-life measurement and well-being from an international and interdisciplinary perspective. The research may be philosophical, empirical, or methodological in nature, and its focus can range from the individual to international systems. Topics covered span many of the sociological specializations, including health, religion, welfare, poverty, stratification, population, mental health, social customs and morality, and more. Indexed in: *Sociological Abstracts, Current Content/Social and Behavioral Sciences, Social Sciences Citation Index,* PsycINFO.

193. **Social Networks.** Vol. 1– , No. 1– . Amsterdam: Elsevier, 1978– . quarterly. $423/yr. (institutions). ISSN 0378-8733. Available: http://www.elsevier.com/wps/find/journaldescription.cws_home/505596/description#description (Accessed: December 22, 2004).

This journal of The International Network for Social Network Analysis publishes three or four articles per issue that make a "theoretical or methodological contribution to the study of social networks" (Web page), or that are case studies of particular networks. Indexed in: *Social Sciences Citation Index, Current Contents/Social and Behavioral Sciences, Sociological Abstracts.*

194. **Social Problems.** Vol. 1– , No. 1– . Berkeley, CA: University of California Press, 1953– . quarterly. $136/yr. (institutions). ISSN 0037-7791. Available: http://www.ucpress.edu/journals/sp/ (Accessed: December 22, 2004).

This is the official journal of the Society for the Study of Social Problems (SSSP). Each issue contains approximately seven articles, often arranged under broad themes (e.g., workplace and neighborhood politics; environmental problems; fear of crime; race, gender and wages; social and cultural capital). Also included is the presidential address given at the SSSP annual conference. Indexed in: *Current Contents/Social and Behavioral Sciences, Sociological Abstracts, Social Sciences Index, Social Sciences Citation Index, Social Work Abstracts,* PsycINFO.

195. **Social Psychology Quarterly.** Vol. 1– , No. 1– . Washington, DC: American Sociological Association, 1937– . quarterly. $120/yr. (institutions). ISSN 0190-2725. Available: http://www.stanford.edu/group/spq/ (Accessed: December 22, 2004).

Formerly titled *Sociometry* and *Social Psychology*, this ASA journal includes upwards of six articles and a few research notes per issue. Articles employ a variety of methodologies and theoretical perspectives, including symbolic interactionism and ethnomethodology. Topics of the articles are varied, though there are occasional theme issues (e.g., race, racism, and discrimination). The focus throughout is on "the study of the relations of individuals to one another, to groups, collectivities and institutions" (Web site). Indexed in: *Social Sciences Index,* PsycINFO, *Sociological Abstracts, Social Sciences Citation Index.*

196. **Social Science and Medicine.** Vol. 1– , No. 1– . Oxford, United Kingdom: Elsevier Science; Pergamon, 1982– . semimonthly in two volumes. $4,393/yr. (institutions). ISSN 0277-9536. Available: http://www.elsevier.com/wps/find/journaldescription.cws_home/315/description#description (Accessed: December 22, 2004).

International and interdisciplinary in scope, this journal is an important one for medical sociologists and medical anthropologists interested in theory, policy, or practice. A range of social factors in the provision and outcome of health care are addressed, and both physical and mental health issues are represented. Journal issues also include book reviews, and specific issues have been devoted to conference papers (e.g., the International Conference on the Social Sciences and Medicine).

197. **Social Science Quarterly.** Vol. 49– , No. 1– . Oxford, United Kingdom: Blackwell, 1968– . quarterly. $195/yr. (institutions). ISSN 0038-4941. Available: http://www.blackwellpublishing.com/journal.asp?ref=0038-4941&site=1 (Accessed: December 22, 2004).

Published on behalf of the Southwestern Social Science Association, this is an interdisciplinary journal with plenty of sociology contributors and topics. Issues include approximately twelve articles on either a range of social science subjects, or on a special theme. Sociologically interesting topics covered in recent issues have included political sociology; causes of unequal educational outcomes; race, class, and inequality; gender and the Internet; affirmative action policy; child care policy reform; sexual harassment training and attitude change; welfare reform; and more. Also included are book reviews, review essays, and research notes. Indexed in: *Current Contents/Social and Behavioral Science, Sociological Abstracts, Sociological Collection,* PsycINFO, *Social Sciences Index*.

198. **Social Science Research.** Vol. 1– , No. 1– . Amsterdam: Elsevier Science, 1972– . quarterly. $534/yr. (institutions). ISSN 0049-089X. Available: http://www.elsevier.com/wps/find/journaldescription.cws_home/622946/de scription#description (Accessed: December 22, 2004).

Spanning a range of social science topics, articles here nonetheless share the journal's focus on methodology and quantitative research. Recent articles have been written on cohabiting couples, flexible staffing, neighborhood distress and school dropouts, job mobility, and women's employment and fertility history, to name a few. Indexed in: *Sociological Abstracts, Social Sciences Citation Index*.

199. **Sociological Focus.** Vol. 1– , No. 1– . Cincinnati, OH: Department of Sociology, University of Cincinnati, 1967– . four issues/yr. $85/yr. (institutions). ISSN 0038-0237. Available: http://www.ncsanet.org/sociological_focus/ (Accessed: December 27, 2004).

The journal of the North Central Sociological Association, this includes both articles and, annually, the text of the presidential address at the NCSA conference. There are approximately four or five articles per issue. Topically, they span the sociological subdisciplines and employ primarily quantitative methodologies. There are occasional theme issues, such as those on the Latino experience and social movements. Indexed in: *Sociological Abstracts*.

200. **Sociological Inquiry.** Vol. 1– , No. 1– . Oxford, United Kingdom: Blackwell, 1930– . quarterly. $120/yr. (institutions). ISSN 0038-0245. Available: http://www.auburn.edu/academic/journals/sociological_inquiry/ (Accessed: December 27, 2004).

This is the journal of Alpha Kappa Delta, the International Sociology Honor Society. Articles and book reviews are included, with recent articles addressing such topics as masculinity, childlessness, emotions, democratization in Weber's political sociology, the effects of free trade on democracy/development/environmental protection, the urban poor, anomie and strain, the Columbine High School shootings and the media, and more. There are occasional special (theme) sections. Indexed in: *Social Sciences Index, Sociological Abstracts, Social Sciences Citation Index*.

201. **Sociological Methods & Research (SMR).** Vol. 1– , No. 1– . Thousand Oaks, CA: Sage, 1972– . quarterly. $538.56/yr. (institutions). ISSN 0049-1241. Available: http://www.sagepub.com/journal.aspx?pid=120 (Accessed: December 27, 2004).

Also known by its acronym, *SMR*, this journal is devoted to clarifying methodological problems and advancing understanding in the areas of research methodology and statistics. There are about four articles per issue, and some book reviews may also be included. Indexed in: *Current Contents/Social and Behavioral Sciences, Sociological Abstracts, Sociology of Education Abstracts.*

202. **Sociological Perspectives.** Vol. 1– , No. 1– . Berkeley, CA: University of California Press, 1958– . quarterly. $251/yr. (institutions). ISSN 0731-1214. Available: http://www.ucpress.edu/journals/sop/ (Accessed: December 27, 2004).

As the Pacific Sociological Association's official journal, this publishes about six articles per issue. The address given by the association's president at the annual conference is also included. A wide range of topics are treated, as reflected in the recent inclusion of articles on socioeconomic status and anger across the life course, value changes among high school students, the effect of single-sex secondary schooling on college choice, and school segregation. A variety of theoretical approaches and methodologies are employed. There are also special theme issues, such as the recent one on gender and sport. Abstracts in Spanish, Chinese, and Japanese are also provided. Indexed in: *Sociological Abstracts, Social Sciences Index, Social Sciences Citation Index,* PsycINFO.

203. **The Sociological Quarterly.** Vol. 1– , No. 1– . Berkeley, CA: University of California Press, 1960– . quarterly. $238/yr. (institutions). ISSN 0038-0253. Available: http://www.ucpress.edu/journals/tsq/ (Accessed: December 27, 2004).

The "Official Journal of the Midwest Sociological Society," this publishes seven or eight articles per issue. Recent articles have addressed such subjects as social movements, gender, social identity, racial segregation and special education, technology and gender, and ethnicity and academic achievement, among others. A range of methodologies and theoretical perspectives are represented. Indexed in: *Social Sciences Index, Sociological Abstracts, Social Sciences Citation Index, Social Work Abstracts,* PsycINFO.

204. **Sociological Research Online.** Guilford, United Kingdom: Department of Sociology, University of Surrey, 1996– . quarterly. £110/yr. ISSN 1360-7804. Available: http://www.socresonline.org.uk/home.html (Accessed: December 27, 2004).

Published out of the United Kingdom, this electronic journal focuses on applied sociology dealing with "theoretical, empirical and methodological discussions which engage with current political, cultural and intellectual topics and debates" (Web page). Each issue includes refereed articles, a review article or two, and book reviews. Additional Internet links of interest to sociologists are also included. There are occasional theme issues, such as those on the Gulf War, adulthood, and sexuality and the church.

205. **The Sociological Review.** Vol. 1– , No. 1– . Oxford, United Kingdom: Blackwell, 1953– . quarterly. $374/yr. (institutions). ISSN 0038-0261. Avail-

able: http://www.blackwellpublishing.com/journal.asp?ref=0038-0261&site=1 (Accessed: December 27, 2004).

This is a British sociology journal published on behalf of Keele University. Its articles reflect primarily qualitative, interpretive, or social constructionist approaches to social analysis, with articles focusing on a range of issues or debates within the field. Recent articles have addressed masculinity, the fact/value debate, social science contract researchers, the environmental movement, teenage pregnancy, the sociology of fear, and much more. There are approximately six articles per issue, as well as a substantial book review section. Indexed in: *Social Sciences Index, Sociological Abstracts, Sociological Collection, Current Content/Social and Behavioral Sciences, Social Sciences Citation Index, Sociological Collection.*

206. **Sociological Spectrum.** Vol. 1– , No. 1– . Basingstoke, United Kingdom: Taylor and Francis, 1981– . quarterly. $534/yr. (institutions). ISSN 0273-2173. Available: http://www.tandf.co.uk/journals/titles/02732173.asp (Accessed: December 27, 2004).

The official journal of the Mid-South Sociological Association, *Sociological Spectrum* publishes five or six articles per issue and covers a range of theories, research methodologies and techniques, and topics in the fields of sociology, social psychology, anthropology, and political science. Recent article topics have included welfare to work; race, class and femininities; sex stereotyping in children's commercials; stigma management among white middle-class singles; employment in low-wage work; and much more. Occasional issues are devoted to special topics (e.g., immigrants in the New South). Indexed in: *Sociological Abstracts, Sociological Collection, Social Sciences Citation Index.*

207. **Sociological Theory.** Vol. 1– , No. 1– . Cambridge, MA: Blackwell, 1983– . quarterly. $202/yr. (institutions). ISSN 0735-2751. Available: http://www.blackwellpublishing.com/journal.asp?ref=0735-2751&site=1 (Accessed: December 27, 2004).

Another of the American Sociological Association journals, articles here predictably focus on sociological theorists, theories, and schools of thought. Recent articles have been on Sigmund Freud, globalization, marriage, ecological-evolutionary theory, Durkheimian solidarity, identity theory, and a theory of movement repression, to name a few. Indexed in: *Sociological Abstracts, Sociological Collection.*

208. **Sociology.** Vol. 1– , No. 1– . London: Sage, 1967– . 5 issues/yr. £232/yr. ISSN 0038-0385. Available: http://www.sagepub.co.uk/journal.aspx?pid= 105783 (Accessed: December 27, 2004).

This is a journal of the British Sociological Association. Issues include both theoretical and empirical research on a wide range of topics. There are anywhere from four to ten articles per issue, as well as research notes, debates, and numerous reviews. Indexed in: *Sociological Abstracts, Social Sciences Index, Social Sciences Citation Index.*

209. **Sociology of Education.** Vol. 1– , No. 1– . Washington, DC: American Sociological Association, 1927– . quarterly. $155/yr. (institutions). ISSN 0038-0407. Available: http://www.asanet.org/pubs/journsub.html#SOE (Accessed: December 27, 2004).

An American Sociological Association (ASA) journal, *Sociology of Education* primarily publishes quantitative research and policy-related articles. It addresses a wide range of topics in the field and does so from a variety of theoretical perspectives, including variants of conflict theory, feminist theory, and social constructionism. There are approximately four to six articles in each issue, with an occasional issue devoted to a special topic (e.g., sociology of school and classroom language). Indexed in: *Sociological Abstracts, Social Sciences Index, Sociology of Education Abstracts, Social Sciences Citation Index.*

210. **Sociology of Health & Illness.** Vol. 1– , No. 1– . Oxford, United Kingdom: Blackwell, 1979– . 7 issues/yr. $685/yr. (institutions). ISSN 0141-9889. Available: http://www.blackwellpublishing.com/journal.asp?ref=0141-9889& site=1 (Accessed: December 27, 2004).

A medical sociology journal, issues include approximately six articles and cover a wide range of topics in the sociology of health, medicine, and illness. For example, recent articles have addressed health and the media, patient rights in mental health care, the illness experience, technology and medical practice, the social organization of health care, and more. A half dozen or more book reviews are included, too, as are occasional rejoinders to earlier articles. In addition to the six regular issues per year, there is a seventh theme issue on current topics and debates, as well as other theme issues (e.g., a retrospective on the journal). Indexed in: *Sociological Abstracts, Social Sciences Citation Index, Sociological Collection.*

211. **Sociology of Sport Journal.** Vol. 1– , No. 1– . Champaign, IL: Human Kinetics, 1984– . quarterly. $208/yr. (institutions). ISSN 0741-1235. Available: http://www.humankinetics.com/products/journals/journal.cfm?id=SSJ (Accessed: December 27, 2004).

International in scope and varied in subject focus, a typical issue includes four or five articles and occasional research notes and book reviews. Recent articles have addressed the subjects of injury time; race and class in neighborhood baseball; sport and communities; masculinity and sports; national sport policy; race relations in school sports; and sport, sexuality, and gender, among others. Also included is the presidential address from the annual conference of the North American Society for the Sociology of Sport, the journal's sponsor. Indexed in: *Sociological Abstracts, Current Contents/Social and Behavioral Sciences, ERIC, Social Sciences Citation Index, Physical Education Index, Sport Discus.*

212. **Symbolic Interaction.** Vol. 1– , No. 1– . Berkeley, CA: University of California Press, 1977– . quarterly. $251/yr. (institutions). ISSN 0195-6086. Available: http://www.ucpress.edu/journals/si/index.htm (Accessed: December 27, 2004).

The official journal of The Society for the Study of Symbolic Interaction (SSSI), this is a major outlet for work in symbolic interactionism and related perspectives. Issues can include six or more articles, sometimes on a central theme, a few book reviews, and an occasional rejoinder to a previous article. There is an author/title index at the end of each volume. Indexed in: *Sociological Abstracts,* PsycINFO, *Sociological Collection, Social Sciences Citation Index.*

213. **Teaching Sociology.** Vol. 1– , No. 1– . Washington, DC: American Sociological Association, 1973– . quarterly. $155/yr. (institutions). ISSN 0092-055X. Available: http://www.asanet.org/pubs/journsub.html#TS (Accessed: December 27, 2004).

The articles in this journal "range from experimental studies of teaching and learning to broad, synthetic essays on pedagogically important issues. The general intent is to share theoretically stimulating and practically useful information and advice with teachers" (Web page). Included are sections for articles, notes, issues, comments and replies, review essays, and book reviews. While a range of teaching topics may be covered, there are also occasional theme issues. The book reviews focus on works that could serve as texts or supplemental texts in courses, and the reviewers' comments emphasize the teaching-related strengths and weaknesses of the book. Indexed in: *Sociological Abstracts, Social Sciences Citation Index,* ERIC, *Current Contents/Social and Behavioral Sciences.*

214. **Theory and Society.** Vol. 1– , No. 1– . Dordrecht, The Netherlands: Kluwer Academic Publishers, 1974– . bimonthly. $503/yr. (institutions). ISSN 0304-2421. Available: http://www.kluweronline.com/issn/0304-2421 (Accessed: December 27, 2004).

Subject areas emphasized here include political sociology and political economy, global development, social change, and sociological theory (particularly as applied to development issues and change). Articles are often theoretical, historical or comparative, and are less likely to make use of quantitative methodologies. A typical journal issue can contain anywhere from four to ten articles and some book reviews. There is an occasional theme issue (e.g., on Pierre Bourdieu). Indexed in: *Sociological Abstracts, Current Contents/Social and Behavioral Sciences, Social Sciences Citation Index.*

215. **Theory, Culture, and Society.** Vol. 1– , No. 1– . London: Sage, 1982– . 6 issues/yr. $808/yr. (institutions). ISSN 0263-2764. Available: http://www.sagepub.com/journal.aspx?pid=106 (Accessed: December 27, 2004).

Recent issues have covered such topics as the Internet, Pierre Bourdieu, Lucie Irigaray, reflexive modernization, and the sociology of knowledge, among others. There is a consistent focus on major contemporary and historical theorists, including Weber, Simmel, Goffman, Bell, Foucault, Habermas, Deleuze, Elias, Lyotard, and Bourdieu, just to name a few. Occasionally, there may be a theme issue (e.g., sociality and materiality), or an interview with a well-known theorist (e.g., Jurgen Habermas). There are approximately eight articles per issue. Indexed in: *Sociological Abstracts, Alternative Press Index, Social Sciences Citation Index*.

216. **Urban Affairs Review.** Vol. 30– , No. 1– . Thousand Oaks, CA: Sage, 1995– . bimonthly. $657.60/yr. (institutions). ISSN 1078-0874. Available: http://www.sagepub.com/journal.aspx?pid=41 (Accessed: December 27, 2004).

Formerly the *Urban Affairs Quarterly*, this includes primarily empirical research articles falling within such areas as urban policy, economic development, residential and community development, governance and service delivery, comparative urban research, and the cultural dynamics of cities. Recent issues have addressed such topics as housing vouchers, the impact of community development corporations, property taxes, access to mental health services among female welfare recipients, and the effect of 9/11 on cities. Issues typically include about five articles, a comparable number of reviews, and an occasional research note. Indexed in: *Sociological Abstracts, Social Sciences Index, Social Sciences Citation Index*.

217. **Work and Occupations.** Vol. 1– , No. 1– . Thousand Oaks, CA: Sage, 1974– . quarterly. $546.24/yr. (institutions). ISSN 0730-8884. Available: http://www.sagepub.com/journal.aspx?pid=162 (Accessed: December 27, 2004).

International in coverage, this journal typically includes four or more articles and as many book reviews. Articles address such topics as labor management relations, organizational culture, socialization processes, work group dynamics, violence, labor force trends, and work and family. There are also occasional special issues devoted to a single theme. Indexed in: *Sociological Abstracts, Current Contents/Social and Behavioral Sciences,* PsycINFO, *Social Sciences Citation Index*.

218. **Work, Employment, and Society.** Vol. 1– , No. 1– . London: Sage, 1987– . quarterly. $314.88/yr. ISSN 0950-0170. Available: http://www.sagepub.com/journal.aspx?pid=301 (Accessed: December 27, 2004).

Recent articles have covered such topics as mental health and absence from work, gender inequality at work, race equality policies, British trade unions, job satisfaction, and self-employed workers, among others. Book reviews are also included. This is a journal of the British Sociological Association. Indexed in: *Sociological Abstracts, Social Sciences Citation Index*.

World Wide Web Sites and Organizations

General

219. **A Sociological Tour through Cyberspace.** Available: http://www.trinity.edu/~mkearl/index.html (Accessed: April 27, 2004).

Created by a sociology professor at Trinity University, this site is incredibly rich in the variety of information it provides and in its links to other useful Web sites. Included here are numerous links to general sociology Web sites, specific sociological subject areas, online journals, methods and statistics, a guide to writing research papers, pop culture analysis and cultural criticism, online data analysis tools, and much more. Links to specific subject areas (e.g., sociology of knowledge, gerontology, family, inequality, social psychology) include explanation and discussion, links to related sites, and occasionally some learning exercises. There are a number of interesting op-ed pieces, as well as an online sociology game, Social Jeopardy.

220. Sociology Central Home Page. Available: http://www.sociology.org.uk (Accessed: May 3, 2004).

This UK Web site provides a wealth of sociological information. The resources section features a variety of useful items from lesson plans and worksheets, to software and videos. A message board is also provided, as are links to evaluated sociology sites, and a bookshop. The site map is very useful for navigating through the Web site's many features.

221. SocioSite: Going Dutch Sociology. Available: http://www2.fmg.uva.nl/sociosite/ (Accessed: May 4, 2004).

Maintained by the Sociological Institute of the University of Amsterdam, this Web site provides links to sociological subjects, sociologists, journals, data archives, departments, research centers, news groups, and more. It is worldwide in coverage and its subject guide includes virtually any specialization in the field of sociology.

222. The SocioWeb. Available: http://www.socioweb.com/~markbl/socioweb/ (Accessed: May 7, 2004).

This is one of the major guides to the wide variety of sociological information on the World Wide Web. It is organized into categories for "Net Indexes & Guides", "Commerial Sites", "Giants of Sociology", "Journals & 'Zines", "Learning Sociology", "Sociological Theory", "Sociological Associations", "Sociology in Action", "Surveys and Statistics", "Topical Research", "University Departments", and "Writings." The bookstore section is also organized into categories: "An Introduction to Sociology," "The Great Theorists", and "Cutting-Edge Sociology." Chat@The SocioWeb, an online discussion list, is also featured.

223. WWW Virtual Library: Sociology. Available: http://socserv.mcmaster.ca/w3virtsoclib/ (Accessed: April 21, 2004).

This resource provides links to a wide range of sociology-related sources on the World Wide Web. Included are links to institutions (including departments of sociology) and to information in related disciplines and fields. An Internet resources category provides links to research centers, resource directories, discussion groups (see below), electronic journals and newsletters, organizations, and more.

224. WWW Virtual Library: Sociology Discussion, Newsgroups, Listservs, Chats. Available: http://socserv.mcmaster.ca/w3virtsoclib/discuss.htm (Accessed: May 4, 2004).

As part of the *WWW Virtual Library: Sociology* site (see above) this resource provides a comprehensive list of discussion and news groups, listservs, and chat services relevant to the field of sociology. The information is arranged as "Indexes to Mailing Lists," "Archived Listservs," and "Newsgroups." Internet addresses for these resources are provided, as well as instructions on how to subscribe.

225. **Yahoo!-Social Sciences: Sociology.** Available: http://www.yahoo.com/Social_Science/Sociology (Accessed: May 5, 2004).

Another of the major guides to World Wide Web sociology sites, this resource provides links to research, organizations, journals, institutes, and papers, as well as to more specific sites in criminology, social psychology, and urban studies.

Organizations

226. **American Sociological Association (ASANet).** Available: http://www.asanet.org/ (Accessed: April 15, 2004).

The *ASANet* provides a guide to the upcoming annual meeting program highlights, as well as an annual meeting archives and information on other meetings. It also includes an employment bulletin, a description of new and existing publications (including ASA journals), media releases, membership information, descriptions of the forty-three ASA sections, and governance and committee information.

227. **Association for Humanist Sociology (AHS).** Available: http://www.humanistsoc.org/index.html (Accessed: April 15, 2004).

The AHS was founded in 1976 with the goal of more actively addressing problems of equality, peace, and social justice. It constitutes a support network for sociologists desiring to make their discipline more relevant to people's needs. This site discusses membership in the association, its journal, *Humanity and Society*, and the newsletter *The Humanist Sociologist*, the annual meetings, the AHS Internet discussion list (AHS-Talk), and links to home pages of AHS members.

228. **The Australian Sociological Association (TASA).** Available: http://www.tasa.org.au/ (Accessed: April 21, 2004).

This home page has information on TASA Online Forums, membership procedures, executive committee, journals (*Journal of Sociology* and *Health Sociology Review*) and newsletter (*NEXUS: The TASA Newsletter*), awards and conferences, sociology careers and study, and the association's constitution and ethical guidelines. The resources section offers a myriad of links to other sociology sites on the Internet.

229. **The British Sociological Association (BSA).** Available: http://www.britsoc.co.uk (Accessed May 7, 2004).

The British Sociological Association (BSA) is the professional organization of British sociologists. This site features an introduction to sociology, professional standards, as well as information on the organization of the BSA and information on the several association prizes. Also available is membership information, including a special section for students; and some thirty different online study groups. Conference information and a list of BSA events is also provided. BSA publishes the academic journals *Sociology*, and *Work, Employment and Society*; a sample issue of the association newsletter, *Network*, is also found on this site.

230. **California Sociological Association (CSA).** Available: http://www.californiasociologists.com/ (Accessed: April 16, 2004).

Included here are news items related to the organization, information about the annual meetings, membership costs and procedures, and details on subscribing to the association's discussion list. The online newsletter archive covers 1998 to the present. There is also information on the organization's officers and history, organization involvement, other conferences, publishing opportunities, and related Web sites (including sociology organizations).

231. **Canadian Sociology and Anthropology Association. La Societe' canadienne de sociologie et d'anthropologie.** Available: http://www.csaa.ca (Accessed: December 27, 2004).

This CSAA/SCSA Web site includes information on awards, membership and subscriptions, sturcture and committees, the 2005 annual meeting, publications, book reviews online, job opportunities, and more.

232. **Culture Section.** Available: http://www.asanet.org/sections/culture.html. Independent section homepage (Culture Web): http://www.ibiblio.org/culture/ (Accessed: April 13, 2004).

One of the American Sociological Association's (ASA) interest groups, the Culture Section maintains a Web site that describes the sections officers, subcommittees, and services. It also includes an archive (1995–present) of the section newsletter, *Culture*. A link to the ASA Theory section's academic discussion list, Theory/Culture/History Discussion, is included. This site also features announcements about section news and member publications, and conference sessions. Links to research networks, and information for student members is also provided. This site can also be found through the ASA's Web site, *ASANet.*

233. **The European Sociological Association (ESA).** Available: http://www.valt.helsinki.fi/esa/ (Accessed: May 4, 2004).

Established in the early 1990s, the purpose of the ESA is "to facilitate sociological research, teaching and communication on European issues" (from the ESA mission statement on the association's Web page). Information on the Web site includes a brief history of the association, its conferences and research networks, as well as its membership and governance information. In addition, there is a description of how to submit material to the association's newsletter, *European Sociologist*, which is available online from 2002–present. Also included is information on how to join the discussion list of the same name, *european-sociologist* (Available: jiscmail@jiscmail.ac.uk). To join the list at this address, type the message *join european-sociology firstname(s) lastname.* Other publication information includes the association's two academic publications, *European Societies*, the ESA journal; and *Studies in European Societies*, the ESA monographic series.

234. ISA (International Sociological Association). Available: http://www.ucm.es/info/isa/ (Accessed: May 7, 2004).

The ISA was founded in 1949 under the auspices of UNESCO, and has members from over 109 countries. The purpose of the association is to promote sociology and represent sociologists throughout the world. This site covers the association's research networks and publications, and provides information on membership (both individual and collective), as well as world congress and conference information. A list of the collective members, and links to their Web sites, is available. ISA UNESCO scholarship information for sociology PhD students, and current employment opportunities, are also provided.

235. Mid-South Sociological Association (MSSA). Available: http://www.midsouthsoc.org (Accessed: April 28, 2004).

Included here is an announcement of the upcoming annual meeting, a list of executive council members and past presidents, a membership form, a membership listing with accompanying Web home-page addresses, and information on the MSSA journal, *Sociological Spectrum.* There are numerous links to other social science Web sites.

236. Midwest Sociological Society. Available: http://www.themss.org (Accessed: May 4, 2004).

Included here is an announcement of the upcoming annual meeting, membership information and a listing of the society's committees, officers, and documents. The publications section highlights the journal *The Sociological Quarterly*, and provides links to the journal's official Web site (http://www.augustana.edu/hosting/tsq/); and also includes back issues of the society's online newsletter, *The Midwest Sociologist.*

237. North Central Sociological Association (NSCA). Available: http://www.ncsanet.org (Accessed: May 7, 2004).

Included here is information about the organization, its officers and members, and its activities, including the annual meeting. There is also a description of the association's journal, *Sociological Focus*, and links to other relevant sociology Web sites. A section for job listings is also provided.

238. Pacific Sociological Association (PSA). Available: http://www.csus.edu/psa/ (Accessed: April 28, 2004).

The *PSA* site includes information on becoming a member of the organization and on attending the annual meeting. There are also lists of the officers and committees, and a special online issue of the PSA's journal,

Sociological Perspectives. Current and back issues of *The Pacific Sociologist*, the PSA's newsletter, are available online (1996–present). In addition, there are links to the Web sites of other sociology associations.

239. **Progressive Sociology Network (PSN).** Available: http://csf. colorado.edu/psn/ and PSN-Café: http://csf.colorado.edu/psn/cafe.html (Accessed: April 22, 2004).

PSN is a moderated discussion list and the information here revolves around concerns with civil rights, women's rights, racial and ethnic minorities' rights, social justice, and related progressive issues. The companion unmoderated list, the *PSN-Café*, includes archives of the *PSN* discussion list, the Progressive Population Network discussion list, the SOCGRAD discussion list, the Racial-Religious-Ethno-Nationalist Violence Studies (REVS) list, and a Homeless list. There is also a link to the ASA Marxist Section's home page as well as links to related sites.

240. **Sociology Association of Aotearoa New Zealand (SAANZ).** Available: http://saanz.rsnz.org (Accessed: April 23, 2004).

The association is a member of the International Sociological Association (see entry above) and the site is hosted by the Royal Society of New Zealand. This site includes association contacts and membership information, the association's constitution and code of ethics, and descriptions of annual meetings and conferences. Also features are links to other New Zealand social science organizations and sociology sites, a list of the organization's officers/representatives/committee members, recent association news, and a 2003–2004 archive of the society's newsletter. SAANZ also publishes *New Zealand Sociology*, and a link to the journal's home page is provided.

241. **Southern Sociological Society.** Available: http://www.msstate.edu/org/ sss/ (Accessed: April 15, 2004).

Included here is membership information and maintenance, an online membership directory, and information on the society's annual meeting. Also included is the society's governance information highlighting its bylaws and constitution, officer and committee information, and the most recent society election results. The conference information includes a description of the program, as well as a means of submitting one's proposal electronically. *Social Forces*, the official journal of the society, is also described; and current and back issues (2001–present) of *The Southern Sociologist*, the society's newsletter, are provided.

242. **Teaching Sociology.** Available: http://www.lemoyne.edu/ts/tsmain.html (Accessed: April 22, 2004).

The American Sociological Association publishes a journal by the same name (see entry in the journal chapter). This site is an offshoot of that and includes information on joining and sending messages to the *Teaching Sociology* listserv/discussion list. Also included here is a list of the editors and editorial board for the journal, a description of the procedures for submitting and processing manuscripts, and information on subscribing to the journal itself—starting in 2004 the print subscription to the ASA journal includes online access at no additional cost. Journal article abstracts from 1998 to the present are also provided. And a link to the *American Sociological Association (ASA)* home page is included.

Directories

243. **1997–98 Biographical Directory of Members.** Washington, DC: American Sociological Association, 1997. 568 p. index. $50.00.

Though somewhat dated now, this is a straightforward directory of about 13,000 U.S. and international members of the American Sociological Association. Members are listed alphabetically, and for each there are many basic categories of information provided. The entry indicates the type of membership, mailing address, degrees, e-mail address, current position, areas of interest, and section memberships within the Association. There is an index by "areas of interest" that is arranged alphabetically by name under each subject area; the subject areas correspond to the areas of interest listed in each faculty member's entry. The only drawback to the index is that there is no initial listing of the subject categories and the page on which each one starts. This work is valuable both for tracking down other scholars and for researching potential graduate programs. In many respects, it is comparable to the Association's *Directory of Members* (see below).

244. **Directory of Departments of Sociology, 1999.** Washington, DC: American Sociological Association, 1999. $10.00 (institutions).

Included here are descriptions of 2,183 institutions in the United States, Canada, and other countries. Information includes institution name, a code number for the highest degree offered, the chairperson, department title, address, phone/extension, fax number, e-mail address, and number of sociology faculty. It also has indexes for state/country and by departmental code.

245. **Directory of Members, 2001.** Washington, DC: American Sociological Association, 2001. 544 p. index. $50.00 (institutions).

This is a biographical edition of the biennially published membership directory of the ASA. It lists approximately 13,000 ASA members alphabetically and includes some fundamental information about them, such as membership category, mailing address, e-mail address (if provided), phone number, degrees held, current position, areas of interest, and ASA section memberships. There is a supplementary geographic index that lists members alphabetically within each state or foreign country, as well as an alphabetical list of members according to their areas of interest (with their state or country noted). Members may indicate up to four areas of interest, and they would be listed alphabetically under all of these. The only drawback to the areas of interest index is that there is no initial listing of the subject categories and the page on which each one starts.

246. **Guide to Graduate Departments of Sociology, 2002.** Washington, DC: American Sociological Association, 2002. 399 p. $50.00 (institutions). ISSN 0091-7052.

This now annual publication gives fairly detailed information on graduate sociology programs in the United States (207) and some foreign countries (39). Programs in the United States are listed alphabetically by the name of the institution. For each program, common categories of information are provided. These include the expected directory information, such as phone, address, e-mail, fax, department chair, director of graduate studies, application deadline, tuition, financial aid, numbers of graduate students (full- and part-time), and number of graduate degrees awarded in a recent year. There is also some indication of whether teacher training is available for graduate students. Another section lists the department's special programs and areas of expertise. There is a list of full- and part-time faculty members with their degree date, appointment level, and specializations. Some departmental entries also include the authors and titles of some recently completed PhDs in the program. The international programs are listed at the end of the volume alphabetically by country, then by institution. The information they provide is comparable to that supplied for U.S. programs. Special programs, PhDs awarded, and faculty are also indexed.

247. **Sociology: Graduate Schools in Australia and New Zealand.** Available: http://www.gradschools.com/listings/Australia/sociology_australia.html (Accessed: July 2, 2004).

The Web page lists more than thirty graduate programs in sociology in Australia and New Zealand. While the descriptions are very brief, there is nonetheless information for addresses, phone numbers, fax numbers, degrees offered, and an e-mail address (that is electronically linked). This is part of the gradschools.com Web site. One can also find the related Web page listing graduate programs in sociology by region of the world, with a breakdown by state for those in the United States (http://www.gradschools.com/listings/menus/sociology_menu.html#USA).

Sociological Fields

Chapter 3

Criminology, Law, and Deviance

Guides

248. Benamati, Dennis C., Phyllis A. Schultze, Adam C. Bouloukos, and Graeme R. Newman. **Criminal Justice Information: How to Find It, How to Use It.** Phoenix, AZ: Oryx Press, 1998. 237 p. index. $59.95. LC 97-39576. ISBN 0-89774-957-X.

This book lays out a roadmap on how to do research in the criminal justice field. Chapter 1 introduces the basic concept of criminal justice, describing its relationship with other fields such as sociology, criminology, law, and so on. It also sets out some basic considerations for the basic and advanced researcher in finding and using information in the criminal justice field. Chapter 2 describes how to identify authorities through the use of biographical resources, listservs, and professional and academic associations. The remaining chapters provide annotations of sources in the following categories: basic information, such as dictionaries and encyclopedias; tools for identifying, locating, and retrieving books, documents, and other information sources, including library catalogs and bibliographies; periodicals, news sources, indexes, and abstracts; statistical sources; government agencies; legal research; international criminal justice information; and Web sites. The legal research chapter is particularly useful in that it includes a guide to understanding legal citations. An index provides additional access to entries throughout the book.

249. Nelson, Bonnie R. **Criminal Justice Research in Libraries and on the Internet.** Westport, CT: Greenwood Press, 1997. 276 p. index. $86.95. ISBN 0-313-30048-8.

Although a bit dated with respect to its descriptions of Web sites and databases, this work still serves its purpose in simplifying and reducing the "drudgery of finding information" (p. xiv). The first section of the book includes an outline of the "information flow" within the field of criminal justice and its cognate disciplines; a primer on creating a "master plan" for doing research; and a discussion of bibliographic and Internet searching. The second section presents annotated descriptions of various types of online and library resources—Web sites, library catalogs, statistics, indexes, and so on. The final section focuses on "special problem" areas of research: research on the nineteenth-century United States using primary sources, legal research, research in forensic science, and research on other countries. Three appendices include listings of Library of Congress Subject Headings for criminal justice topics, directories, and major criminal justice commission reports, respectively. A glossary and several indexes are included.

250. Thurman, Quint C., Lee E. Parker, and Robert L. O'Block. **Criminal Justice Research Sources.** 4th ed. Cincinnati, OH: Anderson, 2000. 171 p. $26.95. LC 99-34074. ISBN 0-87084-860-7.

Intended for undergraduate and graduate students, this useful work is "designed to make criminal justice research less frustrating, more efficient, and more complete than it has been in the past" (p. v). The first chapter presents an overview of the research process: how to select a research topic, how to search for and organize information, and how to lay out a research paper. Chapter 2 discusses descriptive and historical research, as well as the identification of original scholarship in criminal justice. This chapter includes a list of books on aspects of research design and grant proposal writing, as well as an introduction to sources for dissertation and thesis abstracts and grants. Chapter 3 introduces library catalogs, *Books in Print*, interlibrary loan, sources of book reviews, reserve books, and microforms. Chapter 4 discusses the use of indexes and abstracts, and includes an annotated list of abstracts useful in criminal justice. Chapter 5 presents professional and scholarly journals in topical categories (corrections, forensics, etc.). Chapters 6 through 10 consist of annotated entries for reference sources, bibliographies, databases, and government documents, respectively, while chapters 11 through 14 focus on various sources of criminal justice statistics and data. Chapter 15 discusses the use of various secondary and primary sources in the conduct of historical research. Chapter 16 lists members of the Criminal Justice Information Exchange, run by the National Institute of Justice and the National Criminal Justice Reference Service, as well as regional U.S. depository libraries. Chapter 17 overviews legal research; chapter 18 introduces Internet research and useful Web sites. The book concludes with a very brief glossary of library terminology and a list of abbreviations for organizations and government agencies.

Bibliographies

251. National Archive of Criminal Justice Data. **Data Collections Available from the National Archive of Criminal Justice Data.** Ann Arbor, MI: The Archive, 2002. 741 p. index.

The National Archive of Criminal Justice Data is one of several special topic archives under the auspices of the Inter-university Consortium of Political and Social Research (ICPSR). This catalog primarily includes descriptions of studies freely accessible to government and criminal justice researchers or to researchers at ICPSR member institutions through the Archive. The studies are grouped into several broad subject categories: attitude surveys; community studies; corrections; court case processing; courts; criminal justice system; crime and delinquency; official statistics; police; victimization; drugs, alcohol, and crime; and computer programs and instructional packages. Each study description provides the names of the principal investigators, study title, ICPSR study number, sponsor, summary, universe, sampling, extent of collection, extent of processing, and a description of the data file. In many cases, the presence of a weight variable is noted, and publications related to the study are cited. The extent of the collection notes the format of the codebook (e.g., pdf), the number of data files, and the availability of data definition statements for SAS or SPSS and OSIRIS dictionary files. The data file description includes information on record length, number of cases, and number of variables. The catalog also provides a listing of criminal justice–related studies that are available to researchers at ICPSR member institutions or to others for a fee. The catalog includes a listing of studies available on CD-ROM, as well as of studies that appear or have appeared in serial form, such as the National Center for Juvenile Justice's *Juvenile Court Statistics*. Additional access to the study descriptions is provided through indexes of principal investigators, study titles, and study numbers, respectively. A current version of this work is available online at http://www.icpsr.umich.edu/ORG/Publications/NACJD/nacjd02.pdf.

252. Nordquist, Joan, comp. **Race, Crime, and the Criminal Justice System: A Bibliography.** Santa Cruz, CA: Reference and Research Services, 1997. 72 p. (Contemporary Social Issues: A Bibliographic Series, no. 45). $20.00. LC 97-206906. ISBN 0-937855-88-X.

This bibliography provides unannotated entries on the subjects of racism and ethnicity within the United States criminal justice system and race, ethnicity, and inequality as these relate to crime. Entries are drawn from a variety of publication types, and the compiler has made an effort to include items from "alternative publishers, the small presses, the feminist presses and activist organizations" (p. vii). The first section focuses on race, ethnicity, and the criminal justice system, and provides entries on this general topic, as well as on the courts, sentencing, the death penalty, imprisonment, police in the minority community, African Americans, Latinos, Native Americans, minority women, and minority youth, respectively. Section 2 deals with race, ethnicity, inequality and crime, and includes subsections on this topic generally and as it relates to African Americans, Latinos, Asian Americans, Native Americans, minority women, minority youth, and ethnic gangs. *See also* references are provided in each of these two sections. Within each topical subsection, entries are grouped into books, pamphlets, government documents, dissertations and theses, or into articles in periodicals and books. Entries are arranged alphabetically by author within these publication-type groupings. Section 3 is divided into three parts: statistics, bibliographies, and Web sites.

253. O'Shea, Kathleen A, and Beverly R. Fletcher, comps. **Female Offenders: An Annotated Bibliography.** Westport, CT: Greenwood Press, 1997. 264 p. index. (Research and Bibliographical Guides in Criminal Justice, no. 5). $84.95. ISBN 0-313-29228-0.

Intended as a "guide, not only for students and researchers, but for practitioners who are working" with female offenders, this interdisciplinary bibliography attempts to provide comprehensive access to books, book chapters, dissertations and theses, government and nongovernment reports, journal and law review articles, and conference papers on this topic. The entries are arranged in eight distinct chapters: criminology; crimes; arrest, prosecution, sentencing; female juveniles; corrections; probation and parole; political prisoners; and bibliographies. Each entry includes a one- or two-sentence annotation; the annotations for research studies generally give some idea of the research methodology employed and the study sample size. Additional access to the entries is provided through author and subject indexes.

254. Ross, Lee E. **African American Criminologists, 1970–1996: An Annotated Bibliography.** Westport, CT: Greenwood Press, 1998. 108 p. index. (Bibliographies and Indexes in Afro-American and African Studies, no. 36). $62.95. LC 97-52329. ISBN 0-313-30150-6.

This work aims to "document the scholarly contributions of African American criminologists" (p. x), as well as to encourage incorporation of these contributions into criminal justice decision-making processes (p. xii). Ross invited African American criminologists, identified through listserv mailings, professional association membership lists, and personal contacts, to submit three abstracts of their publications for inclusion in this work. For those who failed to respond to this invitation, Ross has included at least one publication. The upper limit for the number of abstracts is four, and in cases where this limit needed to be enforced, the author selected those works that appeared in more mainstream journals or as books.

The first section consists of a reprint of an article entitled "Dual Realities and Structural Challenges of African American Criminologists" (originally published in *ACJS Today* 15, no. 1 [1996]: 1–9), which reflects on the potential of African American criminologists to identify the structural aspects of racism in society and to incorporate this into criminological theory and on the barriers to making such a contribution. The second section provides abstracts for the works of criminologists in alphabetical order by author's last name; where an African Americans may have been a coauthor of a work, this name appears in boldface type. A section on selected references provides citations for each of the entries included in section two. An appendix that provides entries on doctoral dissertations by African American criminologists between 1970 and 1996 is included, as is an author subject index.

255. Russell, Katheryn K., Heather L. Pfeifer, and Judith L. Jones, comps. **Race and Crime: An Annotated Bibliography.** Westport, CT: Greenwood Press,

2000. 192 p. index. (Bibliographies and Indexes in Ethnic Studies, no. 8). $69.95. LC 99-088481. ISBN 0-313-31033-5.

Noting that previous bibliographies with a focus on race and crime excluded research on whites, this work is intended as a "resource guide for those seeking a comprehensive listing of race and crime citations" (p. xi). Entries include monographs, journal articles, research reports, dissertations, government documents, and Web sites. The citations are predominantly to works published during the 1970s, 1980s, and 1990s, although several references to late 1950s and 1960s works are also included. The bibliography focuses on the areas of "race and offending, race and victimization, and race and criminal justice system professionals" in the United States (p. xii). The book is divided into three major sections. Section 1 includes five separate chapters that include race-specific entries on whites, American Indians, Asian Americans, Hispanics, and African Americans, respectively. Section 2 consists of three individual chapters on general race research. The first chapter in this section provides entries from monographs and journal articles in the area of multiracial research on race and crime. The second chapter includes citations to special issues, edited volumes and guides, while the third chapter describes government documents, reports, and commission findings. The final section of the book consists of general criminal justice Web sites. Author and subject indexes are included.

Indexes, Abstracts, and Databases.

256. **Criminal Justice Abstracts.** [electronic resource]. Thousand Oaks, CA: Sage, 1968– . Available: http://www.sagepub.com (Accessed: April 12, 2004).

Based on the print abstracting source of the same name, *Criminal Justice Abstracts* provides coverage of books, book chapters, journal articles, and reports. Coverage is worldwide, including some foreign language sources (though the abstracts are in English), and dates from 1968 to the present. Topics include crime trends, corrections, police, the courts, victims, and sentencing. The descriptive abstracts are detailed and run from one to four paragraphs. Print subscriptions to *Criminal Justice Abstracts* are available through Sage; subscriptions to the electronic version are available through both CSA (http://www.csa.com) and SilverPlatter (http://www.silverplatter.com/catalog/cjab.htm).

257. **Criminal Justice Periodicals Index.** [electronic resource]. Ann Arbor, MI: ProQuest, 1981– . Available: http://www.proquest.com (Accessed: April 12, 2004).

This ProQuest database provides indexing, abstracting, and full text for nearly 200 criminal justice titles, from 1981 to the present. Journals include titles such as the *American Journal of Criminal Justice, Journal of Forensic Sciences*, and *FBI Law Enforcement Bulletin*. Coverage is comprehensive and includes corrections, law enforcement, social work, and law. Subscriptions to the database are available through ProQuest, and the database is also accessible as Dialog File 171.

Handbooks and Yearbooks

258. Altschiller, Donald. **Hate Crimes: A Reference Handbook.** Santa Barbara, CA: ABC-CLIO, 1999. (Contemporary World Issues). 204 p. index. $45.00. LC 98-50275. ISBN 0-87436-937-1.

This handbook provides an overview of the phenomena of hate crimes in the United States. The first section defines the term "hate crime," identifies groups that have been primarily victimized by this type of crime, and discusses hate crime legislation at the state and federal levels. The second section provides a chronology of recent events related to hate crimes, including specific instances of victimization and milestones in advocacy and legislation. The third section includes biographical sketches of key players in the development of hate crimes legislation and awareness. The fourth section consists of a series of statistical tables depicting the extent of hate crimes in the United States, as well as excerpts from landmark governmental and advocacy reports. The remaining sections provide annotated entries for books, articles, videos, Web sites, and other materials. This is a useful introduction to all aspects of hate crimes in the United States.

259. Banks, Cyndi. **Women in Prison: A Reference Handbook.** Santa Barbara, CA: ABC-CLIO, 2003. 225 p. index. (Contemporary World Issues Series). $45.00. LC 2002154379. ISBN 1-57607-929-5.

Women in Prison introduces the unique experience of women in the prison system of the United States. Chapter 1 provides historical background on the topic, including discussions of the reformatory movement and the rise of custodial prisons for women. Chapter 2 looks at policy issues such as women's criminality; the experience of women in prison, including sexual abuse; health and medical issues; and, possible solutions for some of the problems that women prisoners face, including the decriminalization of certain offenses. Chapter 3 is probably unique among works in the Contemporary World Issues Series in that it draws upon the author's own research to present the words of women inmates. Chapter 4 offers a brief chronology of events, while chapter 5 looks at the issues surrounding the guarding of women in prison. Chapter 6 presents brief biographical sketches of reformers and others and describes significant events in prison history. Chapter 7 includes statistical tables on the incarceration of women, while the remaining chapters list and describe agencies, organizations, and print and nonprint resources related to the topic. Includes an index.

260. **Crime in the United States.** Washington, DC: Department of Justice, Federal Bureau of Investigation; distr., Washington, DC: GPO, 1930– . annual. ISSN 0082-7592.

Otherwise known as the Uniform Crime Reports, this is one of the best government sources for crime statistics. The introductory section briefly explains the reporting program and its methods and procedures. Subsequent sections contain statistics on offenses reported, offenses cleared, persons arrested, homicide patterns, and law enforcement personnel. Data are broken down by age, sex, race, ethnic origin, and a large number of other variables. The tables include plenty of explanatory footnotes. In addition, there are appendices dealing with methodology, definitions of offenses, reporting area definitions, state reporting programs, the nation's two crime measures (the National Crime Victimization Survey and the Uniform Crime Reports), a national uniform crime reporting program directory, and a uniform crime reporting publications list. The latest edition of *Crime in the United States* is available online at http://www.fbi.gov/ucr/02cius.htm.

261. **Crime State Rankings.** Lawrence, KS: Morgan Quitno, 1994– . annual. index. ISSN 1077-4408.

More than 500 easy-to-use tables of statistics are drawn from mostly government publications such as *Crime in the United States*, as well as sources like the Bureau of Justice Statistics, the American Correctional Association, and the Bureau of the Census. Both published and unpublished data are included. The tables are arranged under a number of major categories: arrests, juveniles, corrections, drugs and alcohol, finance, law enforcement, offenses, and urban/rural crime. There are also tables of retrospective data. The appendices list urban, rural, and resident state populations. A list of sources is provided, as is a subject index. Though many of these data are available elsewhere, they are conveniently assembled here in a readable format with all source documents cited.

262. **Criminal Victimization in the United States.** Washington, DC: U.S. Department of Justice, Office of Justice Programs, Bureau of Justice Statistics, 1973– . annual. ISSN 0095-5833.

Included here are statistics on crimes reported by their victims on the National Crime Victimization Survey. The data focus particularly on the "personal crimes of rape, robbery, assault, and larceny and the household crimes of burglary, larceny, and motor vehicle theft" (1992 ed., p. iii). There are 120 tables of data divided into five major categories: characteristics of personal crime victims; characteristics of household crime victims; victim-offender relationships and offender characteristics; crime characteristics; and reporting crimes to the police. Each of these categories has tables that break down the data by a number of relevant variables (e.g., race, ethnicity, sex, income, locality, etc.). The appendices include a copy of the survey, as well as a description of the data collection methodology and procedures. There is also an introductory summary of findings, as well as a glossary of basic terms. The latest edition of *Criminal Victimization* is available on the Web at http://www.ojp.usdoj.gov/bjs/abstract/cvusst.htm.

263. **National Criminal Justice Thesaurus: Descriptors for Indexing Law Enforcement and Criminal Justice Information.** Washington, DC: Department of Justice, National Institute of Justice, National Criminal Justice Reference Service, 1900– . annual. ISSN 0198-6546.

This can be used as a guide to indexing terms in the criminal justice and criminology literature, particularly the National Criminal Justice Reference Service database. The descriptors (subject headings) are organized into four major sections: substantive (subject) descriptors, organizational descriptors, geographic descriptors, and a permuted (keyword-out-of-context) index. The first three sections list the preferred terms for searching subjects, organizations, and geographic locations. Broader, narrower, and related terms are listed as well. Some terms are accompanied by a scope note (SN) or definition; others have *use* references that direct the user to the preferred subject heading. The permuted index lists alphabetically every keyword from every descriptor, followed by the full descriptor in which the word appears. Overall, this thesaurus can aid in the search of criminal justice and criminology indexes, abstracts, and databases by identifying potentially fruitful search terms.

264. Phelps, Shirelle, ed. **World of Criminal Justice.** Detroit, MI: Gale, 2002. 2v. index. $150.00. ISBN 0-7876-4959-7 (set).

This book aims to "explain in concise, detailed, and jargon-free language some of the most important topics, theories, discoveries, concepts, and organizations in criminal justice" (p. vii). While some of the more than 1,100 entries, including accounts of sensational murder trials and underworld figures, will prove to be of only marginal interest to sociologists, many of the others provide useful overviews of landmark court cases and basic criminological topics (e.g., class and crime). Each entry contains *see also* references. A list of sources consulted, along with a chronology and indexes, is contained in the second volume.

265. Rafter, Nicole Hahn, and Debra L. Stanley. **Prisons in America: A Reference Handbook.** Santa Barbara, CA: ABC-CLIO, 1999. 226 p. index. (Contemporary World Issues). $45.00. LC 99-35719. ISBN 1-57607-102-2.

Another of the titles in ABC-CLIO's Contemporary World Issues series, *Prisons in America* provides the criminologist with a general introduction to the topic, together with documents, statistics, and resources. Chapter 1 provides historical background on American prisons, focusing on the reformatory movement, the development of prisoner's rights concepts, and the "rejection of the rehabilitative ideal" during the latter half of the twentieth century. Chapter 2 presents brief introductions to controversial policy issues, including prison violence, overcrowding, and private prisons. A chronology details significant events in prison history, including the timing of major court cases, prison openings, and prison-related publications. Chapter 4 provides biographical sketches, which include Sister Helen Prejean, the author of *Dead Man Walking*, and other major figures in U.S. prison history. The documents and statistics section focuses on major court cases and enumerations of prisoner's rights and looks at trends in incarceration rates as well as other topics. The final sections list and describe prison-related agencies and organizations, as well as print and nonprint resources. A glossary is included, and an index provides additional access to the book's content.

266. Schwartz, Martin D., and Michael O. Maume, eds. **Teaching the Sociology of Deviance.** Washington, DC: American Sociological Association, 1999. 184 p. (ASA Resource Materials for Teaching).

Now in its fourth edition, this handbook for teachers of deviance still grapples with how best to teach what has often been a very popular course in the sociology curriculum. Not unlike social problems courses, which have to overcome their "problem of the week" orientation, deviance courses have to confront their stereotype as courses on "nuts, sluts, and perverts." The thirteen class syllabi included in this handbook are provided by faculty from around the country and range from a somewhat typical orientation to the course to more novel approaches. In addition to the syllabi, there is an interesting collection of articles or essays on issues relating to teaching deviance. These are not only how-to articles, but also essays on overcoming challenges in teaching certain deviance topics. There are also sections of class assignments and resources, with the latter including a bibliography, a list of books for student reviews, and a list of Web resources.

267. **Sourcebook of Criminal Justice Statistics.** Washington, DC: Department of Justice, Office of Justice Programs, Bureau of Justice Statistics; distr., Washington, DC: Government Printing Office, 1973– . annual. index. ISSN 0360-3431.

A gold mine of government and nongovernment data on crime, this handbook has hundreds of tables of data arranged under six sections: characteristics of the criminal justice system, public attitudes toward crime and criminal justice-related topics, nature and distribution of known offenses, characteristics and distribution of persons arrested, judicial processing of defendants, and persons under correctional supervision. These categories are comprised of anywhere from 50 to 200 tables of data on various subtopics. In addition, there are appendices defining terms and discussing survey methodologies and sampling procedures. The value of the work is increased by its inclusion, in many tables, of historical data, allowing one to chart trends. A subject index complements the access provided by the detailed list of contents. Along with *Crime in the United States*, this should be one of the first places one looks in trying to locate criminal justice statistics. A Web version of the *Sourcebook* is available at http://www.albany.edu/sourcebook/, and a CD-ROM version is also available.

Dictionaries and Encyclopedias

268. Bryant, Clifton D., ed. **Encyclopedia of Criminology and Deviant Behavior.** Philadelphia: Brunner-Routledge, 2000. 4v. index. $495.00. LC 00-058558. ISBN 1-56032-772-3 (set).

This works represents a summary of scholarship in the field of deviant behavior, which "encompasses both behavior that violates social rules, and behavior and characteristics that fails to meet certain expectations" (p. xii), and in the subfield of criminology, which focuses on the violation of social rules that have been codified into laws. More than 500 entries are included. Entries are meant to "either have some degree of centrality in the study of deviance or are representative of the range of interests among researchers and scholars in the field" (p. vii). Each volume is preceded by an introduction to the general topic.

Entries in volume 1 cover historical, conceptual, and theoretical issues in the study of deviant behavior, including essays on theories of deviance, aspects of social control, and deviance within various contexts. Volume 2 focuses on crime and juvenile delinquency, including essays on crime statistics and data and modalities of crime (against persons, property, etc.). Volume 3 consists of entries on sexual deviance in various contexts (violent, commercial, symbolic, etc.); and, volume 4, self-destructive behavior and disvalued identity, with essays on alcohol use and abuse, drug abuse, and suicide. Each entry consists of an essay, plus a list of references. Each volume is preceded by a table of contents providing a listing of entries in alphabetical order, along with their contributor(s). A secondary table of contents, called a "subject guide," groups entries into categories. Additional access is through author and subject indexes found in volume 4. Biographical sketches of contributors are contained in volume 3. Contributors are from the United States, Canada, Australia, the United Kingdom, and Hong Kong. Entries are arranged alphabetically within each volume and are signed by the author(s).

269. Champion, Dean J. **The American Dictionary of Criminal Justice: Key Terms and Major Court Cases.** 2d ed. Los Angeles, CA: Roxbury, 2001. 405 p. index. $34.95. LC 00-039013. ISBN 1-891487-59-0.

The first section consists of brief alphabetized entries on a wide variety of topics in criminology, criminal justice, corrections, and policing. Distinct is that it also includes entries for noted criminologists. The second section includes U.S. Supreme Court cases. Champion provides a useful introduction to this section, explaining how to understand legal citations and how to make sense of the significance of a case. Cases are presented in alphabetical order by plaintiff. Each case entry includes an official citation, as well as a rendering of this citation in plain English; a list of the legal areas affected by the decision (e.g., civil rights, the Fourteenth Amendment); and, a brief summary of the history and significance of the case. Additional access to the cases is provided by an index. Champion also provides a brief list of Web addresses for criminal justice journal publishers and agencies.

270. Davis, Mark S. **The Concise Dictionary of Crime and Justice.** Thousand Oaks, CA: Sage, 2002. 286 p. $64.95. ISBN 0-7619-2175-3.

This dictionary defines more than 2,000 terms drawn from both the contemporary academic and popular literature of criminal justice. The reader will find brief definitions of terms like "criminal justice funnel," "lex talionis," or "seriousness scaling," alongside others such as "brass knuckles," "Carlo Gambino," and "Zodiac killer." The strength of the dictionary lies in this wide variety of entries and in the lack of jargon used to define terms.

271. **Dictionary of Criminal Justice Terms.** Lanham, MD: American Correctional Association, 1998. 129 p. $12.00. ISBN 1-56991-075-8.

This dictionary is geared for use by criminal justice professionals working in correctional facilities, courts, and so on. As such, it will be useful to sociologists and criminologists who are studying these types of criminal justice environments or working with records produced by such criminal justice-related agencies and organizations. The user will find concise definitions of terms ranging from "juvenile ranch" to "clear and present danger" to "token economy."

272. Dressler, Joshua, ed. **Encyclopedia of Crime & Justice.** 2d ed. New York: Macmillan, 2002. 4v. index. $475.00. LC 2001042707. ISBN 0-02-865319-X (set).

A revised edition of the 1983 *Encyclopedia of Crime & Justice*, this four-volume work focuses on criminal conduct, crime prevention, and punishment. Some essays from the original work have simply been updated for inclusion here; the vast majority, however, have been newly commissioned for the new edition. The encyclopedia contains more than 250 entries on topics ranging from alcohol and crime, to family relationships and crime, to riots. Somewhat oriented towards the United States in focus, Crime & Justice does include several essays on comparative criminal law. Volume 1 includes an alphabetical listing of all essays and of all contributors and their institutional affiliations. Volume 1 also includes a very useful guide to legal citations, including a listing of official abbreviations and explanations of international, United States, New Zealand, and other sources of case law and statutes. Each essay is signed and is several pages in length and includes *see also* references, a bibliography, and, in many cases, a list of relevant legal cases. Volume 4 contains a glossary providing brief definitions of terms found throughout the encyclopedia. There is both an index to legal documents mentioned throughout the work, as well as a general index.

273. Levinson, David, ed. **Encyclopedia of Crime and Punishment.** Thousand Oaks, CA: Sage, 2002. 4v. $600.00. LC 2002001220. ISBN 0-7619-2258-X (set).

Aiming to be a "comprehensive, authoritative, and twenty-first century reference resource on crime and punishment," this four-volume work surveys the field of criminal justice, including "criminology, forensics, penology, police science, criminal law, victimology, and corrections" (pp. xxxi–xxxii). An alphabetical list of the 439 entries is included in each volume, as is a reader's guide, which groups entries into twelve topical categories: crimes and related behaviors, law and justice, policing, forensics, corrections, victimology, punishment, sociocultural context and popular culture, international, concepts and theories, research methods and information, organizations and institutions, and special populations. Individual essays are presented in alphabetical order and are several pages in length, signed, and contain *see also* references and lists for further reading. Tables, illustrations, and excerpts from periodicals accompany many of the essays. Many of the topics are presented in an American context; however, the work also includes essays on the criminal justice systems of many countries and regions. Volume 4 includes appendices on "Careers in Criminal Justice," "Web Resources for Criminal Justice," "Professional and Scholarly Associations," and a "Selected Bibliography." An index provides additional access to the entries. A chronology of significant events in the development of criminal justice as a field is also included. This work represents a very useful survey of the development of criminal justice, including summaries of major concepts and theories, criminal justice programs, and significant events and legal cases.

274. Maguire, Mike, Rod Morgan, and Robert Reiner, eds. **The Oxford Handbook of Criminology.** 3d ed. New York: Oxford University Press, 2002. 1227 p. index. $170.00. ISBN 0-19-925609-8.

This handbook features "state-of-the-art reviews by leading academics covering, as nearly as possible, the full range of issues addressed by criminology" (p. 2). Though the focus is primarily British, this includes much information emanating from and relevant to the United States. The theoretical issues and research findings are important regardless of one's geographic location. In fact, even the discussions of British policies and programs can be instructive for an American audience. The handbook's thirty-one chapters are arranged into five sections or parts: theoretical and historical perspectives, the social construction of crime and crime control, the dimensions of crime, forms of crime, and reactions to crime. The section on crime and crime control addresses the legal, political, and media context of crime. The section on dimensions of crime looks at victims, gender, and mental health, along with other issues. The section, Forms of crime, focuses on violent crime and white-collar crime, among other topics. "Reactions to crime" looks at issues such as prevention, policing, trials, sentencing, probation, and imprisonment. Each essay is written by an expert in that particular area and includes suggestions for further reading and a list of references. A subject index is provided. This is a superb one-volume overview for criminology students.

275. McLaughlin, Eugene, and John Muncie, comps. and eds. **The Sage Dictionary of Criminology.** Thousand Oaks, CA: Sage, 2001. 336 p. index. $99.00. ISBN 0-7619-5907-6.

This work is international in focus and includes contributions from scholars in Australia, New Zealand, the United Kingdom, the United States, the Netherlands, and Greece. Each of the more than 250 entries focuses on a "major theoretical position," "key theoretical position," "central criminological method," or a "core criminal justice philosophy or practice" (p. xi). Each entry is broken down into at least two sections. The first section briefly defines the term. A "distinctive features" section discusses the term's history and significance. All entries for major theoretical positions also include an evaluation section that focuses on how a term in question might be challenged by other theoretical positions, new evidence, and so on. Each entry is signed, includes a list of key readings, and points the reader to associated concepts found elsewhere in the work. Entries address a wide variety of topics, including elements of research design (e.g., cross-sectional design, sampling), theory (conflict theory, individual positivism), and aspects of criminal justice (decarceration, community safety). Subject and name indexes provide additional access to the entries. This is a very useful work for understanding theory in the context of criminology, as well as how research and aspects of criminal justice interrelate with theory.

276. McShane, Marilyn D., and Frank P. Williams, eds. **Encyclopedia of Juvenile Justice.** Thousand Oaks, CA: Sage, 2003. 416 p. index. $125.00. ISBN 0-7619-2358-6.

"[C]ompiled with the belief that everyone should be familiar with the history and current operations of the juvenile justice system" (p. xxi), this work presents signed entries from scholars in the field of criminal justice. Topical entries include gangs, foster care, government programs (e.g., DARE), victimization, prevention strategies, and mental health. Each entry gives historical and contemporary context to a concept, and includes *see also* references and a bibliography. This work should be useful to sociologists looking at the juvenile experience of crime.

277. Rush, George E. **The Dictionary of Criminal Justice.** 5th ed. Guilford, CT: Dushkin/McGraw-Hill, 2000. 444 p. $21.88. LC 99-74549. ISBN 0-07-030709-1.

The fifth edition of this standard work is intended for students, researchers, and practitioners, and includes definitions of thousands of terms drawn from a variety of criminal justice–related disciplines. Concepts, organizations, legislation, and individuals are included, with definitions running from a sentence to half-a-page in length. Organization entries are accompanied by addresses. The second part of the dictionary includes paragraph-long summaries of Supreme Court cases affecting criminal justice. These are arranged under several topical issue areas, including: the First Amendment, Fourth Amendment, Fifth Amendment, Sixth Amendment, Eighth Amendment, due process, equal protection, rights of the incarcerated, juvenile court proceedings, use of illegally obtained evidence, civil rights and constitutional torts, and, habeas corpus in federal courts. Many of these categories, in turn, have more specific subtopics. An index to these court cases is also provided. Appendices include listings of U.S. doctoral programs in criminal justice, forensic agencies and organizations, criminal justice Web sites, and, refereed journals. Overall, the large number of terms included, the interdisciplinary focus, and the inclusion of court cases make this a useful resource.

278. Schmalleger, Frank, and Gordon M. Armstrong, eds. **Crime and the Justice System in America: An Encyclopedia.** Westport, CT: Greenwood Press, 1997. 299 p. index. $79.95. LC 96-10748. ISBN 0-313-29409-7.

This work intends to "include significant terminology, precedent-setting cases, key historical and contemporary figures, notable policy initiatives, and significant findings, studies, agencies, and programs" (p. ix) in the field of criminal justice. Entries are arranged alphabetically and range from a paragraph to a full page in length. Many entries include a short list of recommended readings for further exploration. Each entry is signed by its author, and a list of these contributors and their academic or professional affiliations is included. A table of cases follows the main text of the encyclopedia, and this provides case names, citations, and page numbers for the major cases referred to in the text. A bibliographical essay discusses identifies key works in American criminal justice. While the subjects of some of the entries may now appear dated (e.g., Michael R. Milken), this encyclopedia provides concise overviews of many aspects of criminal justice.

Web Sites and Research Centers

279. **Bureau of Justice Statistics.** Available: http://www.ojp.usdoj.gov/bjs/ (Accessed: January 15, 2004).

The *Bureau of Justice Statistics* Web site provides access to various reports and statistical series within several topical areas: crime and victims, law enforcement, prosecution, the federal justice system, criminal offenders, courts and sentencing, corrections, expenditure and employment, and criminal record systems. Statistics on special topics (e.g., firearms and crime) are also provided. In addition to providing full-text access to entire publications and individual tables, the site also provides summary information for its major topical areas. This is an essential site for criminologists.

280. **National Archive of Criminal Justice Data (NACJD).** Available: http://www.icpsr.umich.edu/NACJD/ (Accessed: January 15, 2004).

One of the topical archives of the Inter-university Consortium for Political and Social Research (ICPSR), the NACJD is sponsored by both the Bureau of Justice Statistics and the National Institute of Justice. The site features a searchable catalog of datasets. A browsing features provides additional access to the datasets and organizes them into several categories, including: attitude surveys; community studies; corrections; court case processing; courts; criminal justice system; crime and delinquency; official statistics; police; victimization; drugs, alcohol, and crime; and computer programs and instructional pages. Each dataset is described in essentially the same manner as are those in the larger ICPSR catalog. The site also features resource guides on hot topics (e.g., capital punishment), as well as an online data analysis tool.

281. **National Criminal Justice Reference Service (NCJRS).** Available: http://www.ncjrs.org/ (Accessed: January 15, 2004).

The *NCJRS* Web site features access to two separate databases. The first, which is also available as Dialog File 21, includes references and abstracts to the NCJRS document collection. Books, journal articles, dissertations, audiovisual materials, reports, empirical studies, and other types of sources are covered. The second database features searching of more than 7,000 full-text publications from NCJRS and its partners. All aspects of criminal justice and law enforcement are addressed in both of these databases, including criminology, corrections, evaluation and policy, human resource development, probation and parole, substance abuse, victim's services, and more. Other features of the

Web site include collections of documents on various issues, including: corrections, courts, drugs and crime, international, juvenile justice, law enforcement, victims of crime and statistics.

282. National Institute of Justice. **Data Resources of the National Institute of Justice.** 15th ed. 2002. Available: http://www.icpsr.umich.edu/ORG/ Publications/NACJD/nij2002.pdf (Accessed: January 14, 2004).

Data Resources provides information about 426 National Institute of Justice datasets that are available for downloading from the Web site of the National Archive of Criminal Justice Data or retrievable from other media formats, such as CD-ROM. It includes a list of data collections, by principal investigator. Study descriptions are arranged in alphabetical order by principal investigator. Notes on file structure are provided, although the extent of processing is not described. Unlike its companion print volume, *Data Collections Available from the National Archive of Criminal Justice Data*, which includes a methodology section that clearly identifies the research design, unit of observation, and description of variables, *Data Collections* incorporates the description of methodology into a summary section. Study descriptions note the inclusion of a study on any CD-ROM product, the sponsoring agency, grant number, and affiliation of principal investigators. Additional access to the study descriptions is provided by a listing of the studies, by principal investigator, as well as by topical and principal investigator indexes. The datasets and codebooks are obtainable in a variety of electronic formats (diskette, CD-ROM, FTP) from the Inter-university Consortium for Political and Social Research (ICPSR); print codebooks are also available for free from the National Archive of Criminal Justice Data (NACJD). Supplementary information includes a list of forthcoming datasets, as well as a list of studies available on diskette and CD-ROM.

Gerontology and Aging

Bibliographies

283. Militech, John J. **Depression in the Elderly.** Westport, CT: Greenwood Press, 1997. 226 p. index. (Bibliographies and Indexes in Gerontology, no. 36). $72.95. ISBN 0-313-30113-1.

With almost 1,000 entries spanning 1970–1996, this annotated bibliography covers an extensive amount of literature on depression in the elderly. Depression is a growing problem as our population ages, and these entries address the problem from a variety of perspectives that are reflected in the book's twelve chapters. These include such topics as causes and diagnosis, memory and cognition, physical illnesses, pharmacological treatments, nonpharmacological treatments, and treatment comparisons. For sociologists, gerontologists, and social workers, some of the other chapters may provide special interest. These included nationality/race/ethnicity, suicide, social aspects, caregivers, and bereavement/anxiety/religiosity. Furthermore, the subject index includes numerous entries under the term "social support," another important subject of sociological research. Major gerontology journals are well represented among the entries. Within chapters, the entries are arranged alphabetically by author. Roughly half of these entries are descriptively abstracted, albeit briefly in a sentence or, at most, a paragraph. Appended are a list of acronyms, an author index, and a subject index.

284. Walker, Bonnie L., comp. **Sexuality and the Elderly: A Research Guide.** Westport, CT: Greenwood Press, 1997. 301 p. index. (Bibliographies and Indexes in Gerontology, no. 25). $82.95. ISBN 0-313-30133-6.

Intended primarily for caregivers of the elderly, this guide annotates 457 books, book chapters, and journal articles dealing with sexuality and the elderly and its subtopics. The descriptively annotated entries are arranged into eighteen chapters. The first three deal with major studies, literature reviews, and texts and text chapters. The remaining chapters focus on specific topics, such as research methods and measurement issues, caregiver attitudes, sexual dysfunction, effects of aging on sexuality, alternative lifestyles, affects of training on caregivers, staff responses to sexual behavior of the elderly, and much more. There is also a chapter dealing with AIDS. While most of the entries are fairly scholarly in orientation, there are some popular works that touch on sexuality and aging as well. These are included as reflections of popular beliefs. Throughout, the paragraph-long, well-written annotations can be quite detailed, often citing sample sizes, research instruments used, and findings. Both author and subject indexes are provided for additional searching.

285. Wheeler, Helen Rippier. **Women and Aging: A Guide to the Literature.** Boulder, CO: Lynne Rienner, 1997. 259 p. index. ISBN 1-5558-7661-7.

This provides a guide to literature on the aging of women from the age of thirty-five on (i.e., midlife and older). Sources are in English and were published between 1980 and 1992. Books, articles, dissertations, and some theses are cited. Subject-focused reference sources are cited, as are selected works of fiction that relate to the topic. Overall, cited works are drawn from the humanities and the social and behavioral sciences. How-to books, comprehensive reference books, and books about men's aging are excluded. The more than 2,200 entries are arranged into thirteen chapters addressing: gerontology, psychological perspectives, sociological perspectives, economic issues, living arrangements, midlife and women, old age and women, ageism/sexism, cross-cultural perspectives, creativity and productivity, biography, fiction and poetry, and women's studies and the aging of females. Each chapter has numerous subtopics, within which entries are arranged alphabetically by author. Abstracts are short and descriptive, though most entries do not have abstracts at all. There are both author and subject/name indexes.

Indexes, Abstracts, and Databases

286. **Abstracts in Social Gerontology.** Vol. 33– , No. 1– . Newbury Park, CA: Sage, 1990– . quarterly. $186/yr. (institutions). ISSN 1047-4862. Available: http://www.sagepub.com/journal.aspx?pid=27 (Accessed: April 25, 2004).

Published in conjunction with the National Council on the Aging (NCOA), this title continues the earlier *Current Literature on Aging*. Each issue includes references to and abstracts of approximately 250 books, journal articles, government documents, pamphlets, reports, and other materials. Entries are arranged by author under an extensive list of some twenty subject categories and many more subtopics. For example, the category "Institutional and Noninstitutional Care" includes subtopics for home care, adult day care, hospitals, and institutionalization/long-term care. In addition to this subject arrangement, every entry is labeled with more specific subject headings that are used in the subject index. The abstracts are lengthy, descriptive, and quite helpful in determining the focus and value of the source. At the end of each issue, there is a supplementary list of "Related Citations." These unannotated references are arranged by author under an additional list of subject categories; they are not indexed. Each issue includes author and subject indexes, which are cumulated in the final issue of each volume. This is an excellent current awareness source for a broad range of literature in the field.

287. **AgeLine Database.** Available: http://research.aarp.org/ageline (Accessed: February 25, 2005).

Provided by the American Association of Retired Persons (AARP), this is the Web equivalent of the AgeLine database available through Dialog File 163. It is freely available and includes some 60,000 abstracts taken primarily from magazines and journals, though it also includes books, chapters, videos, and some sources taken from AARP's Research Information Center. It covers social, economic, health care, and policy aspects of aging. Most of the cited sources date since 1978, though there is selective coverage from 1966–1977. The audience for this database includes researchers, policymakers, the general public, and professionals and service providers in related fields. The subject categorization of entries uses AgeLine's *Thesaurus of Aging Terminology*. Though free, the database allows only a finite number of simultaneous users, thus possibly requiring additional attempts to access. Once connected, the database offers both basic and advanced research interfaces. Up to three terms may be combined using Boolean operators, with additional limits available for data, audience, and document type. Citations and abstracts are available, with occasional links to full text. Other items may be added to a shopping cart for purchase.

Handbooks and Yearbooks

288. **Annual Review of Gerontology and Geriatrics.** Vol. 1– . New York: Springer, 1980– . annual. $58.00. ISSN 0198-8794.

Issues are comprised of chapter-length articles contributed by various experts on those subjects. Typically, each volume focuses on a particular theme, different aspects of which are explored by the contributors. Recent theme issues have addressed such topics as the biology of aging, intervention research, and psychopharmacologic interventions in late life. Articles may focus on medical, management, and social/psychological aspects of the volume's theme.

289. Binstock, Robert H., and Linda K. George, eds. **Handbook of Aging and the Social Sciences.** 5th ed. San Diego, CA: Academic Press, 2001. 513 p. index. (The Handbooks of Aging). $59.95. ISBN 0-12-099194-2.

The twenty-five chapters that comprise this volume touch on many of the major topics of interest to those studying social gerontology and aging and fall within four major categories: theory and methods, social structure, social factors and institutions, and social interventions. The specific topics covered include demography, quantitative and qualitative research methods, social support, stratification, migration, gendered life course, the financing and organization of health care, family relations, end of life, retirement, the social psychology of health, race and ethnicity, role transitions, and much more. In all, there are eleven new topics covered in this edition. As a specialized resource, this is intended for advanced students and researchers in the field. Bibliographic references for further reading are included, as are indexes.

290. **Data Collections from the National Archive of Computerized Data on Aging.** Ann Arbor, MI: Inter-university Consortium for Political and Social Research, 2002. 494 p. Available: http://www.icpsr.umich.edu/ORG/Publications/ NACDA/nacda02.pdf (Accessed: April 25, 2004).

The National Archive of Computerized Data on Aging (NACDA) is a project of the Inter-university Consortium for Political and Social Research (ICPSR) and is funded by the National Institute on Aging. Its purpose is to promote research on aging, in part through the acquisition, preservation, and dissemination of research datasets. This book, which is available in pdf format on their Web site, is the annual guide to NACDA's dataset collection. It provides fairly in-depth descriptions of these datasets arranged under six chapter headings: demographic characteristics of older adults; social characteristics; economic characteristics; psychological characteristics, mental health and well-being; physical health and functioning; and health care needs, utilization, and financing for older adults. The dataset descriptions include the title, principal investigator, ICPSR study number, summary description, study design information (e.g., sampling), technical information (e.g., data format, file structure), and file specifications (e.g., number of cases, record length, cases per record). All datasets are available through the ICPSR. There are supplementary indexes for titles, keywords, and principal investigators, as well as an appended list of data sources in the United States and other countries.

291. Harris, Dan R., ed. **Aging Sourcebook: Basic Information on Issues Affecting Older Americans, Including Demographic Trends, Social Security, Medicare, Estate Planning, Legal Rights, Health and Safety, Elder Care**

Options, Retirement Lifestyle Options, and End of Life Issues. Detroit, MI: Omnigraphics, 1998. 889 p. (Personal Concerns Series, v. 3). $36.00. ISBN 0-7808-0175-X.

Intended primarily for laypersons, this handbook nonetheless has readable and often detailed descriptions of a wide variety of topics related to aging. The fifty-eight chapters are arranged under seven categories: major issues in aging, social security and medicare, legal and financial issues, health and safety, elder care, lifestyle and leisure activities, and end of life. Within each category there are numerous chapters, ranging from four to fifty pages in length, on such topics as social security, medicare, medigap insurance, crime, estate planning, fitness, alcohol abuse, nutrition, medical care, mental health, stroke, assisted living, Alzheimer's, elder abuse, travel trips, funerals, and more. Sources for the various chapters are cited. Lists of resources for further information accompany many of the chapters. Two introductory essays discuss the demographics of aging and "plain talk" about aging. There is an appended list of Web sites arranged according to each of the handbook's seven categories. A detailed name/subject/title index is also provided. While many of the articles here are practical in nature, others do provide an overview of some of the research findings on various aspects of aging. This is suitable for both general readers and undergraduates researching topics in gerontology and aging.

292. Harris, Diana K., ed. **Teaching Sociology of Aging and the Life Course.** 5th ed. Washington, DC: American Sociological Association, 2000. 291 p. (ASA Resource Materials for Teaching).

Included here are forty course syllabi for both general and more specialized courses in aging and gerontology. The general courses have predictable titles and content for what are often survey courses in the area, while the more specialized courses focus on such issues as families, lifestyles and resource management, mental health, politics and policies, spirituality, and race/class/culture. In addition to these syllabi, there are numerous other teaching resources and materials. The second chapter includes class activities or lesson plans on stereotypes, ageism, Facts on Aging quizzes, images of aging, and an Age Period Cohort class exercise. Chapter 3 includes numerous examples of research paper and interview assignments, as well as projects, debate topics, class presentation assignments, and community service activities. The final chapter includes lists of audiovisuals, Web sites, and video series. This is a gold mine of ideas, and the books in this series have become increasingly and appropriately wide-ranging in the kinds of instructional materials they identify (over and above course syllabi).

Dictionaries and Encyclopedias

293. Bettelheim, Adriel. **Aging in America A to Z.** Washington, DC: CQ Press, 2001. 280 p. index. $58.00. ISBN 1-56802-584-X.

Written for a general audience, this encyclopedia nonetheless provides detailed descriptions of well over 250 terms relating to aging. Covered are such broad subject areas as government programs, retirement issues, health and health care, policy issues, court cases, biographies, foundations and think tanks, social problems, organizations, diseases, congressional committees, legislation, and much more. The essays vary from a few paragraphs to a number of pages and are uniformly well written and informative. Within entries, terms that are defined elsewhere are capitalized. A name/subject index further helps in locating relevant essays in what is an excellent work. This would be best suited for undergraduate students and general readers interested in aging and its related topics.

294. **Encyclopedia of Aging.** David J. Ekerdt, ed. New York: Macmillan Reference USA, 2002. 4v. index. ISBN 0-02-865472-2 (set).

As Americans live longer, the research and social service knowledge base on the aging population increases. The purpose of this encyclopedia is to capitalize upon and popularize a good bit of the research done on aging in the last fifty years. Topics covered include various physiological aspects of aging, social and behavioral aspects, economic and financial issues, family relationships, discrimination, abuse, care of the elderly, diseases of old age, retirement, and much more. In all, there are some 400 entries written by academic experts on the various topics covered, ranging in length from two to ten pages. The entries are accompanied by *see also* references, as well as a bibliography. Finally, there is an extensive subject/name index to the set that indexes topics, people, photos, figures, and tables that are included throughout the four volumes. Overall, the entries are well written and the prose is well suited for the intended popular audience, while still being faithful to the scientific research on which the entries are based.

295. **The Encyclopedia of Aging: A Comprehensive Resource in Gerontology and Geriatrics.** 3d ed. George L. Maddox, ed. New York: Springer, 2001. 2v. index. ISBN 0-8261-4842-5.

Now in its third edition, this two-volume set reflects the interdisciplinary nature of gerontology by including entries from the social and behavioral sciences; the biological sciences; and social policy, planning, and practice. This new edition includes approximately 700 entries on key terms, theories, physical conditions, organizations, research instruments, and landmark research studies. The intended audience is the "educated layperson," which in this case means either advanced students or researchers delving into new areas of gerontological research. The essays, written by an international list of 400 experts, range in length from a few paragraphs to a couple of pages. They include references to key theories, theorists, and research, as well as *see also* references to related concepts defined elsewhere in the encyclopedia. Full citations to the works cited can be found in the extensive, 165-page list of references at the end of volume 2. There is an identical and complete subject index in the back of each volume that includes titles and proper names. A list of contributing authors is found at the front of each volume.

296. Howarth, Glennys, and Oliver Leaman, eds. **Encyclopedia of Death and Dying.** London: Routledge, 2001. 534 p. index. $135.00. ISBN 0-415-18825-3.

Over one hundred authors contributed definitions to this interdisciplinary dictionary on death and dying. Entries are drawn from history, philosophy, religion, sociology, psychology, social work, anthropology, medicine, criminal justice, and more. The signed entries can be up to two pages in length and include *see* references, *see also* references, and suggestions for further reading. Words defined elsewhere are indicated in bold print. The definitions themselves vary in readability, as one would expect with so many contributors, though they are mostly quite thorough. Since social science perspectives dominate the dictionary's content, there are many entries of relevance to sociological perspectives on death and dying. These include such concepts as caregiving, bereavement, family, secularization, social death, and more. There is an appended bibliography, as well as name and subject indexes. The content and treatment is sophisticated enough that this dictionary would be best suited to more advanced students of the topic.

297. Kausler, Donald H., and Barry C. Kausler. **The Graying of America: An Encyclopedia of Aging, Health, Mind, and Behavior.** 2d ed. Urbana, IL: University of Illinois Press, 2001. 479 p. index. $49.95. ISBN 0-252-02635-7.

The 470 entries in this encyclopedia reflect the diversity of research interests and findings in the areas of gerontology and aging. Essays range in length from a paragraph to a few pages and cover topics in the areas of health (e.g., exercise, smoking, alcohol, nutrition), specific diseases (e.g., cancer, osteoporosis, Alzheimer's), mental and physical functioning (e.g., memory, reasoning, reaction time), demography, social behavior (e.g., caregiving, elder abuse, grandparenting, friendships), and much more. The essays are well written and appropriate for both general readers and students at various levels. Within definitions, there are cross-references to other definitions in the encyclopedia. However, there are no references for further reading, though specific research studies are alluded to regularly. There is an index of entries and cross-references, as well as an index of entries arranged alphabetically under the fourteen broad topics to which they relate.

298. **Thesaurus of Aging Terminology.** 7th ed. Washington, DC: Research Group, American Association of Retired Persons, 2002. 208 p. $10.00.

Items found in the AgeLine database are indexed using official subject terms ("descriptors") drawn from this thesaurus. The latest edition includes approximately 2,000 subject headings. Terms within the thesaurus may include a definition or "scope note" for clarification, as well as cross-references to narrower, related, or broader terms. The thesaurus also directs the user from unused terms to used or preferred terms. Besides the main, alphabetical listing of terms, there is also a "rotated" display of terms that lists them alphabetically while showing the longer heading or phrase in which they appear. There is also a list of geographical terms that may be used, excluding states in the United States. The introductory matter provides useful and detailed tips on how to search the database, as well as lists of newly added and discarded descriptors. Overall, this is an excellent tool for those wanting to do thorough searches of the AgeLine database.

Directories

299. **National Directory for Eldercare Information and Referral: Directory of State and Area Agencies on Aging.** Washington, DC: National Association of Area Agencies on Aging, 1993/94– . $49.95.

Now in its 2002–2003 edition, this lists state and area agencies providing social services to older Americans and continues the earlier *Directory of State and Area Agencies on Aging*. The volume is organized alphabetically by state. The information for each state includes such details as agency addresses, phone numbers, and contact names. Maps are also included designating each state's planning and service areas, which are served by the different area agencies. Listings for American Samoa, Guam, Puerto Rico, the Virgin Islands, and the Trust Territory of the Pacific and Northern Mariana Islands have also been included.

300. Stepp, Derek D., ed. **Directory of Educational Programs in Gerontology and Geriatrics.** 7th ed. Washington, DC: Association for Gerontology in Higher Education, 2000. 305 p. index. $85.00. ISSN 0148-4508.

This directory lists 774 programs (from more than 350 higher education institutions) that offer undergraduate and graduate credit and postdoctoral training in gerontology, geriatrics, and aging. The entries are arranged alphabetically by state (as well as for Australia, Canada, and Spain), then by institution. For each institution, there may be one or more listings for each organizational unit that offers programs. A description of each unit's activities is provided, along with an address, phone, fax number, e-mail address, Web site, number of teaching faculty, credit courses offered, and special resources available. This information is followed by a description of each individual program offered, including the director's name, the level at which the program is offered (e.g., bachelor's), the credential earned (e.g., degree, certificate, minor), the subject focus, and recent student enrollments and completions. Institutional members of the Association for Gerontology in Higher Education (AGHE) are noted. A second, smaller section of the directory lists sixty-one additional AGHE member schools that provide other offerings, though no formal programs. Finally, there is a list of eight AGHE organizational affiliate members, such as the American Association of Retired Persons (AARP) Andrus Foundation. The indexes include an institutional (name) index, a state index, an educational level index, and a distance learning programs index. This is clearly a valuable resource for those identifying appropriate programs for further study in gerontology.

Web Sites and Research Centers

301. **Ethel Percy Andrus Gerontology Center.** Available: http://www.usc.edu/dept/gero/ (Accessed: May 1, 2004).

Supported by the University of Southern California, the center supports research, training, and graduate education in gerontology and its related disciplines. The site describes the Leonard Davis School of Gerontology, various degree program options, upcoming events, careers in aging, community resources, recent news, affiliated faculty members and their publications, the Gerontology Research Institute, the Andrus Center Online newsletter, and much more.

302. **Gerontological Society of America.** Available: http://www.geron.org (Accessed: May 1, 2004).

Included here is an overview of the society, its annual conference, its publications, its membership procedures, and professional job opportunities. For a subscription fee, one can access online copies of its journals, *The Gerontologist* and the *Journals of Gerontology* (Series A and Series B). There are also links to two related sections: the National Academy on an Aging Society, and the Association for Gerontology in Higher Education. The *GSA* also has a number of special interest sections, including the "Behavioral and Social Sciences" section, the "Biological Sciences" section, the "Clinical Medicine" section, the "Social Research, Policy and Practice" section, and a student organization. Each section has its own Web page here, with additional information and numerous links to its officers, activities, committees, and membership information.

303. **Institute of Gerontology.** Available: http://www.iog.wayne.edu (Accessed: May 1, 2004).

Part of Wayne State University, the institute supports teaching and research in gerontology and its various areas of focus (e.g., work, family relations, caregiving, health care, policy). Its graduate student organization also maintains a Web site (*GeroWeb*) that is an excellent guide to other Web sites on gerontology. There is information here from *Transitions Online*, an electronic newsletter, and from *Aging Well*, an Institute-sponsored radio program. There are lists and descriptions of research projects, training programs, degree programs, a colloquium schedule, and more.

304. **The National Archive of Computerized Data on Aging (NACDA).** Available: http://www.icpsr.umich.edu/nacda (Accessed: April 25, 2004).

Located at the Inter-university Consortium of Political and Social Research (ICPSR) and funded by the National Institute on Aging, this site identifies and provides access to information and research data on aging. It includes information about NACDA, its publications, related conferences, and new data releases. There is also online data analysis available for some selective data collections. Beyond this, there are numerous links to research centers, organizations, surveys (e.g., Panel Study of Income Dynamics), government resources (e.g., the National Institute on Aging), and other related Web sites, services, and programs. There are also links to and descriptions of cooperative initiatives and datasets on aging in Europe, Latin America, and other parts of the world.

305. **National Council on the Aging.** Available: http://www.ncoa.org/index. cfm (Accessed: May 1, 2004).

Established in 1950, the NCOA provides information, training, and research on issues related to aging. There is a section with news items on both political and health issues, an advocacy page for those wanting to express their views in the political arena, information on research, descriptions of programs, workforce development training and programs, and lists of available publications. Besides its many publications and research reports, the NCOA also publishes an important guide to the literature on aging, *Abstracts in Social Gerontology*.

306. National Institute on Aging (NIA). Available: http://www.nia.nih.gov/ (Accessed: April 25, 2004).

Part of the National Institutes of Health, the National Institute on Aging is intended to undertake research on aging, to provide resources to advance and support research efforts, to provide training to researchers, and to disseminate information. The Web site includes a calendar of events, press releases, texts of the *Work Group on Minority Aging Newsletter*, links to related government Web sites, publication lists, resource directories, descriptions of research programs, lists of forthcoming conferences and workshops, training opportunities, sources of funding, and more.

307. Research Center. Available: http://research.aarp.org (Accessed: May 1, 2004).

Part of the American Association of Retired Persons (AARP) Web site, the center supports research in social gerontology, health care, retirement, nursing care, public policy, and almost any other area related to aging. AARP is the provider of the *AgeLine Database* (see above). It also provides statistics (e.g., the annual *A Profile of Older Americans*), research reports, and policy documents or position papers. There is information here on such topical areas as health and long-term care, economic security and work, independent living, consumer issues, demographics and reference, public policy institute, Age-Source worldwide (for international information), and the AgeLine Database. Each of these pages has numerous links to other documents, research, and policy statements.

308. Social Gerontology & the Aging Revolution. Available: http://www. trinity.edu~mkearl/geron.html (Accessed: May 1, 2004).

This Web site is another superb offshoot of Michael Kearl's larger sociological site, *A Sociological Tour through Cyberspace*. It provides wide-ranging coverage of issues related to gerontology and aging. There are links to government data, for starters, as well as overview documents discussing the demographic implications of our aging societies. After that, the page provides an overview outline, with links to the aging revolution as it relates to biology, psychology, social psychology, other cultures, and other historical periods. There are also categories for the various institutional impacts of the aging revolution on politics, economics, family, religion, social services, the mass media, and more. Each topic provides dozens of links for further research. The Web site also has links to academic programs for the study of gerontology.

Industrial Sociology/Sociology of Work

Handbooks and Yearbooks

309. Derks, Scott. **The Middle Class: Working Americans, 1880–1999. Vol. 2.** Lakeville, CT: Grey House, 2001. 591 p. index. $135.00. ISBN 1891482726.

310. Derks, Scott. **The Upper Class: Working Americans, 1880–1999. Vol. 3.** Millerton, NY: Grey House, 2001. 567 p. index. $135.00. ISBN 193095638X.

311. Derks, Scott. **The Working Class: Working Americans, 1880–1999. Vol. 1.** Lakeville, CT: Grey House, 2000. 558 p. index. $135.00. ISBN 1891482815.

These three volumes provide qualitative, historical accounts of what life was like for working Americans from various social classes and occupations. Each of the volumes begins in the late nineteenth century and proceeds through the years and decades to the end of the twentieth century. For any particular year in that time span, there is profile of a specific working individual or family. There is some discussion of their annual income, budget, home life, work life, and community life. An added historical snapshot provides a social and economic context for that individual's life, and there is also an economic profile of typical jobs, incomes, and consumer product prices. Plenty of historical photographs are provided as well. While the individual portraits may seem a bit anecdotal for social science research, they can provide valuable snapshots on working life for students. The fact that the three volumes focus on different social classes can allow for valuable comparisons of experiences across class lines. All three volumes append a list of sources consulted, and volumes 2 and 3 also include an index.

312. **Research in the Sociology of Work.** Vol. 1– . Greenwich, CT: JAI Press, 1981– . annual. ISSN 0277-2833.

Each volume in this series is devoted to a special topic, and the volume itself is edited by a scholar and expert in that field. The contributing authors are also scholars specializing in the volume's subject matter. Recent topics have included work and family, job training, the transformation of work, the globalization of work, high-tech work, the meaning of work, and unemployment, among others. These are primarily research articles, with accompanying data and analysis, so the target audience would be advanced scholars in that field.

Web Sites and Research Centers

313. **International Labour Organization.** Available: http://www.ilo.org (Accessed: February 22, 1004).

This site addresses many policy aspects of work or labor on an international level. One can find here documents on international standards and rights at work, international agreements or conventions on important topics like child labor, statistics, labor legislation guidelines, and more.

314. **Organizations, Occupations, and Work.** Available: http://campus.north park.edu/sociology/oow/ (Accessed: February 23, 2004).

This is the Web page of the American Sociological Association's interest group section on the sociology of work and organizations. Included here are announcements, position openings, fellowships and grants information, current and back issues of the section newsletter, award committees, officers and committee members, and calls for papers for both the annual ASA conference and other conferences.

Marriage and the Family

Bibliographies

315. Nordquist, Joan, comp. **Gay and Lesbian Families: A Bibliography.** Santa Cruz, CA: Reference and Research Services, 2000. 68 p. (Contemporary Social Issues: A Bibliographic Series, no. 57). $20.00. ISBN 1-892068-12-5.

Approximately 700 books, monographs, book chapters, pamphlets, dissertations, Web sites and articles are identified on this topic of growing interest. These are far more references than even a broad search in *Sociological Abstracts* retrieves. The entries here are arranged into eleven chapters addressing gay or lesbian families, their parents, their children, violence, same-sex marriage, domestic partnership, and reference sources (i.e., handbooks and guides, bibliographies, and Internet resources). Within subject chapters, there are subchapters for books/monographs or articles, with titles arranged alphabetically by author or, occasionally, by title within each section. The Internet resources include both organizations and many full-text publications, including some court decisions.

Indexes, Abstracts, and Databases

316. **Australian Family and Society Abstracts.** [electronic resource]. Melbourne: Australian Institute of Family Studies, 1980– . monthly. $561.00. ISSN 1032-4003. Available: http://www.aifs.org.au/institute/info/infodev.html#afsa (Accessed: April 18, 2004).

This database includes more than 50,000 citations, abstracts, and selective full-text books, book chapters, research reports, conference papers, journal articles, and other documents on the many facets of family research. Topics covered include child development, adolescence, services to the aged, domestic violence, child abuse, marriage and divorce, children's rights, and more. The database is available online through the Informit Online database service, as well as on CD-ROM from other providers. For the online version, approximately 30 percent of the titles indexed are electronically linked and available full text. Other items may be borrowed via interlibrary loan from the Australian Institute of Family Studies research library. The content of this source is also included in the Family and Society Studies Worldwide database, cited below.

317. Family and Society Studies Worldwide. [electronic resource]. Baltimore, MD: National Information Services Corporation, 2001– . monthly. Available: http://www.nisc.com/frame/NISC_products-f.htm (Accessed: April 18, 2004).

Available in both CD-ROM format and on the Web through its BiblioLine interface, this database includes a number of well-regarded sources for literature-searching on the family. These include the former print source *Inventory of Marriage and Family Literature*, as well as the *Australian Family and Society Abstracts*, the National Clearinghouse on Family Violence from Health Canada, and the U.S. Military Family Resource Center Documents Database, and the Family and Society Studies database (1970–). The database includes references to journal articles, books, book chapters, documents, Web sites, dissertations, and more. Overall, it includes approximately 600,000 references to useful literature in the field on such topics as family therapy, foster care, social work, divorce and remarriage, blended families, family law, family violence, gender roles, and more. The online version of the database is updated monthly, while the CD-ROM is updated quarterly. An accompanying thesaurus, *Family Thesaurus: Subject Terms Used in Australian Family & Society Abstracts* (6th ed., 2001), helps in searching the database.

318. Family Index Database. [electronic resource]. Colombia, MO: Family Scholar Publications, 1995– . monthly. $199/yr. (institutions). ISSN 1089-6147. Available: http://216.119.116.241/fsp/fidinfo.cfm (Accessed: April 18, 2004).

This database is the Web-based equivalent of the print source, *Family Index*. The database includes articles from over 2,000 journals, with approximately 6,000 article citations added to the database each year. Articles are drawn from the fields of education, sociology, psychology, and nursing/medicine, social work, family therapy, and more. Article citations fall within such broad categories as family problems; education, therapy, and family services; diverse families; family relationships; sexuality and reproduction; institutions and policy; individual development; foundations (e.g., history, methodology, demography, theory), among others. Though not included in the database, abstracts and full text may be retrievable from local collections using supplementary software. Access may be either through a username and password or from a registered IP address. The database publisher's home Web site, www.familyscholar.com, also includes descriptions of and links to over a dozen family-related organizations, descriptions of family studies academic programs, faculty members in the field, listservs, and journals, among other items.

319. Sage Family Studies Abstracts. Vol. 1– , No. 1– . Thousand Oak, CA: Sage, 1979– . quarterly, with annual cumulative index. $680/yr. (institutions). ISSN 0164-0283. Available: http://www.sagepub.com/journal.aspx?pid=141 (Accessed: April 18, 2004).

Approximately 250 journal articles, books, and book chapters are descriptively abstracted in each issue. The entries are arranged alphabetically by author within a large number of subject categories and subcategories. These include such subjects as sexual attitudes, gender roles, reproduction, singlehood/mate selection/marriage, early socialization, child care, late socialization, family relations, life cycles, family services, divorce, economics, minority relations, theory, and more. All citations include subject headings, which are used in the subject index. Each index issue also provides subject and author indexes, which are cumulated annually. A source list of over one hundred journals consulted is listed in the last issue of the volume. The contents of this title are also available through some database providers, such as EBSCO online, OCLC First-Search, and others, though there may be embargo periods in providing the most recent abstracts.

Handbooks and Yearbooks

320. Chadwick, Bruce A., and Tim B. Heaton, eds. **Statistical Handbook on the American Family.** 2d ed. Phoenix, AZ: Oryx Press, 1999. 326 p. index. $69.95. ISBN 1-57356-169-X.

Both government and nongovernment data comprise this handbook's 340 tables, charts, and illustrations on the family. Government sources include ongoing publications such as the *Current Population Reports* and the *Statistical Abstract of the United States*. Nongovernment sources include books and journal articles (including the *Gallup Poll Monthly*), as well as research studies such as the *General Social Survey* and the *National Survey of Families and Households*. Retrospective data are included in some, though not all tables. The data are arranged into nine subject chapters: marriage; quality of marriage and family life; divorce and separation; children; sexual attitudes and behavior and contraceptive use; living arrangements and kinship ties; working women, wives, and mothers; demographic and economic context; and child care. Chapters on family violence and the elderly have been removed in this edition, though some relevant tables on these topics are now found under different chapters. Each of the current edition's chapters has numerous subtopics with many tables of data for each. The data source for each table is fully cited in the supplementary "List of Sources." Every chapter begins with a brief overview of each subtopic. A fairly detailed subject index complements the list of contents and the more thorough "List of Tables and Figures."

321. Henderson, Helene, ed. **Domestic Violence and Child Abuse Sourcebook.** Detroit, MI: Omnigraphics, 2000. 1064 p. index. (Health Reference Series). $78.00. ISBN 0-7808-0235-7.

The incidence of various kinds of abuse or violence within family settings is in the millions, and these are only the reported cases of what is a typically underreported social problem. This abuse can include spousal or partner abuse, child abuse, sibling abuse, parent abuse, and elder abuse. Within these various categories, there can be multiple causes of the abuse, with further variations by population group. Given such a complex and multifaceted problem, this sourcebook provides invaluable information on the incidence, causes, consequences, and treatments or interventions for such types of abuse. At over 1,000 pages, the volume covers a wide variety of sources and material.

The book is divided into eight parts or large topical categories, and then further subdivided by chapter and section. The parts include: historical background; spousal and partner abuse; child abuse; sibling abuse; parent abuse; elder abuse; prevention and treatment; research; and additional help and information. Material comprising the various chapters and sections are reprints of or excerpts from various books, chapters, articles, or government publications on the topic. Many of the reprinted items are accompanied by bibliographies or lists of works cited. The concluding chapters provide lists of hotlines and organizations, a topically arranged bibliography of further readings, and a glossary of key terms used throughout the work. Finally, there is a combined name/title/subject index. Overall, this would be an excellent starting point for students or interested general readers, with enough issues, data, and suggested readings to answer questions or prompt further study.

322. Kaul, Chandrika. **Statistical Handbook on the World's Children.** Westport, CT: Oryx Press, 2002. 544 p. index. $65.00. ISBN 1-57356-390-0.

Data describing the condition and well-being of children were, until recently, either not readily collected or scattered in a wide variety of sources. This handbook proceeds on the assumption that tending to the needs of children requires, among other things, good data describing the nature of their existence. It pulls together data from government and nongovernment sources, including the U.S. Census Bureau, the World Health Organization, UNESCO, UNICEF, the United National Food and Agriculture Organization (FAO), the World Bank, and more. There are approximately 270 tables of data arranged under eight broad chapter headings: demographics and vital statistics; education; health and nutrition; disease, hunger and malnutrition; AIDS; economics; family, social environment and behavior; and crime, violence, and war. Each of these chapters, in turn, contains data on subtopics within that general subject area. The data are reproduced from their original sources, with some editing, and the source documents are fully cited. Web addresses for the documents are cited as well. Important international documents relating to the well-being of children are appended full text. There is also a glossary of key terms, as well as a subject index.

323. Kinnear, Karen L. **Single Parents: A Reference Handbook.** Santa Barbara, CA: ABC-CLIO, 1999. 263 p. index. (Contemporary World Issues). $45.00. LC 98-47236. ISBN 1-57607-033-6.

Like other titles in this series, Kinnear's work provides an excellent overview of a very hot topic in the social sciences, social services, and social policy. A wide variety of information is included in seven chapters that not only introduce the reader to the topic and its issues, but also foster further study of the topic. Chapter 1 provides an overview of single parents, including definitions, causes, consequences, demographic characteristics, social policy debates and concerns, research findings, legal issues, sources of data, and much more. Chapters 2 and 3 provide a chronology of key events and biographical sketches of notable activists, scholars, and politicians involved in the issue. Chapter 4 presents statistical data arranged topically and also includes descriptions of key Supreme Court decisions. Chapter 5 is an annotated directory of organizations, including addresses, phone numbers, and Web addresses. Chapter 6 is an annotated bibliography of books and articles, while Chapter 7 does the same for videos and Internet resources. A detailed subject index aids access. High school and college students would be the target audience for this handbook.

324. Stebbins, Leslie F. **Work and Family in America: A Reference Handbook.** Santa Barbara, CA: ABC-CLIO, 2001. 247 p. index. (Contemporary World Issues). $45.00. ISBN 1-57607-224-X.

For both alternative (e.g., single-parent) and dual-income families, balancing family life with work is difficult. This is made all the more so because of both the cost of child care and the sluggish response of employers in accommodating new work-family realities.

The volume begins with a historical overview of the relationship between work and family, with subsections addressing women, men, low-income and minority groups, caregiving, and strategies for resolving work-family conflicts. Subsequent chapters provide: a chronology of events (dating to the eighteenth century); biographical sketches of key individuals; statistics on the work-family relationship (including some international data); key legislation and Supreme Court decisions; an annotated directory of organizations; and annotated listings of relevant books, journals, videos, and Web sites. A glossary of key terms is appended, as is a name/subject index.

As with other volumes in this series, this is an excellent introduction to an increasingly hot topic (as reflected by over 400 citations since 2000 in *Sociological Abstracts*). Students and general readers should find this an excellent starting point for further research.

325. Sussman, Marvin B., Suzanne K. Steinmetz, and Gary W. Peterson, eds. **Handbook of Marriage and the Family.** 2d ed. New York: Plenum Press, 1999. 822 p. index. $110.00. ISBN 0-306-45754-7.

This second edition includes twenty-eight chapters, ranging from twenty to fifty pages, under five major topical headings: family diversity, theory and methods, changing family patterns and roles, the family and other institutions, and changing family patterns and roles (with different essays). The twenty-eight chapters address such topics as demography, ethnic variation, postmodernism, socializing children and parents, marital dissolution, methodology, families and law or work or economics, family abuse, family communications, adolescence, family and health, family dynamics, sexuality, and more. Experts from a variety of social science disciplines authored these chapters. The chapters often review the historical development of each topic, its major issues and subtopics, its key theories and theorists, and significant data and research. Authors were encouraged to focus on new developments since the first edition. The new edition treats varieties of family structures in a single chapter, yet numerous chapters also specifically address diverse family forms. Because all of the chapters are still quite thorough and somewhat historical, they would be an excellent starting point for students beginning to do research on subtopics within marriage and the family. For more recent references on these topics, one could consult current bibliographies (cited elsewhere in this section), *Sage Family Studies Abstracts, Sociological Abstracts*, or the Family and Society Studies Worldwide database, to name a few sources. There is an extensive subject index for tracking topics across essays.

326. Touliatos, John, Barry F. Perlmutter, and Murray A. Straus, eds. **Handbook of Family Measurement Techniques.** Thousand Oaks, CA: Sage, 2001. 3v. index. $431.95. ISBN 0-8039-7250-4.

Intended for clinicians and researchers, this book describes 1,343 research instruments available for various aspects of family research. Volume 1 is a reprint of the earlier edition and includes descriptions of instruments published between 1929 and 1986; volume 2 abstracts 367 instruments published between 1987 and 1996. The descriptions are arranged by author under a classification scheme of thirteen major categories across the first two volumes, which are devoted to abstracts. The categories are the dimensions of marital and family interaction; intimacy and family values; parenthood; roles and power; adjustments; measuring family relations; measuring parent-child relations; measuring family adjustment, health, and well-being; and measuring family problems. Each major category is introduced by an essay that attempts to integrate "conceptual development and measurement concerns" (p. ix). Over half of the instruments have been cited since 1975 and are given more detailed descriptions in the first part of volume 1. For each instrument, there is information including the author(s), title, availability, variables measured, type of instrument, instrument description, sample items (if permission was granted), comments (e.g., validity, reliability, Cronbach's alpha), and references that describe the instrument. The older research instruments that have not been recently cited are given abbreviated abstracts in the last, smaller section of volume 1. Almost half of the newer instruments abstracted in volume 2 are reproduced in their entirety, with permission, in volume 3. These are arranged alphabetically by instrument name under the five subject categories used to classify instruments in volume 2. There are instrument author, title, and subject indexes, as well as an introductory essay on the evolution of family research principles and techniques.

327. Turner, Jeffrey Scott. **Families in America: A Reference Handbook.** Santa Barbara, CA: ABC-CLIO, 2002. 351 p. index. $45.00. (Contemporary World Issues). ISBN 1-57607-628-8.

Like other books in this series, this is an excellent overview of a range issues, facts, events, and people connected to family life in America. The content is divided into eight major chapters: history and scope of American families (from Colonial times to the present), diversity of family life (covering structural and multicultural variations), family issues and controversies (e.g., family planning, work, single-parent families, gay and lesbian families, caregiving for aging family members, abusive relationships), chronology, biographical sketches (covering twenty-four individuals spanning the nineteenth and twentieth centuries), facts and statistics, agencies and organizations (a directory), print resources (an annotated bibliography), and nonprint resources (an annotated bibliography). The first three major sections have well-written discussions of the history of the family, variations in its form, and many of the major issues relating to the family. The biographies are for key individuals, including Benjamin Spock, Sigmund Freud, Alfred Kinsey, Erik Erikson, and others who have had substantial impacts on family life. The various chapters with annotated resource listings are excellent. The content and presentation of information here is perfectly suited to high school, college, and general reader audiences. Major sociological concerns, such as family structures, abuse, divorce, and female-headed households are covered.

Dictionaries and Encyclopedias

328. Balter, Lawrence, ed. **Parenthood in America: An Encyclopedia.** Santa Barbara, CA: ABC-CLIO, 2000. 2v. index. (The American Family). $185.00. ISBN 1-57607-213-4.

Like other titles in this encyclopedia series (including infancy, boyhood, girlhood, family, and adolescence in America), this is a well-written and valuable overview of topics related to parenthood. Topics covered include theories, key concepts, important individuals, controversies, health and medical issues, and organizations. Not surprisingly, since all of the encyclopedias in this series revolve around the family and its constituent members, roles, and evolution, there is some overlapping of topics from one set to the next. However, these common topics are authored by different scholars, making for additional insights into and information on the subjects. The over 200 signed entries range from one page to over ten pages, and include *see also* references and bibliographies for further reading. There are historical topics and biographies of important historical figures (e.g., Maria Montessori, Erik Erikson, Theodore Geisel, Fred Rogers, and Jean Piaget). There is a wealth of important social science topics covered, including acculturation, alienation, immigrant families, transition to fatherhood, interracial families, and much more. One can also find entries on important health conditions and diseases that impact family life and parenting, such as sudden infant death syndrome (SIDS), anorexia and bulimia, AIDS, chronic illness, and sleep deprivation. A lengthy bibliography is appended, as is a subject/name/title index. Overall, this is an excellent encyclopedia for both general readers and students.

329. Bankston, Carl L., ed. **Encyclopedia of Family Life.** Pasedena, CA: Salem Press, 1999. 5v. $380.00. ISBN 0-89356-940-2.

Aimed at general readers, this encyclopedia provides an overview of the wide variety of topics, people, organizations, legislation, court cases, and controversies that are relevant to the field of marriage and the family from social science and policy perspectives. The 452 entries range from 250 words to 4,000 words. Longer entries are accompanied by bibliographies, while the longest entries have annotated bibliographies. All of the essays include numerous *see also* references, and the text is often complemented by statistical tables, charts, graphs, and photographs. Besides entries on topics, there are also biographical entries on important individuals, both historical and contemporary (e.g., Jane Addams, John Bradshaw). There are also entries on key organizations, court cases, legislation, and programs, such as Aid to Families with Dependent Children (AFDC) or the Family and Medical Leave Act. There is an accompanying list of the entries arranged under twenty-eight broader terms, including such categories as court cases, economic issues, education, health and medical issues, laws, marriage and couples, organizations and government programs, religion, and much more. Also, there are two time lines relating to (1) important legislation and court cases and (2) other developments relating to family life (primarily in the United States since the seventeenth century). An annotated list of support groups, a glossary, and an annotated selective bibliography are also provided. The index includes subjects, people, acronyms, organizations, legislation, government programs, and court cases.

330. Clark, Robin E., and Judith Freeman Clark, with Christine Adamec. **The Encyclopedia of Child Abuse.** 2d ed. New York: Facts on File, 2001. 344 p. index. $71.50. ISBN 0-8160-4060-5.

Surprisingly, child abuse is not a simply defined and unchanging social problem. Definitions of what constitutes abuse or neglect can vary across cultures and can evolve with changing social, economic, and political factors, as well as changes in medicine. This does not make child abuse a social construction; it does make it a multifaceted and moving target. Abuse can be physical or psychological, or may even be marked by more subtle patterns of neglect, coercion, or exploitation. This encyclopedia endeavors to explore and explain many of these features of child abuse. The selective list of entries, which are fairly concise, includes key terms, laws, medical conditions and diseases, country information, organizations, programs, court cases, and more. Appended are directories of various agencies, organizations, and resources centers. There are also data tables, the text of the Child Abuse Prevention and Treatment Act, a bibliography of further readings, and a subject index.

331. Hawes, Joseph M. **The Family in America: An Encyclopedia.** Santa Barbara, CA: ABC-CLIO, 2001. 2v. index. (The American Family). $185.00. ISBN 1-57607-232-0.

Comprising over 180 entries, this encyclopedia provides substantial essays on both contemporary and historical aspects of the family. The signed essays, written by scholars in the various specialty areas, cover key concepts, legislation, major individuals, important organizations and events, controversial debates, and more. The essays range from one page to over ten pages, include *see also* references to related entries, and provide a lengthy bibliography of references and suggestions for further reading. Some of the classic and contemporary social science topics on the family include theories of birth order, child development, twins, demography, gender roles, child abuse, family therapy, drug and alcohol abuse, varieties of families, and more. Landmark individuals for whom biographies are provided include Sigmund Freud, Robert and Helen Lynd, Magaret Sanger, Benjamin Spock, and Ellen Richards, among others. Entries on legislation and related topics include, for example, the Family and Medical Leave Act and the Earned Income Tax Credit, as well as the White House conferences on children. There is treatment of important historical subjects, such as the Oneida community, eugenics, the Shakers, White House conferences on children, and the internment of Japanese American families during World War II. There are even entries on medical conditions with major effects on the family, such as AIDS, venereal disease, polio, and syphilis. Throughout, the essays are well written and, as a result, are well suited for both general readers and academic researchers. Supplementary information includes both a substantial bibliography, and a combined name/title/subject index.

332. **International Encyclopedia of Marriage and the Family.** 2d ed. James J. Ponzetti, Jr., ed. New York: Macmillan Reference USA, 2003. 4v. $450.00. ISBN 0-0286-5672-5.

Now comprising four volumes, the second edition of this encyclopedia represents a "significant expansion and revision" (p. viii) of the first edition. This edition still takes a multidisciplinary approach to studies of marriage and the family, drawing heavily from scholars in fields such as sociology, psychology, social work, gerontology, law, medicine, and more. The most significant change in this edition, over and above the updating of earlier entries, is the addition of an international perspective. This is reflected both in the entries on various countries, and in the internationalization of other topics (e.g., abortion, childhood). While not comprehensive in its coverage of other countries, this encyclopedia nonetheless includes information on fifty countries from all regions of the world. In all, there are now approximately 400 entries, more than twice the number of the earlier edition. There are entries on countries, particular ethnic groups, and certain religions (e.g., Buddhism, Catholicism), as well as on more predictable topics in the field of marriage and family studies. These would include subjects such as child abuse, conflict, family assessment, single parent families, divorce, birth order, family roles, family systems theory, homeless families, poverty, social networks, spouse abuse, and mate selection, among others. There is also an attempt here to treat marriage and family in an inclusive way, with entries on such topics as lesbian parents and gay parents. In addition, there are some topics covered from a medical or health sciences perspective, including birth control, abortion, and assisted reproductive technologies. Entries typically range from two to eight pages and include both a bibliography of cited sources and *see also* references to related topics. The contributing authors are experts in their topics and are drawn from around the world. Few of the entries are just reprints from the earlier edition. Most are either new or have been more substantially revised. The writing is good throughout and seems aimed at students, scholars, or more advanced general readers. The accompanying index includes proper names, subjects, acronyms, court cases, and some titles (mentioned in entries).

Web Sites and Research Centers

333. American Sociological Association Family Section: Home on the Web.
Available: http://www.asanet.org/sectionfamily/ (Accessed: April 25, 2004).

The site describes what the ASA family section does and what family sociologists do, lists officers, describes section awards for scholarships (for students and faculty), and provides information on why and how to join. Other links to graduate programs, ASA conference sessions, and family resources were not functional.

334. ChildStats.gov. Available: http://www.childstats.gov (Accessed: April 25, 2004).

A product of the Federal Interagency Forum on Child and Family Statistics, this official Web site helps meet the agencies goals of enhancing data collection on children and youth, as well as disseminating those data to the general public and policy community. Included here is the Forum's annual report, *America's Children: Key National Indicators of Well-Being.* This includes data on a number of indicators of child well-being, including health, education, economic security, and more. International comparative data are also provided on many of the same subject categories that are covered in *America's Children.* The category of economic security, for example, has data on youth unemployment, childhood poverty, and child labor, among other subjects. The Web site also includes a report on *Counting Couples*, with accompanying data, as well as links to other Web sites related to the same major categories explored on this site.

335. Family Development Page. Available: http://www3.uakron.edu/hefe/fam1.html#link (Accessed: April 25, 2004).

This includes links to a range of Web sites related to the sociology of the family, touching on such topics as marriage, divorce, remarriage, human sexuality, family economics, death/widowhood/bereavement, family violence, women's issues, and the media. Academic and government Web sites are listed too. Many of these subject categories are briefly annotated.

336. Marriage and Family Processes. Available: http://www.trinity.edu/~mkearl/family.html (Accessed: April 25, 2004).

Part of Professor Michael Kearl's Web site, *A Sociological Tour through Cyberspace*, this page provides a wealth of information and a wide variety of links on the sociology of the family and related topics. There are thoughtful discussions of key issues and controversies, usually with links to Web sites with additional and, when appropriate, contrary points of view. Additionally, there are numerous links to charts and statistics, as well as full-text reports on aspects of marriage and the family. There is an initial discussion of what constitutes a family, followed by some facts and related Web sites on the personal benefits of family. The site then breaks itself down into various subtopics, including: cultural factors shaping family structures and processes, parenting, coupling, relationships between husbands and wives through time, other family players (e.g., grandparents), marital disunions, and institutions affected by family systems. Each page is thought provoking and skillfully prompts the reader to explore further at critical points in the page. Overall, this is an excellent and well-conceived site that is deserving of its numerous Web site awards.

337. **National Council on Family Relations (NCFR).** Available: http://www.ncfr.org (Accessed: April 25, 2004).

Founded in 1938, the NCFR provides support and services for researchers, educators, and practitioners working with families. It has thousands of members and regional, state, and local groups. Besides publishing the *Journal of Marriage and the Family* and *Family Relations*, the NCFR sponsors an annual conference, gives awards, fosters dialogue between specialists in the field, and publishes an online newsletter. There is information on the site on becoming a certified family life educator (CFLE). The Web site also now includes research-based practical tips related to family life arranged under eleven categories (e.g., family law, parenting, family dynamics, personal relationships). In addition, there are policy-related Web pages with fact sheets, policy briefs, and more.

338. **Public Agenda Online: Family.** Available: http://www.publicagenda.org/issues/frontdoor.cfm?issue_type=family (Accessed: April 25, 2004).

Public Agenda Online provides discussion, insights, data, and public opinion on a variety of important, and often controversial, public policy issues. The subsection on family, as with other topics, provides a number of links for understanding the issue, the controversies around it, different perspectives and their policy implications, the key players in the debate, relevant facts, recent news stories, and more. Some of the controversies or policy issues discussed here include changes in the role and influence of the family, parental responsibilities, and gay marriage and adoption. The discussion of various perspectives, with accompanying policy implications, should be particularly useful for demonstrating to students the connection between theory and its implications for practice. Another collection of pages provides findings from public opinion surveys (conducted by Public Agenda) on the family and related policy issues. This is an interesting, policy-oriented site that could complement students' readings in the sociology of the family.

339. **Sociology of Family and Children.** Available: http://www2.fmg.uva.nl/sociosite/topics/familychild.html (Accessed: April 25, 2004).

This is a section of the Dutch Web site, *SocioSite*, and it includes an extensive number of links to Web sites on the sociology of the family and on children and youth. Included among the sites are organizational Web pages from around the world, full text of some online publications, college course Web pages, publisher Web pages, interactive tutorials, glossaries of terms, support groups, resource directories, statistical sources, and much more.

Medical Sociology

Indexes, Abstracts, and Databases

340. **CINAHL.** [electronic resource]. Peabody, MA: EBSCO Publishing, 1982– . weekly updates. ISSN 0146-5554. Available: http://www.epnet.com/academic/cinahl.asp (Accessed: March 15, 2004).

CINAHL, Cumulative Index to Nursing and Allied Health Literature, indexes and abstracts articles in approximately 2,000 serial publications in the fields of nursing and allied health. Books, dissertations, conference proceedings, and other materials are also included in the database, which now has over 700,000 records. Because the database deals with the provision of health care, there may be much of interest here for medical sociologists and sociologists studying health care professions, caregivers, emotional labor, stress and burnout, and so on. Some full-text material is included, and subscribers to additional EBSCO services will also get access to additional full-text articles for almost 400 of the journals indexed here. The database is also made available from other providers, such as Ovid and OCLC.

341. **MEDLINE.** [electronic resource]. Bethesda, MD: National Library of Medicine, 1966– . daily updates.

The MEDLINE database is equivalent to three print sources: *Index Medicus*, *Index to Dental Literature*, and *International Nursing Index*. It also now includes the *AIDSLine*, *BioethicsLink*, and *HealthSTAR* (management) databases for research related to those specialized fields. Overall, some 4,500 journals from 70 countries are indexed and abstracted, though almost 90 percent are English language. For medical sociologists, it is an excellent source for citations dealing with health care accessibility; health care policies; the treatment and epidemiology of various conditions (e.g., AIDS); aspects of the work of health care professionals; treatment related to race, ethnicity, and gender; and much more. Numerous online and CD-ROM versions of the MEDLINE database are also available from such publishers as Ovid/SilverPlatter and EBSCO, with options for accompanying full text. The NLM version of the database, PubMed, is also available at their Web site (Available: http://www.ncbi.nlm.nih.gov/pubmed; accessed: June 28, 2004).

Handbooks and Yearbooks

342. Albrecht, Gary L., Ray Fitzpatrick, and Susan C. Scrimshaw, eds. **Handbook of Social Studies in Health and Medicine.** Thousand Oaks, CA: Sage, 2000. 545 p. index. $143.00. ISBN 0-7619-5617-4.

The social sciences, and most certainly sociology and anthropology, have much to offer in the analysis of health and illness. This handbook, with its thirty-two articles, highlights these contributions and the various analytical levels to which they contribute. The first part of the book ("Social and Cultural Frameworks of Analysis"), comprises eleven articles that address how social structure and social processes affect one's chances of suffering ill health. They also address, somewhat, how these factors affect perceptions of health. Included are chapters on socioeconomic inequalities in health, gender and health, health and aging, the social causation of health and illness, the social construction of medicine and the body, and much more. Part 2 of the book focuses on "The Experience of Health and Illness." Here, the articles are more focused on social factors that affect how individuals or groups (e.g., family) experience health and illness. This is a more micro-level analysis, reflecting interpretive and ethnographic research, and it clearly has implications for how people seek help and respond to interventions. Chapters include such topics as the personal experience of illness, cultural variation in the experience of health and illness, and health care utilization and barriers to health care, among others. Part 3 takes a macro-level approach and looks at "Health-Care Systems and Practices." There are chapters on health care markets, equity in health policy, comparative health systems, the medical profession, and more. The authors of the chapters are experts in their specialties and are drawn primarily from the fields of sociology and anthropology. Author and subject indexes are provided.

343. Andrulis, Dennis P., and Nanette J. Goodman. **The Social and Health Landscape of Urban and Suburban America.** Chicago: AHA Press, 1999. 403 p. $200.00. ISBN 1-55648-260-4.

Medical sociologists, policymakers, and researchers interested in health in urban areas should find this compilation of data valuable. The focus here is on collecting data that allow one "to compare both the health care system and the social health status of one city to another" (p. 1). To give a full picture of these geographic areas, both demographic data and health-related data are included. Also, data are often presented for cities, counties, and metropolitan areas (excluding the cities), in order to make other comparisons. The book is divided into nine chapters. The first two chapters present data for cities, counties, and Metropolitan Statistic Areas, or MSAs (excluding central cities) on such demographic features as poverty, unemployment, crime, and child welfare, among others. Chapters 3 through 5 present data on hospitals, community health centers, and health departments, respectively. Chapter 6 presents data on HIV/AIDS, syphilis, and tuberculosis. Chapter 7 recombines data from earlier chapters to create a deprivation index and a child welfare index for cities and counties. The last chapter includes poverty maps for many metropolitan areas, as well as collections of key data for those same cities, and for counties and metropolitan areas (both excluding the city). Data are drawn from a variety of public and private sources, including the Bureau of the Census, the American Hospital Association, the FBI, the Department of Commerce, and the National Center for Health Statistics, among others. There is an extensive introductory chapter that discusses a broad range of demographic, health, and welfare data that are featured throughout the volume.

344. Bird, Chloe E., Peter Conrad, and Allen M. Fremont, eds. **Handbook of Medical Sociology.** 5th ed. Upper Saddle River, NJ: Prentice Hall, 2000. 438 p. index. $73.00. ISBN 0-1301-4456-8.

Now in its fifth edition, this handbook continues to track ongoing changes in the field of medical sociology. This latest edition includes twenty-nine chapters, all of which were newly written. In keeping with its past practice of marking the evolution of this field, this edition includes essays on both traditional topics (e.g., doctor-patient relationships, professions, medical education) and newer, cutting-edge topics (e.g., gender, disability, alternative medicine, managed care). The contributions, written by experts in the field, run from ten to twenty pages and are not written as overviews, but rather as provocative essays. The twenty-nine articles are divided into six categories: introduction and history, social contexts of health and illness, health and illness behavior and experience, organization of health services, medical care, and areas of collaboration and future directions for medical sociology. This last category includes articles discussing contributions from related fields that closely mirror concerns of medical sociologists, including fields like medical anthropology and health psychology. All articles are accompanied by a substantial list of references. There is also a name index and a rather brief subject index.

345. Cockerham, William C., ed. **The Blackwell Companion to Medical Sociology.** Malden, MA: Blackwell, 2001. 518 p. index. $124.95. ISBN 0-631-21703-7.

Medical sociology has been a growing subdiscipline within the field of sociology. It is also multidisciplinary and international in its scope and influence. According to the editor, this volume is the first effort to reflect all of these factors in a state-of-the-art overview of the field, covering developments since the 1950s. There are two major parts to this handbook: part 1 covers substantive topics; part 2 covers regional perspectives. Part 1 is divided into nine chapters with essays covering such topics as medical sociology and sociological theory; social stratification; work stress and health; health professions and occupations; sociology of the body; gender analysis of health; migration, health, and stress; health and culture; and modern health care systems. Part 2 is divided into subsections for regions of the world, each with a number of chapters on specific countries or regions. These essays may be either overviews of the state or history of medical sociology research in that country, such as the essay on Great Britain, or a medical sociological analysis of a large health issue in that country, such as the impact on Poland's health system of its move from communism. An international group of scholars, experts in their topic or country, have contributed the essays. A substantial subject/name index is also provided.

346. Darnay, Arsen J., ed. **Statistical Record of Health & Medicine.** 2d ed. New York: Gale Research, 1998. 1029 p. index. $130.00. ISBN 0-7876-0093-8.

Included here are 950 tables of data profiling the health status of Americans and the provision of health care primarily in the United States. The data are organized into eleven chapters: summary indicators; health status of Americans (e.g., causes of death, incidence of diseases, mental health); the health care establishment (e.g., clinics, hospitals); lifestyles and health (e.g., obesity, smoking, and drugs); health in the workplace (e.g., occupational health and safety); health expenditures and funding; health care programs (e.g., Medicaid, Medicare, HMOs); medical professions (including compensation and education); medical practices and procedures; politics, opinion, and law (e.g., Family and Medical Leave Act, malpractice); and international comparisons. The data are assembled from both government and nongovernment sources, covering information from the early to mid-1990s. While government sources are a major source of data here, there are also data from popular magazines, journals, and newspaper articles, as well as public opinion polls. A list of source documents is included. There is also an extensive keyword index that includes both keywords and keywords as subtopics under the names of cities, metropolitan areas, or states. The only blemish under these subtopics is the undifferentiated listing of entries for medical facilities, the numbers for which can run into the dozens. Overall, however, this is a fairly comprehensive, albeit now somewhat dated compilation.

347. Eisler, Richard M., and Michel Hersen, eds. **Handbook of Gender, Culture, and Health.** Mahwah, NJ: Lawrence Erlbaum, 2000. 531 p. index. $125.00. ISBN 0-8058-2638-6.

As stated in the preface, "the quality and effectiveness of our disease prevention and health promotion activities are dependent on our understanding of how gender, ethnicity, age, and sexual orientation are related to health practices and outcomes" (p. ix). This volume is dedicated to addressing, at least in part, the concerns identified in this statement. The twenty articles are divided into four parts or sections, each focusing on a different theme: stress in diverse populations, differences in health issues (including culture, ethnicity, aging), specific health problems (e.g., cancer, heart disease, substance abuse, eating disorders, HIV), and health problems of special populations (e.g., lesbians; widows; gender and culture in aging; intimate partner violence). The authors come from the fields of psychology, health, and related fields, but the articles themselves should appeal to the broad range of social and health sciences. Articles range from ten to twenty pages in length and are accompanied by an extensive list of references. Author and subject indexes are included.

348. Gochman, David S., ed. **Handbook of Health Behavior Research.** New York: Plenum, 1997. 4v. index. $275.00. ISBN 0-614-30711-2.

One of the more important goals of this four-volume set is to help establish health behavior research "as an important area of basic research, worthy of being studied in its own right" (p. x). Towards that end, the editor has brought together numerous state-of-the-art essays reviewing what is known on different aspects of health behavior. Though interdisciplinary, health behavior research is still distinctly oriented towards the social sciences. The four volumes in this set each have a different focus: personal and social determinants (volume 1); provider determinants (volume 2); demography, development, and diversity (volume 3); and relevance for professionals and issues for the future (volume 4). Early on, the editor makes the point that a major emphasis of these volumes is the interaction of health behavior with various systems, including families, institutions, communities, and culture. A glossary of key terms, a volume-by-volume list of contents, and a cumulative subject index are found in the back of all four volumes.

349. **A Handbook for Teaching Medical Sociology.** 4th ed. Robin D. Moremen, comp. and ed. Washington, DC: American Sociological Association, 2001. 321 p. (ASA Resource Materials for Teaching).

This is part of a series of titles put out by the American Sociological Association intended help sociology faculty improve their teaching. It is a collection of a few different types of materials. First, it contains syllabi for survey courses in medical sociology at the undergraduate level. These syllabi were contributed by faculty at various universities. After that there are syllabi for courses on special topics, such as health and inequality, the human side of medicine, disability studies, and much more. Second, there is a small section of "basic teaching materials" that includes a list of books about medical school and residency, as well as a copy of an ASA conference presentation on "Addressing Lesbian and Gay Issues in the Medical Sociology Curriculum." Third, there is a collection of special assignments, such as a sick-role memoir, the social construction of illness, a disability-role assignment, and more. Fourth, there are some classroom exercises on topics such as abortion, HIV, hearing the elderly, and reproductive technologies, among others. Contributors are listed at the end. This could be a valuable source for those teaching new courses in medical sociology.

350. Thomas, Richard K., ed. **Health and Health Care in the United States: County and Metro Area Data.** 2d ed. Lanham, MD: Bernan, 2001. 401 p. $135.00. ISBN 0-89059-278-0.

The editor argues that even common health data are often located in a variety of sources, forcing users to do more digging for these data than one might anticipate. This work attempts to correct that problem by assembling some 80 statistics on health and health care for 3,000 counties and 329 metropolitan areas in the United States. These data are drawn from both government sources, such as the Census of Population and Housing and the National Center for Health Statistics, and private companies. Furthermore, the data are recent, covering 1997 through 2000, with retrospective data from 1990 and projections to 2005 included in some tables. The data in the section labeled "table A" are arranged alphabetically by state, then by counties within each state. Over twenty tables initially cover general demographic data, such as population, households, age groupings, race/ethnicity, and income. Following these data are almost sixty tables of health-related data under the categories of vital statistics (e.g., births, deaths, causes of death), health care resources (e.g., number of physicians, nursing homes, dental clinics, home health agencies), and Medicare (e.g., Medicare enrollment, Medicare cases, Medicare programs). Many of the same categories of data are covered in the section labeled "table B," which presents data for metropolitan areas, counties, and central cities. A list of sources identifies the various government and nongovernment data sources, and there are definitions of key terms arranged under the headings from each section of the book.

351. Wright, Eric R., and Michael Polgar, eds. **Teaching the Sociology of HIV/AIDS: Syllabi, Lectures, and Other Resources for Instructors and Students.** Washington, DC: American Sociological Association, 1997. 205 p. (ASA Resource Materials for Teaching).

Since the first ASA volume on teaching about HIV/AIDS, the number of such courses has grown significantly, as has the epidemic. Furthermore, "there is a growing body of sociological research around which to develop courses" (p. 2). This growth in research, as well as in courses and instructional modules, is reflected here. The volume has four parts. Part 1, course syllabi, includes eleven examples drawn from a variety of disciplines and institutions around the country. Part 2 includes six lectures on HIV/AIDS, focusing on such specific topics as women and AIDS, the social construction of HIV/AIDS, social movement aspects of AIDS, outreach interventions, and the perceived risk of health care workers. Besides the text of the lecture, there is often a list of references or recommended readings. Part 3 covers related teaching resources and includes class assignments, discussion exercises, an annotated list of filmed images of HIV/AIDS, Internet resources, and the introduction to a book on service learning and the AIDS epidemic. Finally, part 4 includes several articles on teaching about HIV/AIDS taken from Teaching Sociology.

Dictionaries and Encyclopedias

352. Cockerham, William C., and Ferris J. Ritchey. **Dictionary of Medical Sociology.** Westport, CT: Greenwood Press, 1997. 169 p. index. $79.95. ISBN 0-313-29269-8.

Intended for both medical sociologists and researchers in related fields, this dictionary includes hundreds of terms for both practical and theoretical concepts. To be included, terms had to be either generic or "descriptive terms created by medical sociologists" (p. x), or else terms from other fields that are regularly part of the discourse in medical sociology. Terms that are more readily identified with other fields, and defined in their specialized dictionaries, are not included. The definitions here are typically a paragraph long, though occasionally they extend to a couple of pages. When needed, multiple definitions of a term are provided, as is a discussion of the theoretical and practical import of the term. Fairly descriptive terms are included (e.g., "ambulatory care," "crude birth rate"), as well as theoretically oriented terms with more significant implications for analysis and research (e.g., "medicalization," "labeling theory"). There are also a few biographical entries on key contributors to medical sociology, such as Talcott Parsons and Erving Goffman. More typically, the contributions of theorists are discussed in the context of some of their ideas or theories. Throughout, the definitions, even on the more difficult concepts, are very clear and straightforward. A bibliography of important references is appended, as is a fairly detailed subject index.

Web Sites and Research Centers

353. **eSocHealth.** Available: http://www.latrobe.edu.au/telehealth/esochealth/ (Accessed: December 29, 2004).
This is an extensive Web site for the health section of The Australian Sociological Association. Included here are links to health-related Web sites and associations, health journals and new books, an archive of past issues of the newsletter (*eSocHealth*, the association's health sociology online newsletter and interest group Web site), and a discussion forum, among others. There is also a link to and information about *Health Sociology Review* (a paid subscription journal), as well as news and announcements. In all, this is a solid Web site with numerous leads for scholars in this field.

354. **Health Statistics.** Available: http://www.trinity.edu/mkearl/health.html (Accessed: December 29, 2004).
Though not a medical sociology Web site per se, this nonetheless has excellent links to data and information sources that could be of interest to medical and health sociologists. Mounted on the Web site, *A Sociological Tour through Cyberspace*, this page includes links to the National Center for Health Statistics, *Health, United States*, the *Morbidity and Mortality Weekly Report*, Center for Disease Control datasets, and much more. There are additional categories of links for the medical profession, ethics, international health, the history of medicine, alternative medicine, and medical journals.

355. **The Medical Sociology Section Homepage.** Available: http://dept.kent. edu/sociology/asamedsoc/ (Accessed: December 29, 2004).
As mentioned on the American Sociological Association medical sociology Web page, the purpose of this interest group is to examine "the phenomena of health and illness, the social organization of health care delivery, and differential access to medical resources" (http://www.asanet.org/sections/medical.html). There is a wealth of information here, including links to: Web pages for related journals, data sources on the Web, publishing opportunities in journals or monographs, upcoming conferences, online discussion groups in the field, recent relevant publications in medical sociology (e.g., the *Handbook of Medical Sociology*), links to the British and Australian medical sociology Web sites, descriptions of and links to graduate programs in the field, and much more.

356. **Medical Sociology Study Group.** Available: http://www.britsoc.co.uk/ bsaweb.php?link_id=55&area=item2 (Accessed: December 29, 2004).
One of the interest groups of the British Sociological Association (BSA), this study group's site makes available information on the medical sociology annual conference, book reviews, the group newsletter (*Medical Sociology News*), its regional and study groups, journals in the field, and prizes for writing in the

field. There are also links to the BSA's other study groups, news items, related Web sites, and much more.

Population and Demography

Bibliographies

357. Agyei-Mensah, Samuel, comp. **Fertility Decline in Developing Countries, 1960–1997: An Annotated Bibliography.** Westport, CT: Greenwood Press, 1999. 140 p. index. (Bibliographies and Indexes in Geography, no. 3). $69.95. LC 98-51612. ISBN 0-313-30242-1.

Intended for "population experts and students interested in carrying out research on fertility decline in the developing world" (p. viii), this bibliography includes nearly 500 references from journals, dissertations, monographs, and research reports. These works are arranged into chapters on general concepts and theories of fertility decline; fertility decline in major areas of the developing world, including Latin America, Asia, and Sub-Saharan Africa; and, fertility decline in the developing world as a whole. References are listed alphabetically by author within each chapter and are briefly annotated. Subject and author indexes are provided, as is a list of journals consulted.

Indexes, Abstracts, and Databases

358. **POPLINE.** Available: http://db.jhuccp.org/popinform/basic.html (Accessed: December 29, 2004).

POPLINE is a freely accessible database maintained by the INFO Project at the Johns Hopkins Bloomberg School of Public Health and Center for Communication Programs. The database contains more than 300,000 citations with abstracts to books, articles, and reports on population, demography, family planning, fertility, AIDS, health care, public policy, and related issues. Some of the references are historical, dating back to the nineteenth century. The database features instant searches of popular topics such as population and environment; index, keyword, and expert searching; a thesaurus ("Keyword Guide"); and limiting by peer-reviewed journals. POPLINE also provides links to nearly 4,000 full-text versions of documents cited. Free CD-ROM versions of POPLINE are available to users in developing countries.

359. **Population Demographics.** New York: Market Statistics, 1990– . annual updates. Dialog File 581.

Though probably intended as a marketing database, this nonetheless provides ready access to 1990 and 2000 Census data, current-year estimates, and projections on population, households, income, education, and occupation. Data in these categories are easily broken down by numerous other variables, such as age, race, gender, metropolitan area, county, state, and so on.

360. **Population Index on the Web.** Available: http://popindex.princeton.edu/ (Accessed: December 29, 2004).

Population Index on the Web is maintained by the Office of Population Research at Princeton University. *Population Index on the Web* provides access to more than 46,000 abstracts that appeared in the print version of *Population Index* between 1986 and 2000, when the *Index* ceased publication; no new citations have been added to the database since 2000. The database features searching by author, subject, geographic region, keyword, and date; researchers can also browse through individual issues by date and number. Each issue contains approximately 900 annotated citations "designed to cover the world's demographic and population literature, including books and other monographs, serial publications, journal articles, working papers, doctoral dissertations, and machine-readable data files" (from the *User's Guide*). Within each online issue, items are arranged alphabetically by author under an extensive list of topics and subtopics. Each citation receives a number code which refers to the index volume and citation number; these codes are used in the author and geographical indexes. The bibliography is international in scope, including source documents in other languages; however, citations and abstracts are in English. Each entry also includes an address for correspondence and the location of at least one holding library for that item. The author and geographical indexes in each issue are cumulated yearly. The 1937 through 1985 issues of the *Population Index* are available through JSTOR.

Handbooks and Yearbooks

361. **American Incomes: Demographics of Who Has Money.** 3d ed. Ithaca, NY: New Strategist, 1999. 404 p. index. (American Money Series). $89.95. ISBN 1-885070-24-1.

Like other New Strategist publications, this book is geared towards marketing staff but is also useful for social science research. Tables and charts drawn from both government and private sources are accompanied by a brief analysis. Topics covered in this volume include household income, men's income, women's income, discretionary income, wealth, and poverty. A glossary and index are also included.

362. Anderton, Douglas L., Richard E. Barrett, and Donald J. Bogue. **The Population of the United States.** 3d ed. New York: Free Press, 1997. 693 p. index. $150.00. ISBN 0-684-82774-3.

Although somewhat dated (the book was published before the 2000 decennial census), this work remains valuable for the variety and historical detail of the tables and charts included. Each topical chapter includes an overview, definitions of terms, comprehensive analyses of subtopics, and tables. Subjects covered include size and growth of the U.S. population; source of U.S. population data; mortality; marriage and marital status; fertility and reproduction; health and disability; spatial movement and regional geographies; race, ethnicity, and ancestry; aging and gender; household and family; educational enrollment and attainment; labor force and employment status; occupation, industry, and class of worker; and, income, wealth, and poverty. The source for each table is provided in an accompanying note; an index is also included.

363. **Demographic Yearbook.** New York: Department of Economic and Social Affairs, United Nations, 1948– . annual. ISSN 0082-8041.

For comparative research into population and demography, the *Demographic Yearbook* is an invaluable tool. It presents country-by-country data on such areas as population; birth and death rates; fetal, infant, and maternal mortality; natality; nuptiality; and divorces. Each of these broad categories includes a handful of subcategories of data, with each table listing countries alphabetically within their world region. In addition to the recurring categories of data, every issue of the yearbook has a special topic section with data on a particular subject. Many of these should be of use to sociologists since they touch on subjects like fertility and mortality, population aging, marriage and divorce, international migration, and household composition. Furthermore, these special topics are revisited periodically. There are extensive technical notes explaining the content and limitations of the data tables, with all notes and table headings in both English and French. Finally, there is a subject index that identifies which volumes in this series contain data on a particular subject. Researchers should note that there is approximately a two-year lag between the year of the data and the publication year of the volume.

364. Gilbert, Geoffrey. **World Population: A Reference Handbook.** Santa Barbara, CA: ABC-CLIO, 2001. 223 p. index. (Contemporary World Issues). $45.00. LC 2001-002707. ISBN 1-57607-229-0.

This work aims to be a "starting point for research" and to "give the reader an appreciation of the *controversial* aspects of population" [italics in original] (p. xii). Chapter 1 provides an overview of world population, describing how fertility and mortality affect growth rates and how social phenomena such as urbanization and migration affect where growth occurs. It also summarizes the views of "modern Malthusians" and "population optimists," and analyzes public policies towards population growth, especially in light of the age structure of national populations. Chapter 2 presents a chronology of milestones in population studies and population growth. Chapter 3 consists of short biographical sketches of leading figures in population research, including Thomas Malthus. Chapter 4 presents tables and graphs depicting population growth over time, national population rankings, and other statistical measures. Chapter 5 reprints landmark pieces of population literature including the first two chapters of Malthus's *Essay on Population* and reports from the United Nations and the U.S. government. Chapter 6 identifies and describes organizations involved in population research and advocacy, while Chapters 7 and 8 present monographs, videos, and Web sites for further information. A glossary of key terms in population research and a subject index are included.

365. Mitchell, Susan. **American Generations: Who They Are, How They Live, What They Think.** 2d ed. Ithaca, NY: New Strategist, 1998. 473 p. index. $79.95. ISBN 1-885070-14-4.

Intended more as a guidebook for market researchers or marketing students, this work focuses on generational differences in such areas as attitudes and behavior, education, health, households, housing, income, labor force, population, spending, and wealth. Each chapter consists of tables, charts, and graphs—drawn from both government and private sources of statistics—that illustrate patterns between or within generations. Many of these representations are accompanied by a short analysis of the statistics. The book includes lists of the tables and charts; a glossary of demographic and economic terms; a bibliography, with a focus on statistical sources that are available online; and an index. This is a very useful resource for sociologists looking for a wide variety of statistics on generational differences in the United States.

366. Russell, Cheryl. **Americans and Their Homes: Demographics of Homeownership.** Ithaca, NY: New Strategist, 1998. 313 p. index. (American Consumer Series). $79.95. ISBN 1-885070-16-0.

Another New Strategist publication intended for marketing professionals, *Americans and Their Homes*, contains sets of tables and charts on the following housing-related topics: the demographics of homeownership, homeowners and their homes, homeowners by region, owners of new homes, homeowners who have moved, owners of upscale homes, affluent homeowners, and spending of homeowners. Many of the tables and charts depict trend lines and all include a note on the source(s) consulted (e.g., *American Housing Survey, Current Housing Reports*). This is a useful work on an important demographic group within American society.

367. Russell, Cheryl. **Demographics of the U.S.: Trends and Projections.** Ithaca, NY: New Strategist, 2000. 570 p. index. $89.95. ISBN 1-885070-31-4.

One of many New Strategist publications intended for marketers, this volume presents tables depicting trends and projections. Subjects covered include attitudes and behavior, education, health, housing, income, labor force, living arrangements, population, spending, and wealth. The dates vary from table to table: some of the trend tables reach back to the 1950s, others to the 1970s; some projections are for 2008, others for 2050. A glossary, bibliography, and index are also provided.

368. **The Sourcebook of County Demographics.** Vienna, VA: ESRI Business Information Solutions, 1990– . irregular.

Though intended primarily for market researchers, this nonetheless has useful data for students of population and demography. It may be particularly suitable as a current data source for courses doing statistical analysis on select population and demographic variables. The data are arranged alphabetically by state, then by county. For each county one finds data on population, population composition, households, income, and spending potential. The population section of the latest edition (15th) includes projections to the year 2008, annual change from 2000–2003, and percentage by race. Population composition covers percentage Hispanic origin, age distribution, median age, and the ratio of males to females. Household data include the number of households (with projections), the annual percentage change from 2000 through 2003, the number of families, and median household income. Income data include per capital income, household income base, household income distribution, and home value base and distribution. The spending potential indices show potential demand for various categories of products. Summary data are included for metropolitan statistical areas (MSAs), as well as Nielsen market areas (DMAs); business data by county are also provided. County maps are included, as are appendices for state, MSA, and DMA codes and definitions.

369. Wright, Russell O. **Life and Death in the United States: Statistics on Life Expectancies, Diseases, and Death Rates for the Twentieth Century.** Jefferson, NC: McFarland, 1997. 139 p. index. $28.50. ISBN 0-7864-0320-9.

This short work looks at life expectancy (or life expectation), leading causes of death, cardiovascular diseases, and cancer in the United States. Each of these major sections includes an overview of the concept, along with charts and tables. The figures presented are for the twentieth century, and include numbers as recent as 1993; the statistics themselves are largely derived from the *Statistical Abstract of the United States*, as well as the American Heart Association and American Cancer Society. A final section of the book presents leading causes of death by age group and includes recommendations for prevention.

Dictionaries and Encyclopedias

370. Ciment, James, ed. **Encyclopedia of American Immigration.** Armonk, NY: Sharpe Reference, 2001. 4v. $399.00. ISBN 0-7656-8028-9 (set).

This useful four-volume encyclopedia looks at immigration to the United States from a number of angles. The first volume includes sections on the history of immigration and on immigration issues (wars, civil unrest), processes (human smuggling, the marriage market). Volume 2 deals with the political, economic, and social dimensions of immigration. Volume 3 looks at the place of immigration in popular culture, including the media, and at the religious and geographical characteristics of immigration; it also examines specific groups of immigrants. Volume 4 continues this look at immigrants from specific geographic regions; it also includes reproductions of key documents in immigration history, such as laws and treaties, executive orders, court cases, and government and nongovernmental reports. A glossary and bibliography are included in the final volume, as are several indexes.

371. Ness, Immanuel, and James Ciment, eds. **The Encyclopedia of Global Population and Demographics.** Armonk, NY: Sharpe Reference, 1999. 2v. $185.00. ISBN 1-56324-710-0 (set).

This is a very useful encyclopedia that provides statistical data on demographic topics ranging from identity (i.e., ethnicity, language, and religion) to health for nearly every country. Volume 1 also includes several essays on basic demographic subjects, including: resources and the environment, general population and vital statistics, families and households, cultural identity, labor and the economy, migration, transportation and communications, and health care and education. Each essay includes a list of further readings. The country profiles section takes up the remainder of the two volumes. This section is prefaced by a user guide, a brief bibliography of sources, and several comparative regional tables. Each country profile includes a short geographical description, along with tables of statistical data. Volume 2 includes an extensive bibliography of sources used and an index. This work will appeal to sociologists looking for comparative data on a wide range of demographic topics.

Web Sites and Research Centers

372. **CensusScope.** Available: http://www.censusscope.org (Accessed: January 15, 2004).

CensusScope is another project of the Social Science Data Analysis Network (SSDAN), which is based at the Population Studies Center, University of Michigan. It aims to be an "easy-to-use tool for investigating U.S. demographic trends . . . [using] eye-catching graphics and exportable trend data." The charts and trends section presents basic tables and graphs on population growth, race, age distribution, household and family structure, educational attainment, and other topics. A "change location" feature allows tables and charts on this same set of topics to be displayed for metropolitan areas and states. The maps section depicts the geography of various geographic topics. The rankings section presents ranked lists of states or counties within states for several main demographic variables. Finally, the segregation section shows "dissimilarity indices" and "exposure by race" charts for metropolitan areas or cities; it also features ranked lists of dissimilarity indices by cities and metropolitan areas. This is a very useful tool for students of contemporary U.S. demographic trends.

373. **Migration Information Source.** Available: http://www.migration information.org/ (Accessed: January 15, 2004).

The *Migration Information Source* attempts to "chronicle global migration movements, provide perspectives on current migration debates, and offer the tools and data from numerous global organizations and governments needed to understand migration." Although many of the data tools featured on the Web site are geared to the United States, the *Migration Information Source* also provides statistical profiles of Australia, the United Kingdom, Japan, Turkey, and many other countries. The statistical data are generally presented in tabular form; additional analysis is included in the spotlights and data insights sections. This is a useful clearinghouse for contemporary migration issues.

374. **Office of Population Research at Princeton University (OPR).** Available: http://opr.princeton.edu/ (Accessed: January 15, 2004).

In addition to maintaining the *Pop Index*, the Office of Population Research also provides online access to its catalog of demographic datasets, including the Little Village Survey of Chicago's south side, the World Fertility Survey, and Demographic and Health Surveys, and the Organisation for Economic Co-operation and Development (OECD) tables of deaths and registration data. Direct access to the codebooks, data files, and questionnaires associated with these datasets is available. The site also features online working papers, as well as information about the OPR's programs, courses, and sponsored events.

375. **Population Reference Bureau (PRB).** Available: http://www.prb.org/ (Accessed: January 15, 2004).

The *Population Reference Bureau's* mission is to inform "people about the population dimensions of important social, economic, and political issues." Its Web site provides access to research on population trends, education, fertility, gender, marriage and the family, urbanization, mortality, and many other topics; the *PRB's* scope is international. The DataFinder tool allows users to select countries or regions of the world and then to pick a variable or set of variables in order to generate statistical data. For the United States, this feature is also available at the state level. The *PRB* also sponsors the *PopNet* Web site (http://www.popnet.org/), which aims to present a comprehensive annotated listing of population-related Web sites, and the *AmeriStat* Web site (http://www.ameristat.org/), which focuses exclusively on the U.S. population.

376. **United Nations Population Fund (UNFPA).** Available: http://www.unfpa.org (Accessed: January 15, 2004).

In addition to providing information about the population programs of the United Nations, the UNFPA provides access to a useful set of "population and reproductive health country profiles." Each profile includes a narrative overview along with a summary set of statistics. Users can also select up to five countries for purposes of statistical comparison. Online access to the current and previous years' versions of the *State of the World Population* report is also available. Each report includes topical essays, such as HIV/AIDS and adolescents; graphs and tables are also included.

377. **United Nations Population Information Network (POPIN).** Available: http://www.un.org/popin/ (Accessed: January 15, 2004).

POPIN "strives to make international, regional and national population information, particularly information available from United Nations sources, easily available to the international community." *POPIN* serves as a clearinghouse for various UN publications related to population, including *World Population Prospects, Statistical Data on Children*, and *World Urbanization Prospects*, as well as for UN member state publications. *POPIN* is a useful starting point for identifying and retrieving worldwide and comparative trend data.

378. **United States Census Bureau.** Available: http://www.census.gov (Accessed: January 15, 2004).

The U.S. Census Bureau is the most significant source of demographic information about the U.S. Population, and its Web site provides access to online versions of many of its popular print products (e.g., the *Statistical Abstract of the United States*). The site also features access to statistical data collected via its various programs through the American FactFinder. The FactFinder supports searching for a range of demographic topics at different geographic levels (e.g., block group, census tract, metropolitan area). Data are drawn from the 1990 and 2000 decennial census, population estimates, the economic census, and the American community survey. Other interactive data tools include Censtats, QuickFacts, Tiger Maps, the US Gazeteer, 1990 Decennial Census Lookup, and DataFerrett. Links to other governmental sources of statistical data are also provided.

Race and Ethnic Relations

General Sources

Bibliographies

379. Wheeler, Albert J., ed. **Racism: A Bibliography with Indexes.** Huntington, NY: Nova Science Publishers, 2000. 319 p. index. ISBN 1-56072-856-6.

This is a relatively unprocessed bibliography of books, journal articles, manuscript collections, and other documents relating to racism around the world. There is no introduction describing the parameters of the bibliography, so this must be discerned by browsing the entries. Book citations appear to have been drawn from OCLC since the details on many books match perfectly with the content and layout of the WorldCat database. Besides the bibliographic citation, there are notes, subject headings, LC classifications and Dewey class numbers. Article entries include abstracts and descriptors, though again there is no indication of how these were identified or which, if any, databases were searched to retrieve them. The entries are arranged alphabetically by author under nine subject chapters: racism-general, racial attitudes, racism and poverty, hate groups, racial justice, racism and politics, racial discrimination, racial identity, and racism and education. Numerous entries cover other countries (with some in foreign languages), and there does not appear to be a date restriction on inclusion since some entries date to early in the twentieth century. There are author, subject, and title indexes to aid in searching the entries. While the coverage of this bibliography must be inferred, the entries are nonetheless intriguing. Racism is covered from a variety of perspectives, and there are important topics, controversies (e.g., *The Bell Curve*), and authors reflected in the bibliography. While it is vague on its scope, this bibliography does have lots of interesting citations, both current and historical, on the problem of racism worldwide.

Indexes, Abstracts, and Databases

380. **Ethnic Newswatch.** [electronic resource]. Stamford, CT: Softline Information, 1992– . bimonthly. ISSN 1068-1272. Available: http://enw.softlineweb.com/ (Accessed: February 9, 2004).

This subscription Web-based database provides full-text articles from 271 ethnic and minority magazines and newspapers in the United States, with both an English and Spanish language interface. Coverage is from 1990 to the present, and there are both basic and advanced search screens with different searching capabilities. Both options allow for searching words in articles. They vary, however, in the additional indexable fields one can search in. The basic screen allows searching by subjects, publication name, and ethnic group, while the advanced screen adds words in title, publication date, author, type of article, and language. Each field has a drop-down menu of options to pick from. The full text of articles is included, and these can be printed or downloaded. Virtually any subject of interest to sociologists is covered, including drug use, crime, religion, health care, inequality, AIDS, social change, and more. Also, important current controversies in the academy, or in public policy, are addressed.

381. **Sage Race Relations Abstracts.** Vol. 1– . London: Sage, 1975– . quarterly. $723/yr. ISSN 0307-9201. Available: http://www.sagepub.com/journal.aspx?pid=63 (Accessed: February 9, 2004).

Published in association with the London-based Institute of Race Relations, each quarterly issue includes abstracts of approximately 250 books, articles, and conference papers. Coverage is multidisciplinary and international, with most citations coming from England, the United States, and Canada. Entries are arranged alphabetically by author under approximately thirty-six broad subject categories such as bibliographies, area studies, community relations, culture and identity, demographic studies, education, family and adoption, housing, immigrant communities, and more. Some abstracts are accompanied by *see also* references to other abstracts. Cumulative author and subject indexes are provided in the last issue of each volume. Each issue also includes a bibliographic essay and often contains an "extended views" section that deals with a specific issue. This publication is also available for subscribers on the Web via Ingenta from volume 25 (2000) to the present. However, the online version, while full text, does not provide any index to the contents of the numerous abstracts in each issue.

Handbooks and Yearbooks

382. Aguirre, Adalberto, Jr. **Racial and Ethnic Diversity in America: A Reference Handbook.** Santa Barbara, CA: ABC-CLIO, 2003. 277 p. index. $50.00. (Contemporary World Issues). ISBN 1-57607-983-X,

As with other books in this series, this volume provides a wide-ranging overview of its topic, in this case racial and ethnic diversity. The first three chapters are historical and provide a review of immigration to this country and the subsequent diversification of its immigrant populations. The third chapter addresses the challenges of contemporary diversity in this country, including issues of racial profiling, hate crimes, nativism, immigration restriction, and more. There is also an overview of noteworthy court cases related to these themes. Subsequent chapters follow the format of other books in the series, focusing on a chronology; biographical sketches; statistics, laws, and quotations; a directory of organizations; print resources (i.e., a bibliography); and nonprint resources (primarily videos). The entries in most of these chapters are thoroughly annotated and quite informative. There is a glossary of key terms, and a subject index that includes proper names and titles. Overall, this is an excellent source for students exploring the history, evolution, and contemporary context of racial and ethnic diversity in this country.

383. Cunnigen, Donald, comp. and ed. **Teaching Race and Ethnic Relations: Syllabi and Instructional Materials.** 4th ed. Washington, DC: American Sociological Association, 2001. 464 p. (ASA Resource Materials for Teaching).

Intended for novice instructors of race and ethnic relations, the forty-six syllabi included here are divided into six sections based upon their area of focus. These sections include: general (i.e., interdisciplinary), race and society, race and theory, race and gender, international perspectives, and graduate seminars. The international section reflects the growing number of syllabi submitted by colleagues in other countries and includes numerous British and Canadian examples. Throughout, class projects, assignments, and other teaching activities are included within the syllabi themselves. There is no separate listing of such activities, as is found in some other titles in this series. A short introductory outline, "Checklist for Constructing a Syllabus," is included and should provide some useful guidance to new teachers.

384. Fischetti, P. R. **The Ethnic Cultures of America: A Reference Source for Teachers, Librarians, Administrators, and Human Resource Directors.** Revised ed. Washington, DC: Educational Extension Systems, 2000. 388 p. index. $29.95. ISBN 0-8108-4253-X.

This is a quirky but surprisingly readable overview of over one hundred ethnic groups in the United States. For most ethnic groups, the author provides a sort of demographic overview that includes not only population growth, but also factors that prompted immigration in the first place. There is also some discussion of settlement patterns, as well as a brief section identifying holidays and customs. Not surprisingly, the general background information is more extensive on the larger ethnic or immigrant populations. The chapter on African Americans is broader in coverage than the others. There are helpful introductory and summary chapters, as well as a subject/name/title index. The ethnic group overviews are fairly superficial, so these would not be well suited for college students studying race or ethnic relations. However, this treatment might prompt further interest from K–12 students. At the very least, students may find the wide-ranging introduction of interest.

385. Heaton, Tim B., Bruce A. Chadwick, and Cardell K. Jacobson. **Statistical Handbook on Racial Groups in the United States.** Phoenix, AZ: Oryx Press, 2000. 355 p. index. $65.00. ISBN 1-57356-266-1.

The categorization of individuals by race is not without problems, as noted by the authors in the introduction. Race, they argue, is primarily a social construction, not a biological category. Yet as a social category, race is profoundly influential. That said, this statistical compilation presents hundreds of data tables illustrating both differences and commonalities among the various racial and ethnic groups in the United States. These data are drawn primarily from government sources (e.g., Bureau of the Census) and publications (e.g., *Current Population Reports*) or, in some cases, datasets (e.g., National Educational Longitudinal Survey, General Social Survey). The tables and charts are organized into nine major subject chapters: demographic context; education; economics and employment; health, well-being, and lifestyles; family; sex, fertility, and contraception; religion and religiosity; crime and delinquency; and political participation. Each of these subject categories has a half dozen or so subtopics with as many as a dozen data tables. For example, education includes a subtopic for enrollment, with six tables detailing enrollment in various levels of schooling (e.g., college), programs (e.g., Head Start), and courses (e.g., high school science and mathematics). All of the tables highlight data focusing on race and ethnicity, and they may cover anywhere from 1980 to 1997. A detailed subject index is also included. Overall, those researching the comparative well-being of various racial and ethnic groups in America should find this valuable.

386. Levinson, David. **Ethnic Groups Worldwide: A Ready Reference Handbook.** Phoenix, AZ: Oryx Press, 1998. 436 p. index. ISBN 1-57356-019-7.

Levinson is prolific in writing on ethnic groups around the world, and this volume provides a readable overview of such groups in every country. The volume is sensibly arranged into four regions of the world (i.e., Europe, Africa, Asia and the Pacific, the Americas), with countries listed alphabetically under their region. For each country, there is brief information on its geographic location and political evolution, followed by discussion of its ethnic composition and ethnic relations. This information runs from one to two pages and is clear and well written. Entries on Russia, the United Kingdom, the United States, and China, for example, are much longer. Though there is little in the way of sociological analysis of ethnic relations, the background information may nonetheless be useful in exploring ethnic diversity in those countries or in the United States. A substantial subject index is provided, though its entries primarily locate ethnic groups in various countries. Maps, an introduction, and a bibliography are included at the beginning of each of the four regional sections.

387. Russell, Cheryl. **Racial and Ethnic Diversity: Asians, Blacks, Hispanics, Native Americans, and Whites.** 4th ed. Ithaca, NY: New Strategist, 2002. 974 p. index. (American Consumer Series). $99.00. ISBN 1-885070-45-4.

This is an excellent and well-constructed guide to a variety of data on racial and ethnic groups in the United States. Drawn primarily from Census and other government data sources, this volume presents hundreds of tables, charts, and graphs detailing the similarities and differences between major racial and ethnic groups. The book is divided into eight chapters, with most focusing on the different groups identified in Census data: American Indians and Alaska natives, Asians, blacks, Hispanics, native Hawaiians and other Pacific Islanders, whites, total population, attitudes and behavior. For chapters on groups, there are standard subtopics on which data are presented: business, education, health, housing, income, labor force, living arrangements, populations, spending, and wealth. Most of the data are drawn from the 2000 Census, but other data are drawn from additional sources, such as the 1997 Economic Census or the Current Population Report. The last chapter, on attitudes and behavior, provides responses to questions on diversity that were asked in the 2000 administration of the General Social Survey, an ongoing national attitudinal survey. Throughout, the data are nicely presented and address core areas of interest to social scientists studying race and ethnicity. Appended are a listing of addresses and Web sites for additional information, a glossary of key terms, a bibliography, and a subject index.

Dictionaries and Encyclopedias

388. **Gale Encyclopedia of Multicultural America.** 2d ed. Detroit, MI: Gale, 2000. 3v. $205.00. ISBN 0-7876-398-9 (set).

There are 152 ethnic and Native American cultures included in the second edition of this multivolume set, reflecting a 50 percent increase from the first edition. The essays are substantial, ranging anywhere from 3,000 to 20,000 words, and are arranged alphabetically by the name of the group. Essays feature not only the history of the group's immigration or settlement in the United States, but also the group's experiences and contributions relating to the major social institutions, such as family, religion, politics, culture, and employment. Also found in the essays are a demographic and geographic overview of the originating country, a brief history of the group in that country, immigration and settlement patterns into the United States, and some of the other social and cultural features mentioned above. Notable contributors are also identified, as are media, organizations, museums and research centers, and suggested readings for additional study. Addresses, e-mails, contact names, Web site addresses, mailing addresses, and phone and fax numbers are also added wherever available. An expanded subject index is included that covers subjects, people, events, places, and more. Finally, the encyclopedia includes 250 images sprinkled throughout the volumes. These concise and readable overviews of racial and ethnic groups should provide an excellent introduction to general readers and students interested in social and cultural features of these groups.

389. Herbst, Philip H. **The Color of Words: An Encyclopaedic Dictionary of Ethnic Bias in the United States.** Yarmouth, ME: Intercultural Press, 1997. 259 p. $24.95. ISBN 1-877864-42-0.

This dictionary is a collection of 851 racial and ethnic slurs and epithets. The author, an anthropologist, provides definitions, etymologies, and cultural contexts for most of the words included here. In the introduction, Herbst states that "the book should serve to emphasize that the entries are labels for the classifications people make in society, and that these classifications are often made for reasons of manipulation or mischief" (p. xiii). Words are powerful in framing their subjects, and the words included here are particularly so. Their examination and dissection is an antidote, somewhat, against their usage. Mostly excluded from the dictionary are epithets referring to social class differences and, to a lesser extent, religious differences. Exceptions are made when there are distinct racial and ethnic overtones to the words. The dictionary makes extensive use of cross-references and *see also* references to preferred terms and related terms, respectively, which are found elsewhere in the dictionary. The definitions themselves can range in length from a paragraph to more than a page. Appended is a list of "Core Works Consulted" and a short essay on ethnic epithets in society.

390. **Racial and Ethnic Relations in America.** Pasadena, CA: Salem Press, 2000. 10v. index. ISBN 0-89356-629-2 (set).

Included here are almost 900 entries on the full range of topics that relate to racial and ethnic relations in this country. For sociology students, this includes a gold mine of essays on such topics as anglo-conformity discrimination, ability testing, classless society, the culture of poverty, race as a concept, poverty and race, social mobility and race, the power elite, racism, racial formation theory, economics and race, and many equally compelling sociologically related issues. The encyclopedia also includes entries on historical events, court cases, legislation, countries, and popular culture, among others. The essays are well written and include both *see also* references and, occasionally, a bibliography of core resources. A number of entries also include introductory statements on the social or historical significance of the topic. Entries range in length from a few paragraphs to three or four pages. Appended are a biographical section of "pioneers of intergroup relations" (subdivided by racial or ethnic group), a time line, a bibliography subdivided by major topics, a categorized list of entries, a personages index, and an index that includes subjects, names, titles, organizations, and court cases. This would be an excellent source for undergraduate students and general readers studying racial and ethnic relations and its constituent issues.

Web Sites and Research Centers

391. **Centre for Research in Ethnic Relations.** Available: http://www.warwick.ac.uk/fac/soc/CRER_RC/ (Accessed: February 16, 2004).

Focusing on the United Kingdom and Western Europe, the Centre pursues a research agenda focusing on such general areas as refugees, cultural identity, nationalism, racial discrimination, and citizenship, among others. Specific current projects include Muslims in prison, women refugees, and national employment strategies towards migrants and ethnic minorities. For each, a project description and contact information are provided. There is also a *Resources Centre* with a searchable database of "grey literature" (i.e., pamphlets, reports, etc.) in the field. Contact information is provided for this service as well. The Centre also offers fellowships and courses in the subject area, as well as studentships approved by Britain's social science data consortium, ESRC.

392. **Section on Racial and Ethnic Minorities.** Available: http://www.asanet.org/sectionrem/ (Accessed: February 16, 2004).

This is the American Sociological Association's page for its section on racial and ethnic relations. Over and above information on joining the ASA or this section, the Web site includes copies of past section newsletters, news on section awards (e.g., the Oliver Cromwell Cox Award), available fellowships, calls for papers or manuscripts, job announcements, information on the annual ASA conference, and more.

393. **SocioSite: Ethnicity, Migration, and Racism.** Available: http://www2.fmg.uva.nl/sociosite/topics/ethnic.html (Accessed: December 29, 2004).

A subsection of the *SocioSite* Web site, this provides links to a variety of Web sites dealing with race, ethnicity, racism, and more. Coverage is international, and electronic journals and discussion lists are included. There are also links to the corresponding *Yahoo* categories for these topics.

African Americans

Bibliographies

394. Strickland, Arvarh E., and Robert E. Weems, Jr., eds. **The African American Experience: An Historiographical and Bibliographical Guide.** Westport, CT: Greenwood Press, 2001. 447 p. index. $105.00. ISBN 0-313-29838-6.

This is a collection of bibliographic essays on African American life and culture. Among the seventeen chapters are numerous ones of sociological interest, including migration and urbanization, families, education, slavery and freedom, intellectual and political thought, sexuality and race, civil rights, the press, and religion. These essays are approximately twenty pages each and are accompanied by complete bibliographic references at the end of the essay, over and above their mention in the text itself. A comprehensive index to names, titles, and subjects is included.

395. Tischauser, Leslie V. **Black/White Relations in American History: An Annotated Bibliography.** Lanham, MD: Scarecrow Press; Pasadena, CA: Salem Press, 1998. 189 p. index. $45.00. (Magill Bibliographies). ISBN 0-8108-3389-1.

Race relations in this country cannot be fully understood separated from the context of their development. As the author states, the focus here is on "historical and sociological treatments of the topic of race relations that have been published since 1945" (p. xi). Entries include both books and articles and go back to the beginnings of slavery in the seventeenth century. The book is organized into eleven chapters that proceed, for the most part, in chronological order. The first two chapters identify general overviews of race relations and slavery in the United States, respectively. After that, the remaining chapters address the following subjects or time periods: state and local studies of slavery; free blacks and slave revolts; pre–Civil War; Reconstruction; race, riots, and lynching; segregation, 1877–1920; the Depression and War, 1920–1960; civil rights, 1961–1995; and the costs of prejudice and discrimination. Within chapters, entries are arranged alphabetically by author, with each entry getting an informative paragraph-long annotation. The authors include renowned historians, sociologists, other social scientists, as well as some popular writers. Author and subject indexes are provided.

Indexes, Abstracts, and Databases

396. G. K. Hall Index to Black Periodicals. New York: G. K. Hall, 2000– . annual. price on request. ISSN 0899-6253.

This continues the *Index to Periodical Articles By and About Blacks*, which in turn continued some earlier titles that date back to the 1950s. Some thirty-four journals focusing on black Americans are indexed, with the exact volumes and issues cited in the "List of Periodicals Indexed." Both popular (e.g., *Jet, Ebony*) and scholarly (e.g., *Race and Class, The Journal of Black Psychology*) journals are included. The citations themselves are arranged alphabetically in one list by either author or subject. Book, fiction, film, music, and theater reviews are included among the entries and are indexed by author, reviewer, and subject. The subjects covered span all of the social sciences and humanities, with many references on sociological topics such as class and race identity, aging, health care, the production of educational inequality, families, gender, and more.

Handbooks and Yearbooks

397. Horner, Louise L. **Black Americans: A Statistical Sourcebook.** 2002 ed. Palo Alto, CA: Information Publications, 2002. 307 p. index. $55.00. ISBN 0-929960-32-7.

Assuming a diverse user audience, this sourcebook presents statistical data that should appeal to a range of users. Data are drawn from a variety of United States government sources, including the Bureau of the Census, the *Statistical Abstract of the United States*, the *Digest of Education Statistics*, the *Handbook of Labor Statistics, Health United States, Employment and Earnings*, and the *Current Population Reports*. These data are arranged into eight subject chapters: demographics and characteristics of the population; vital statistics and health; education; government, elections, and public opinion; crime, law enforcement, and corrections; labor force, employment and unemployment; earnings, income, poverty, and wealth; and special topics. Special topics includes such subjects as Social Security, farm operators, housing, black-owned firms, and general mobility. All data tables include the source, notes, and units used in measurement; Web addresses are included whenever a government Web page was the source of the data. While the source for many tables is the *Statistical Abstract of the United States*, the author notes that this is due to the unique content and presentation of some of the data there. The introduction does discuss the usage of "blacks" instead of "African Americans," and it also draws the user's attention to the fact that the category "Hispanic" is not a racial classification. A glossary is appended, as is a modest subject index. This source is published annually, so it should be a good source of longitudinal data, provided it covers categories of interest.

398. Lehman, Jeffrey, ed. **The African American Almanac.** 9th ed. Detroit, MI: Gale, 2003. 1500 p. ISBN 0-7876-4020-4.

Formerly *The Negro Almanac*, this award-winning book provides an excellent one-volume overview of important people, events, and historical developments in the African American experience. There are now twenty-nine chapters covering a wide range of topics in history, the arts, social and economic conditions, politics, and popular culture. Of particular interest to sociologists may be the chapters on population, religion, education, the family and health, employment and income, the law, black nationalism, music and popular culture, politics, and the civil rights movement. The chapters make liberal use of illustrations, charts, and statistical tables. Many chapters also include historical overviews of their topic, as well as biographies of key individuals. Of the approximately 1,000 biographies, over half were updated for this new edition. All chapters have been revised to contain current data, timely new entries, updated directory information, and new images to reflect developments since the last edition. An extensive chronology is provided, with fifty new entries added, as are copies of or excerpts from significant historical documents. There is an appended list of African American award winners, a bibliography, and a subject index; picture and text credits are provided in the front of the volume.

399. Schomburg Center for Research in Black Culture. **The New York Public Library African American Desk Reference.** New York: John Wiley & Sons, 1999. 606 p. index. ISBN 0-471-23924-0.

This is an excellent source for general readers and students researching the cultural, social, and historical features of the African American experience. The Schomburg Center, part of the New York Public Library, also has a superb collection that adds breadth and depth to this one-volume source. Included here are statistical tables and charts, both current and retrospective, chronologies of events, biographies, organizational directories, media outlets, and much more. Topically, the desk reference covers such major and sociologically interesting subject areas as slavery, civil rights, family, religion, education, business, the military, law, music, literature, and health, among others. While not ostensibly a sociological reference source, it nonetheless includes data and history that provide a critical context for various sociological concerns. There is an extensive name/subject index. Overall, this is a superb source for beginning social science investigations.

400. Smith, Jessie Carney, and Carrell P. Horton, eds. **Statistical Record of Black America.** 4th ed. Detroit, MI: Gale, 1997. 1064 p. index. ISBN 0-8103-9252-6.

Statistical information on black Americans is spread across a wide range of government and nongovernment sources. This handbook pulls together data from many of those sources and reproduces them in 996 tables. These tables are arranged under fifteen subject categories: attitudes, values, behavior; business and economics; crime, law enforcement, legal justice; education; health and medical care; housing; income, spending, wealth; labor and employment; miscellany; politics and elections; population; social and human services; sports and leisure; the family; and vital statistics. Most of these chapters include anywhere from four to over a dozen subtopics for the further categorization of the data. Many of the tables include historical data, and all fully cite the source document. A bibliography of the reference sources that were consulted is appended, as is a subject index.

Dictionaries and Encyclopedias

401. **The African American Encyclopedia.** 2d ed. R. Kent Rasmussen, ed. New York: Marshall Cavendish, 2001. 10v. index. ISBN 0-7614-7208-8 (set).

Included here are over 3,500 entries on African American history, politics, social and cultural life, business and economic life, performing arts and artists, and more. This constitutes a substantial update, revision and expansion of the previous edition and its supplement. The entries, which range in length from a few paragraphs to approximately 5,000 words, include biographies, concepts, historical events, institutions and organizations, court cases, and social issues, among others. The new entries, as well as the longer entries from the earlier editions, are signed and include a bibliography of suggested readings. Sociology students may find useful overview essays on a variety of topics, including family life, health, black nationalism, civil rights and race relations, religion, and virtually any other subtopic in the discipline. To aid access to the encyclopedia's many biographical entries, a supplementary list of people by profession is provided. There is also a bibliography arranged by broad topical area (e.g., black nationalism, performing arts, health, etc.), as well as a subject index. Other appended materials include directories of relevant research centers and libraries; a bibliography of books for children; a time line; and a list of Web sites and digital resources. The writing is excellent throughout, making this an excellent starting point for those researchers new to some of these topics.

Asian Americans

Bibliographies

402. Nordquist, Joan, comp. **The Asian American Woman: Social, Economic, and Political Conditions: A Bibliography.** Santa Cruz, CA: Reference and Research Services, 1997. 72 p. (Contemporary Social Issues: A Bibliographic Series, no. 48). $15.00. ISBN 0-937855-94-4.

As with others bibliographies in this series, this work identifies references from mainstream and alternative indexes and databases on its subject. Included here are over 700 unannotated references to books, articles, and Web sites on a variety of Asian American groups and topics. The first seven of the twenty-one chapters focus on Asian American women in general, then Chinese-, Korean-, Japanese-, Filipina-, East Indian-, and Indochinese-American women (including Cambodian, Vietnamese, and Hmong). Following these chapters are subject chapters addressing such topics as education, health, employment, family, violence against women, sex roles, elders, feminism, and more. Each chapter is subdivided for books and, if available, articles; citations are then listed alphabetically by author. Bibliographies, directories, and Web sites are listed in the final "Resources" chapter. Many chapters include an index by nationality. This is a tremendous resource for sociologists studying Asian American women from the constituent ethnic groups. The quality of the citations more than compensates for the lack of abstracts.

Hispanic Americans, Latinos/Latinas, Chicanos/Chicanas, Mexican Americans

Indexes, Abstracts, and Databases

403. **Chicano Database.** [electronic resource]. Berkeley, CA: Ethnic Studies Library Publications Unit, University of California, Berkeley. Available: http://eslibrary.berkeley.edu/ (Accessed: June 28, 2004).

Also available on CD-ROM, this database is primarily available in Web format through RLG Citation Resources. Both the CD-ROM and Web versions incorporate a number of print publications, including: the *Chicano Periodical Index*, the *Chicano Index*, the *Chicano Anthology Index*, *Arte Chicano: A Comprehensive Annotated Bibliography of Chicano Art, 1965–1981*, the *Chicana Studies Index: Twenty Years of Gender Research, 1971–1991*, and *Hispanic Mental Health Research: A Reference Guide*. The database also incorporates records from the Spanish Speaking Mental Health database. The database includes citations from a wide variety of sources, including both popular and scholarly periodical titles in both English and Spanish. Many of the records include abstracts. This database provides useful coverage of social science research focusing on Chicanos and on the wider Hispanic American population.

404. **HAPI Online.** [electronic resource]. Los Angeles: UCLA Latin American Center, University of California Los Angeles. $1,400/yr. Available: http://hapi. gseis.ucla.edu/ (Accessed: June 28, 2004).

This is the electronic equivalent of the *Hispanic American Periodicals Index*. The database provides access to citations from more than 400 journals dealing with Latin America, Hispanics in the United States, and the United States–Mexico border region, from 1970 to the present. The subject headings are drawn from the *HAPI* thesaurus (available online at http://hapi.gseis.ucla. edu/hapi/html/free/thesaurus-help.shtml). Article citations are presented in their original language. The journals covered span the social sciences and humanities, and important sociological concepts are indexed. These include the family, sex roles, population, cultural identity, social change, social classes, old age, religion, educational sociology, mobility, and many more.

Handbooks and Yearbooks

405. Nguyen, Manthi, ed. **Hispanic Americans: A Statistical Sourcebook.** Palo Alto, CA: Information Publications, 2003. 262 p. index. ISBN 0-929960-35-1.

Like its companion volume, *Black Americans: A Statistical Sourcebook*, this volume draws its statistics on Hispanic Americans from U.S. government documents, such as *Employment and Earnings*, *Current Population Reports*, *Health United States*, *Statistical Abstract of the United States*, *Digest of Education Statistics*, the *Handbook of Labor Statistics*, and the *Sourcebook of Criminal Justice Statistics*, among others. The tables of data are arranged into eleven chapters covering demographics; social characteristics; household and family characteristics; education (pre-primary through grade 12); education (postsecondary); government and elections; labor force, employment, and unemployment; earnings, income, poverty, and wealth; crime and corrections; vital statistics and health; and special topics (e.g., AIDS, health care coverage, death by various causes). While most tables use only "Hispanic" as a category, some include categories for "Mexican," "Puerto Rican," "Cuban," "Central/South American," and "other Hispanic." Source documents for all tables are cited, and explanatory notes and units of measure are included as well. Numerous tables are retrospective to the 1970s or 1980s. Both "complete count" data and sample survey data are used, depending on the table. A supplementary glossary defines many key terms encountered in the tables and their data categories, and a very brief subject index is also provided.

Native Americans

Guides

406. Klein, Barry T. **Reference Encyclopedia of the American Indian.** 9th ed. Nyack, NY: Todd Publications, 2000. ISBN 0-915344-90-4.

Included here are thousands of reference and information sources for those researching Native Americans in the United States and Canada. The materials are divided into four sections. Section 1, the largest, contains directories or lists on such topics as federally recognized tribes, reservations, government agencies, regional or state organizations, college courses and programs, financial aid, health services, libraries and research centers, communications, audiovisual aids, and periodicals, among others. Complete addresses and phone numbers are provided where appropriate. Section 2 focuses exclusively on Canada and has listings of first nations and bands, national and regional associations, museums, libraries, periodicals, colleges, and media. Section 3 is a bibliography of 4,500 books that is arranged alphabetically by title. Each entry includes a complete bibliographic citation; most include prices, and some include brief descriptions. These titles are listed again in a subject section that includes topics and tribes. An alphabetical directory of publishers completes this section. Section 4 is a collection of 2,500 biographies.

Bibliographies

407. Nordquist, Joan, comp. **Native American Woman: Social, Economic, and Political Aspects: A Bibliography.** Santa Cruz, CA: Reference and Research Services, 1999. 68 p. $15.00. (Contemporary Social Issues, no. 56). ISBN 1-8920-6810-9.

Drawing on a diverse set of sources, Nordquist has identified approximately 700 references addressing key social science features of the experiences of Native American women. Included here are books, book chapters, journal articles, dissertations, government documents, Web sites, and other sources that speak to this topic. The entries are arranged into sixteen subject chapters: social and economic conditions, gender roles, sexuality, family, violence against women and children, education, political activity, health and health care, mental health, drug and alcohol abuse, crime and the law, history, testimonials, literature, literature anthologies, and resources. Within each chapter, entries are grouped by books or articles, and then they are listed alphabetically by author. The "Resources" chapter includes a list of bibliographies and directories as well as Web sites. As with other volumes in this series, Nordquist has drawn references from mainstream and alternative indexes, abstracts, and databases. This provides a theoretically and politically diverse set of references on these social, cultural, and policy issues.

408. Nordquist, Joan, comp. **Native Americans: Social, Economic, and Political Aspects: A Bibliography.** Santa Cruz, CA: Reference and Research Services, 1998. 76 p. $15.00. (Contemporary Social Issues, no. 50). ISBN 0-937855-98-7.

Almost 1,000 books, articles, chapters, dissertations, government documents, and other items are included in this sweeping guide to social science aspects of Native American life. The unannotated citations are divided into twenty-one subject chapters. Some of the most sociologically oriented chapters include ethnic and cultural identity, social conditions, stereotypes, political institutions, education, health, drug and alcohol abuse, crime, women, and the elderly. Within chapters, entries are subdivided by books and articles, and then listed alphabetically by author. Nordquist has scanned a diverse set of indexes, abstracts, and databases to identify these resources. Consequently, there is broad representation of different theoretical and political viewpoints on the subjects under discussion. The next to last chapter identifies testimonials, while the final chapter lists bibliographies, directories, and Web sites as additional resources. This is an excellent guide to social science literature on Native Americans, and it is suitable for all levels of students and general readers.

Web Sites and Research Centers

409. **American Indian History and Related Issues.** Available: http://www. csulb.edu/projects/ais/ (Accessed: April 17, 2004).

This is a gateway site provided by the American Indian Studies program at California State University, Long Beach. The site is an Internet Scout Project award winner in the social sciences category. There are links here to sites related to Indians of North American, as well as a few sites related to Indians of Central America and Mexico. There are also links to specific tribes, social issues, historical events, culture, social movements, organizations, individuals, and much more.

Research Methods and Statistics

Guides

410. Silver, N. Clayton, and James B. Hittner. **A Guidebook of Statistical Software for the Social and Behavioral Sciences.** Boston: Allyn & Bacon, 1998. 461 p. index. $56.00. ISBN 0-205-20063-X.

Designed to "aid those researchers who have statistical problems that [SAS, SPSS, SYSTAT] do not handle at this time," this sourcebook provides information on various statistical software programs. Entries are arranged alphabetically by type of statistical procedure accomplished by the software programs (e.g., "Adaptive Testing—Bayesian," "Agreement," etc.). Each entry includes the name of the software program, author(s), a citation to a review of the program, description, language used to create the program, compatibility and memory requirements, cost of program, and information on how to obtain a copy of the program. Additional access to the entries is provided by an alphabetical table of contents, as well as by keyword and personal name indexes. This is a very useful tool for researchers who need to perform statistical analyses of data using procedures that are unavailable in some versions of commercial statistical software.

Bibliographies

411. Walden, Graham R., comp. **Survey Research Methodology, 1990–1999: An Annotated Bibliography.** (Bibliographies and Indexes in Law and Political Science, no. 28). Westport, CT: Greenwood Press, 2002. 432 p. index. $94.95. ISBN 0-313-30597-8.

The author of two previous bibliographies on survey research which focused on the 1935–1979 and 1980s time periods, respectively, Walden here describes 617 research items published during the 1990s. The entries were drawn from a wide variety of disciplines, including: business, criminology, mass media, political psychology, and religion, among many others. The bibliography purposefully excludes research that focuses exclusively on the self-administered questionnaire method; instead, the entries deal with research on the methods of face-to-face and telephone interview (p. xiv). The entries are drawn primarily from books, book chapters, dissertations, ERIC documents, government documents, and journal articles. The author has excluded from consideration publications by non–U.S. authors, as well as non–U.S. publications; thus, works by American authors appearing in journals such as *Survey Methodology* do not appear in the bibliography (p. xiv). The entries are organized into broad subject categories within the field of survey research: history, reference sources, instructional materials, cognitive aspects of survey methodology, design, sampling, interviewers, interviewing, data collection methods, respondents, responses, analysis, reporting, and discipline-oriented studies and applications to specific areas. Entries are further arranged by subcategory within these broader themes, where warranted—for example, the interviewing category is subdivided into topics such as confidentiality, ethnographic, and so on. Each entry provides complete bibliographical information, as well as short, descriptive summary and a total of the number of references appearing in the work. Includes an appendix that lists source journals with corresponding entries, and another that features a brief directory of organizations involved in survey research. Additional access to the entries is provided by author and subject indexes.

Handbooks

412. Ballard, James David, comp. and ed. **Qualitative Research Methods: Syllabi and Instructional Materials.** Washington, DC: American Sociological Association, 2001. 220 p. (ASA Resource Materials for Teaching).

There are many approaches to doing qualitative research, and the syllabi and teaching materials included here reflect that diversity. As the editor mentions in the introduction, those approaches include the Chicago school, feminism, and postmodernism, to name some important theoretical orientations. The ten undergraduate and seventeen graduate syllabi presented also reflect the teaching of qualitative research methods in various disciplines, including sociology, public administration, and nursing, among others. Besides the two sections containing course syllabi, there is also a section of teaching assignments and exercises. Also included is an institutional affiliation and address for all contributors to the volume. This handbook is useful not just for instructors of qualitative research, but also for advanced students seeking additional information and research on this methodological technique.

413. Mulvey, Kevin P., ed. **Research Methods Courses: Syllabi, Assignments, and Projects.** 4th ed. Washington, DC: American Sociological Association, 1997. 172 p. (ASA Resource Materials for Teaching).

Instructors who care about their teaching are always looking for better ways to convey the material and to engage students in their learning. One source for new instructional ideas is course syllabi developed by colleagues teaching the same subject. This handbook includes eleven undergraduate and graduate research-methods course syllabi from sociology faculty around the country. The editor selected these syllabi because they not only reflect different teaching styles, but also are complete and original. While it is not obvious that the "teaching styles" diverge noticeably, nonetheless many of the course assignments are well constructed and reveal a thoughtful and systematic approach to teaching research methods. All of these syllabi are new to this edition and are reproduced in their entirety so the reader can appreciate how the course design and materials are integrated.

Dictionaries and Encyclopedias

414. Everitt, B. S. **The Cambridge Dictionary of Statistics.** 2d ed. New York: Cambridge University Press, 2002. 410 p. $50.00. ISBN 0-5218-1099-X.

This dictionary provides the definitions for more than 3,000 statistical terms, along with brief biographical information for roughly 100 significant statisticians. Although many of the entries are geared towards researchers in other disciplines such as biomedicine, sociologists will find concise meanings for terms like "Bayesian inference," "panel study," "student's *t*-distribution," and so on. Formulae and graphs, as well as *see also* references are included in the definitions, where appropriate.

415. Lewis-Beck, Michael S., Alan Bryman, and Tim Futing Liao, eds. **The Sage Encyclopedia of Social Science Research Methods.** Thousand Oaks, CA: Sage, 2004. 3v. index. $550.00. ISBN 0-7619-2363-2.

Sage, of course, is well known for its extensive series of excellent books on various research methods and techniques. Consequently, this work comes with a good pedigree. It is arranged alphabetically and includes approximately 900 entries on various terms, techniques, and methods in social science research. These entries can be either shorter definitions on fundamental terms, or longer essays or more substantial methods and techniques. Some of the topics covered include traditional ones such as factor analysis, historical research, ethnography, analysis of variance, or multiple regression. There are also more specialized entries on a similarly wide variety of methods, including feminist methodology, loglinear models, time series, and sampling in qualitative research. Recommended readings are also included, as is an index.

416. Schwandt, Thomas A. **Dictionary of Qualitative Inquiry.** 2d ed. Thousand Oaks, CA: Sage, 2001. 281 p. $34.95. ISBN 0-7619-2166-4.

This work is intended as a "commentary on the meaning of approximately 300 selected words" in the field of qualitative inquiry, with an emphasis on how these words are interpreted differently "within and across the various theoretical perspectives and philosophies" (p. xvii). The book's preface reinforces this idea of commentary by suggesting clusters of terms that might be explored in common, for example: "criteria," "authenticity criteria," "trustworthiness criteria," "reliability," and "validity" (p. xix–xx). Entries vary in length from a single paragraph to several pages. Entries typically include references to related terms or to terms that are necessary for a greater understanding of the entry in hand. Key reference(s), referring readers to articles or monographs that are standard works on or representative of a given term, are supplied at the conclusion or each entry. References to other works and authors are sometimes made in the text of the entries themselves. This is a useful work for researchers or students in methods courses who require a sophisticated understanding of qualitative methods and concepts, such as epistemology, deconstructionism, positivism, and postmodernism, including a discussion of various interpretations and challenges to these aspects of qualitative inquiry.

417. Upton, Graham, and Ian Cook. **A Dictionary of Statistics.** New York: Oxford University Press, 2002. 420 p. $16.95. ISBN 019-280100-7.

This is another useful dictionary of statistics for those in the social sciences, although some of the terms belong more properly to the fields of operations research and probability. Each of the more than 1,500 entries provides a concise definition, along with *see also* references and formulae. More than 150 biographical entries are also included. The sixteen appendices include information on Greek letters used in statistical formulae; percentage points for the t-, f-, and chi-squared distributions; critical values used in other formulae; and sources for further help.

418. Vogt, W. Paul. **Dictionary of Statistics & Methodology: A Nontechnical Guide for the Social Sciences.** 2d ed. Thousand Oaks, CA: Sage, 1999. 318 p. $93.95. LC 98-25411. ISBN 0-7619-1273-8.

This considerably expanded second edition maintains the author's focus on providing relatively jargon-free definitions of key statistical and methodological terms in the social sciences. The author explains statistical concepts in familiar terms, rather than through the use of mathematical equations (although numerical examples of statistical concepts are found throughout the text). Basic terms are more fully elaborated than are advanced ones. Many definitions include cross-references, marked with asterisks, referring readers to related terms found elsewhere in the dictionary. A nice feature of the dictionary is its use of examples. These greatly clarify definitions that, though well written, may not have been fully understood. This is an excellent and quite helpful dictionary from a publisher that is well-known and respected for publishing monographs and book series on social science research methods and statistics.

Web Sites and Research Centers

419. The Web Center for Social Research Methods. Available: http://www. socialresearchmethods.net/ (Accessed: December 29, 2004).

This well-established site is maintained by William M. Trochim, a professor in the Department of Policy Analysis and Management at Cornell University. Several features of this Web site will appeal to sociologists, including *Selecting Statistics* and the *Knowledge Base.* The former attempts to provide the appropriate statistical measure based on a user's answers to a series of questions. For example, the feature asks, "How Many Variables Does the Problem Involve?" After selecting two variables, it then asks, "How Do You Want to Treat the Variables with Respect to Scale of Measurement?" After providing several more answers, the feature suggests using the regression coefficient for a statistical test; it suggests a book title for further information and notes the SPSS and SAS functions for this test. The *Knowledge Base* is an online manual for research design. It includes sections on sampling, validity, reliability, survey research, types of research designs, and statistical analysis.

420. How to Do Ethnographic Research: A Simplified Guide. Available: http://www.sas.upenn.edu/anthro/CPIA/methods.html (Accessed: April 4, 2004).

Created by Barbara Hall of the Public Interest Anthropology program at the University of Pennsylvania's Department of Anthropology, this guide to ethnographic research presents the basic aims of this type of qualitative research, noting how these aims differ from those of other research methods, describes the process of site selection and some of the ethical problems inherent in fieldwork, outlines how to take field notes and conduct interviews, discusses the analysis of data within a theoretical context, and, provides guidance on the development of a thesis and argument and on drafting a paper. This is a very useful guide for students who are in the process of developing a research design.

421. HyperStat Online: An Introductory Statistics Textbook and Online Tutorial for Help in Statistics. Available: http://davidmlane.com/hyperstat/ (Accessed: January 14, 2004).

Maintained by David Lane, a professor at Rice University, this Web site covers much of the same material that would be found in an introductory statistics textbook. Topics covered include basic probability theory, distributions, confidence intervals, hypothesis testing, and chi-square. The site also provides links to other statistical sites, including sources of free statistical analysis software.

422. ICPSR Summer Program in Quantitative Methods, Syllabi, and Reading Lists from Past Programs. Available: http://www.icpsr.umich.edu/training/ summer/biblio/index.html (Accessed: April 1, 2004).

Each summer, the Inter-university Consortium for Political and Social Research (ICPSR) offers courses and workshops in quantitative research methods and techniques. ICPSR makes available outlines for these courses, as well as bibliographies of required and supplementary readings, from 1995 to the present on its Web site. The outlines provide insights into the major problems associated with various statistical methods, while the bibliographies are sources of some of the most current research in these areas. These courses, offered by experts from U.S. and Canadian universities, are intended to provide state-of-the-art information on approximately forty topics. These include regression analysis, LISREL models, event history analysis, social network analysis, time series analysis, and spatial data analysis, among others. There are also classes focusing on quantitative research in particular subject areas, such as health and crime.

423. **International Institute for Qualitative Methodology.** Available: http://www.ualberta.ca/~iiqm/ (Accessed: April 4, 2004).

Hosted by the University of Alberta, this site is a clearinghouse for a wide variety of information on qualitative research in the social sciences. There is information on workshops, conferences, training, ongoing research, publications, journals (e.g., *Qualitative Health Research*, or *International Journal of Qualitative Methods*, an online journal), dissertation awards, cooperating sites, and much more.

424. **The Qualitative Report.** Available: http://www.nova.edu/ssss/QR/index. html (Accessed: April 4, 2004).

This is an online journal devoted to qualitative research, hosted by the online and distance education university, Nova Southeastern University. Of particular note here are links to qualitative research Web sites, journal descriptions, texts, and syllabi. There are also links to practitioner-oriented, how-to articles in a special section titled "Practicing Qualitative Research." Back issues of the journal itself are available full text online all the way back to the first issue in 1990.

425. **Question Bank: Social Surveys Online.** Available: http://qb.soc.surrey. ac.uk/ (Accessed: January 14, 2004).

Funded by the UK Economic and Social Research Council, the *Question Bank* is a source for "questionnaires for large scale social surveys which have a nationally representative sample and are generally conducted by a large and professional survey organisation." As such, the *Question Bank* does not contain any data sets. Rather, researchers can quickly access the surveys used in nearly fifty longitudinal studies from throughout the United Kingdom. Examples include the General Household Survey for England, Wales, and Scotland, and the Church Attendance Surveys for the United Kingdom. The overview of each study includes links to the survey organization, background information, a note on sampling and methodology, a listing of main topics, and a guide to both the data collected by and reports derived from the survey. The questionnaires themselves are available in pdf format. Access to the surveys is provided through both a search engine and a general listing of surveys. A number of bibliographies are also available on the site, as is a well-organized set of links to outside resources.

426. **Social Science Information Gateway: Research Methods.** Available: http://www.sosig.ac.uk/roads/subject-listing/World-cat/meth.html   (Accessed: January 14, 2004).

This set of links to research methods Web sites is maintained by librarians at the Exeter University Library. The links are organized into several categories including "editor's choice," bibliographic databases, books/book equivalents, data, educational materials, journals, mailing lists/discussion groups, organizations/societies, papers/reports/articles, reference materials, research projects/centers, resource guides, and software. Annotations are provided for each linked Web site.

427. **SocioSite, Research Methodology and Statistics.** Available: http://www2.fmg.uva.nl/sociosite/topics/research.html (Accessed: January 14, 2004).

International in scope, this sub-site is sponsored by the University of Amsterdam. Annotated links are provided in the following categories: methodology, qualitative research, software, research institutes, survey method, statistics, statistical journals, and data archives.

428. **Surfstat.australia.** Available: http://www.anu.edu.au/nceph/surfstat/surf stat-home/surfstat.html (Accessed: January 14, 2004).

Intended as the "primary learning resource for students taking STAT101 at the University of Newcastle, Australia," this established site functions as an introductory textbook on statistics. Topics covered include types of variable, data presentation, measures of variability, research design, probability, and statistical inference. The site also features an excellent glossary of statistical terms and sets of exercises.

429. **United States General Accounting Office, Special Publications: Evaluation Research and Methodology.** Available: http://www.gao.gov/special. pubs/erm.html (Accessed: April 25, 2004).

The United States General Accounting Office (GAO) utilizes a wide variety of social science methodologies in preparing its reports to Congress. GAO makes available a number of special publications that describe these methodologies on its Web site. Most of these publications have been collected on the page "Special Publications: Evaluation Research and Methodology," and include: *Designing Evaluations, Using Structured Interviewing Techniques, Quantitative Data Analysis: An Introduction, Case Study Evaluations, Prospective Evaluations Methods: The Prospective Evaluation Synthesis*, and, *The Evaluation Synthesis.* Several reports are available elsewhere on the site: *Content Analysis: A Methodology for Structuring and Analyzing Written Material* (http://161.203.16.4/d48t13/138426.pdf), *Using Statistical Sampling* (http://161.203.16.4/t2pbat6/146859.pdf), *Developing and Using Questionnaires* (http://161.203.16.4/t2pbat25/130587.pdf), and, *Evaluation and Analysis to Support Decisionmaking* (http://161.203.16.4/f0302/096894.pdf). Each of these pdf-format publications presents an in-depth introduction to a respective methodology or methodological issue. While some of the reports will appeal most directly to those working in the field of applied sociology, others are useful to anyone working in the social sciences.

Rural Sociology

Indexes, Abstracts, and Databases

430. **World Agricultural Economics and Rural Sociology Abstracts.** Vol. 1– , No. 1– . Wallingford, Oxfordshire, United Kingdom: CABI Publishing, 1959– . monthly. $725/yr. ISSN 0043-8219. Available: http://www.cabi-publishing.org/ AbstractDatabases.asp?SubjectArea=&PID=83 (Accessed: March 9, 2004).

While the bulk of this source's entries are on agricultural economics, there is a section in each issue on rural sociology. This includes articles, books, book chapters, and reports on such topics as demography, stratification, rural communities, conflict and political movements, rural families, and more. There are few rural sociology entries per issue, but they are international in coverage. Copies of cited documents can be obtained through a photocopy service. Besides the topical arrangement of the abstracts, access is provided by author and subject/geographical indexes, which cumulate annually. The online version has a backfile of ten years and 80,000 records, with approximately 13,000 new items added to the database per year.

Dictionaries and Encyclopedias

431. Goreham, Gary A., ed. **Encyclopedia of Rural America: The Land and People.** Santa Barbara, CA: ABC-CLIO, 1997. 2v. 861 p. index. $175.00. ISBN 0-87436-842-1.

This is not an encyclopedia of rural sociology, yet sociological concerns and issues are infused throughout. Approximately 230 entries are included in these two volumes. Many of these do revolve around agriculture, agricultural economies and business, the environment, and so on. However, one also finds essays on various minority and ethnic groups, crime, health care, the family, homelessness, the elderly, inequality, mental health, rural sociology, sense of community, poverty, and urbanization, to name a few. The essays generally run to three or four pages in length and are accompanied by *see also* references to related entries and a list of cited and recommended references for further reading. Appended to the end of volume 2 is a list of 230 contributing authors that is well populated by sociologists and social scientists. Also included are a selective bibliography and an extensive index. This should have wide-ranging appeal to students, faculty, and individuals working in and providing service to rural communities.

Web Sites and Research Centers

432. **International Rural Sociology Association.** Available: http://www.irsa-world.org/ (Accessed: March 9, 2004).

The Association is devoted to advancing the field, improving rural life through sociological inquiry, and fostering exchanges between rural sociologists. Toward that end, the Web site highlights the association's upcoming and past world congresses on rural sociology, with conference registration information, themes, program information, and much more. The site also includes the association's history and bylaws and constitution, membership information, key people, affiliated societies, news, minutes of association meetings, and dates of related conferences or meetings.

433. Rural Policy Research Institute (RUPRI). Available: http://www.rupri. org (Accessed: March 9, 2004).

As a policy institute, RUPRI focuses on a number of key policy issues that are also central to interests of sociologists. These include rural poverty, rural health policy, welfare reform, rural telecommunications, rural entrepreneurship, community policy analysis, rural hospital flexibility, and more. In these and other areas, RUPRI may provide news items, editorials, policy studies, or reports (or their executive summaries), notices of events, bibliographies of research, and much more. One can sign up for the e-mail newsletter, and there is also information on fellowships of various kinds (e.g., doctoral, postdoctoral). There is also a lengthy list of pdf documents for research papers and presentations.

434. Rural Sociological Society. Available: http://www.ruralsociology.org/ index.html (Accessed: March 9, 2004).

The stated mission of the Rural Sociological Society is almost identical to the International Rural Sociology Association, namely the "generation, application and dissemination of sociological knowledge" towards the end of enhancing "the quality of rural life" (Web page). This Web site includes information on the society's upcoming annual conference, membership information, professional opportunities (e.g., elections of officers, other requests for papers and proposals, meetings, organizations, teaching/research/administrative positions available). There is also information on scholarships, research and interest groups, committees, and so on. Overall, this is a valuable site for practicing and prospective rural sociologists.

435. Rural Sociology. Available: http://www2.fmg.uva.nl/sociosite/topics/ rural.html (Accessed: March 9, 2004).

Part of the Dutch Web site, *SocioSite*, this Web page has links to six categories of information: general information, journals, professional associations, directories, research centers, and discussion groups. Entries in each category are briefly described and have links to the site or information being described. All of the categories reflect the international coverage of the site, with links to resources in the United Kingdom, Canada, the United States, Scotland, Italy, German, Austria, Australia, Sweden, Holland, Norway, and Latin America, to name a few.

Social Change, Movements, and Collective Behavior

Bibliographies

436. Garner, Robert, and John Tenuto. **Social Movement Theory and Research: An Annotated Bibliographical Guide.** Lanham, MD: Scarecrow Press; Pasadena, CA: Salem Press, 1997. 274 p. index. (Magill Bibliographies). $39.50. ISBN 0-8108-3197-X.

This is an excellent bibliography due to both the detailed overview of social movement theory in the introduction and the obvious care with which entries were selected. Approximately 600 books, book chapters, and journal articles are annotated. The introduction provides a lengthy overview of what the compilers of the bibliography identify as three distinct periods in social movement theory and research. The features and historical origins of each period are discussed. As a result, this introduction is fairly theoretical and addresses broad trends in social movement theory. Following this, the bibliography itself focuses more on "research studies of specific movements and research methods for studying movements, as well as activists' memoirs of their experiences in movements" (p. 1). The bibliography is thus broken down into thirteen chapters: theory; movements in temporal context; movements in spatial context; conservative ideologies and movements; varieties of liberalism; the left; populism; movements of faith; nationalism; the far right; gender and sexual orientation; environmental movements; and social movements in films, documentaries, and novels. Each of these chapters gets a brief introduction, and the entries themselves receive informative, paragraph-long annotations. Works from the 1950s through mid-1990s are included. Both name and subject indexes are provided.

Handbooks and Yearbooks

437. Moore, Kelly, ed. **Syllabi and Teaching Resources for Courses on Collective Behavior and Social Movements.** Washington, DC: American Sociological Association, 1997. 189 p. (ASA Resource Materials for Teaching).

Included here are a total of thirty-three syllabi, bibliographies, and assignments for courses in both collective behavior and social movements. The handbook is actually divided into four parts for syllabi on four different areas of focus: social movements, collective behavior, special topics, and revolutions. The special topics include course syllabi on social movements related to feminism, religion, the Vietnam War and the 1960s, social justice, collective identity and activism, and conservatism and anti-immigration. As the editor points out, however, a close inspection of the syllabi indicates a large amount of overlap between the four sections. Faculty members who contributed these syllabi are from universities across the United States and Canada.

Dictionaries and Encyclopedias

438. Barbuto, Domenica M. **American Settlement Houses and Progressive Social Reform.** Phoenix, AZ: Oryx Press, 1999. 270 p. index. $74.95. ISBN 1-57356-146-0.

Sociologists interested in social movements, social change, urban sociology, and social history may find value in this encyclopedia of the settlement house movement. This social reform movement at the turn of the twentieth century was a significant effort to address various social problems of the time, "including public health, political reform, public education, protective legislation for women and children, and improved living and working conditions for urban dwellers" (p. vii). Included here are approximately 230 entries on major individuals (e.g., Jane Addams, Jacob Riis), events (e.g., the Triangle Shirt Waist Company fire), organizations (e.g., Charity Organization Society, Hull House), and publications (e.g., *How the Other Half Lives*) that comprised this movement. Entries can run from a few paragraphs to over a page in length, each with an added citation to a bibliographic source. Appended are both a bibliography of resources and a comprehensive subject/name/title index.

439. Buhle, Mari Jo, Paul Buhle, and Dan Georgakas, eds. **Encyclopedia of the American Left.** 2d ed. New York: Oxford University Press, 1998. $125.00. ISBN 0-19-512088-4.

The "American left" in this volume refers to far more than the social and political movements of the 1960s. In fact, this encyclopedia is historical in nature and the second edition now goes back to the pre–Civil War period to find examples of and precursors to the American left. This new edition is 25 percent larger than the first, with an additional seventy articles. It covers organizations, social movements, individuals, key concepts, major events, legislation, and much more. The entries themselves are written and signed by subject experts, and they include suggestions for further reading as well as *see also* references to other relevant entries. While there are some biographies included here, much biographical information is integrated into the subject entries that reflect an individual's contributions. Throughout, the encyclopedia continues its previous editorial focus on the radical American left instead of more reformist groups and initiatives. Appended are a selective glossary and general bibliography, an outline of contents, and an excellent and detailed name/subject/title index. Overall, this is an excellent historical work that should interest researchers of social movements and social change.

440. Halsey, Richard S. **The Citizen Action Encyclopedia: Groups and Movements that Have Changed America.** Westport, CT: Oryx Press, 2002. 385 p. index. $64.00. ISBN 1-57356-291-2.

People and organizations that pursued their interests in organized social movements provided much of the dynamism of twentieth-century American history. These included movements organized around principles such as civil rights or women's rights, around events such as the Vietnam War, or around broader political and religious beliefs, such as political conservatism or fundamentalist Christianity, among others. These are the causes and actors that have changed and continue to change the country. This encyclopedia provides a concise but fascinating overview of many of these people, organizations, and movements. The hundreds of entries here can be spot read, based upon one's interests, or can be identified thematically in the introductory "Guide to Related Topics." The list of entries includes many organizations (e.g., the National Rifle Association), people (e.g., Malcolm X), court cases (e.g., *Roe v. Wade*), and much more. The guide to related topics includes almost forty large topics, such as abortion, activist think tanks, Native American rights, the senior movement, the anti–nuclear power movement, antiwar movements, and more. Various entries are listed under each topical category. The entries themselves can range from a few paragraphs to a few pages and include both *see also* references and suggestions for further reading. Appended are a directory of organizations (with address, phone numbers, and e-mail/Web addresses), a bibliography, and an extensive name/subject index.

441. Khan, Veryan B., ed. **Beacham's Encyclopedia of Social Change: America in the Twentieth Century.** Nokomis, FL: Beacham Group, 2001. 4v. $350.00. ISBN 0-933833-62-8 (set).

This encyclopedia of social change is organized around forty-one topical chapters that are used as barometers of change in American history in the twentieth century. Those forty-one topics include issues such as advertising and consumerism, cities, crime, education, family life, food, the automobile, inventions, leisure, morality, music, race and class, religion, sex and gender, war, and the workplace, among others. Within these chapters, the essays are arranged chronologically. There are usually accompanying tables and photographs, as well as an appended bibliography and list of Internet resources. The bibliography entries are often drawn from academic books and journals, making the list a good academic resource for further reading. Each chapter begins with a time line that identifies important historical periods within that subject area, as well as milestone events related to that period. The topics covered here are clearly important, and they do have implications for the study of social or cultural change. However, sociological considerations of social change are not drawn out, leaving this up to the reader. Appended is a time line from 1500 to the present, as well as an index to subjects, names, court cases, organizations, book/magazine/film titles, and legislation. This is a fascinating read and would be suitable for general readers and students of social change and twentieth century history.

442. Luker, Ralph E. **Historical Dictionary of the Civil Rights Movement.** Lanham, MD: Scarecrow Press, 1997. 331 p. $68.00. ISBN 0-8108-3163-5.

The civil rights movement has spanned decades and consisted of scores of individuals (e.g., Ralph Abernathy, A. Philip Randolph, Eldridge Cleaver, Angela Davis), events (e.g., Birmingham, Alabama Movement, Selma to Montgomery March), organizations (e.g., the NAACP Legal Defense and Educational Fund, Student Nonviolent Coordinating Committee), legislation (e.g., Voting Rights Act of 1965), and court cases (e.g., *University of California Regents v. Bakke*). This work presents concise descriptions of these topics, with its strength being its major coverage of both individuals and court cases. The definitions are well written and quite detailed, ranging in length from a paragraph to a few pages. There is a lengthy chronology at the beginning of the dictionary covering from 1941 to the mid-1990s, with many of the cited people, events, and court cases also receiving substantial entries within the dictionary. At the end, there is a long bibliography of both primary and secondary sources.

443. Meier, Matt S., and Margo Gutierrez. **Encyclopedia of the Mexican American Civil Rights Movement.** Westport, CT: Greenwood Press, 2000. 293 p. index. $76.95. ISBN 0-313-30425-4.

This work is intended to help fill a scholarly gap by providing concise descriptions of key individuals, events, organizations, legal cases, and legislation that have helped shape the Mexican American civil rights movement. Entries range from a paragraph to a few pages, and many of the entries are accompanied by references for further reading. There are *see also* references to direct the reader to additional relevant entries. At first glance, the introductory essay does not appear to be robust enough to provide a good context for the entries that follow. However, the entries themselves are extremely well written and, in a sense, provide the context for each of their subjects. Appended are a chronology of the movement since 1836, the Bill of Rights, the Fourteenth Amendment, the Treaty of Guadalupe Hidalgo, a list of acronyms, and some notes on Spanish pronunciation. There is also a subject/name index. Overall, this is a thoughtful and very well-constructed guide to the people and events that comprise the civil rights movement for Mexican Americans.

Web Sites and Research Centers

444. **Collective Behavior and the Social Psychologies of Social Institutions.** Available: http://www.trinity.edu/mkearl/socpsy-8.html (Accessed: December 30, 2004).

As with other Web pages at Michael Kearl's site, *A Sociological Tour through Cyberspace*, this is an incredibly rich guide to background information and other Web pages related to collective behavior and social movements. There are links to full-text documents, overviews of important historical events (e.g., the 1921 Tulsa race riots), excerpts from scholarly writing on the subject, an annotated bibliography, and much more.

445. **Havens Center.** Available: http://www.havenscenter.org/index.htm (Accessed: December 29, 2004).

Erik Olin Wright directs the A. E. Havens Center for the Study of Social Structure and Social Change, which is located at the University of Wisconsin. It focuses on the study of social change and social movements from critical theoretical perspectives. The center sponsors conferences, such as RadFest and the Real Utopias Project (which also generates monographs), as well as a visiting scholars program. It also offers an interdisciplinary graduate minor in social theory, cultural studies, feminist thought, and radical political economy.

446. **Section on Collective Behavior and Social Movements.** Available: http://www.asanet.org/sectioncbsm/ (Accessed: December 29, 2004).

This is the World Wide Web site for one of the American Sociological Association's interest groups. Included here is information on the interest group section itself (e.g., elections, bylaws, officers, award nominations, meetings at conferences, etc.); links to resources such as journals and listservs; links to related sociology organizations worldwide; and notifications of various professional calls for papers, workshop notices, or fellowship announcements. Also included are the full text of the interest group's newsletter, *Critical Mass Bulletin*, links to sociology department Web pages, and an electronic directory of members, among other items.

Social Indicators

Handbooks and Yearbooks

447. **Gale Country & World Rankings Reporter.** 2d ed. Detroit: Gale, 1997. 953 p. index. ISBN 0-7876-0060-1.

Comparative country data on demographics, education, health, family, criminal justice, and labor could be useful as social indicators of development and policy priorities, among other things. This volume provides some of those data, albeit in a slightly quirky format. There are more than 3,000 tables of data included here, covering not only social life as reflected in the categories above, but also agriculture, environment, economics, geography, energy, communications, infrastructure, transportation, politics, law, industry, markets, and more. While there are a wealth of topics covered, and numerous tables on many of them, the data presented are abbreviated. That is, countries or regions are ranked on the indicator in question, but most tables only rank from four to forty countries or regions. Furthermore, the topics covered in some of the tables (e.g., fast-food establishments such as Dunkin' Donut) may seem fairly quirky at first glance. However, many of these tables may have their uses. This makes for intriguing reading, but it will be up to the user to put such data in a meaningful context. Data come from a wide variety of sources, including government publications, agencies, and Web sites; newspapers; magazines; and journals. Appended are a list of sources, a location index, and a keyword index.

448. Kurian, George Thomas, ed. **The Illustrated Book of World Rankings.** 5th ed. Armonk, NY: M. E. Sharpe, 2001. 471 p. index. $149.00. ISBN 0-7656-8026-2.

This work attempts to rank the performance of countries on 300 indicators which have been grouped under larger topical headings, including population, vital statistics, race and religion, labor, consumption and housing, health and social services, education, crime and law enforcement, women, and so on. Each entry is prefaced by a paragraph explaining the indicator's significance. This is followed by a tabular and/or graphical representation of the national rankings for that indicator. The source of the data is included at the foot of each table; most of the data derive from 1998. An appendix includes a listing of major international statistical publications and publishers. Additional access to the entries is provided by a topical index. A companion CD-ROM is also available. This is a useful work for fairly up-to-date comparative indicators of social and economic development.

449. Muth, Anmarie, ed. **Statistical Abstract of the World.** Detroit, MI: Gale, 1997. 1,134 p. index. ISBN 0-8103-6434-4.

This is a repackaging of country data from a variety of sources, including the United Nations and its various agencies (e.g., UNICEF, UNESCO, International Labor Organization), the United States and a number of its agencies (e.g., the CIA, Bureau of the Census), and other major sources (e.g., World Bank, OECD, Organization of American States). Data cover 185 countries in the United Nations, as well as Switzerland, Hong Kong, and Taiwan. For each country, one can find data on geography, demographics, health, education, science and technology, government and law, labor force, production sectors, manufacturing sector, and finance/economics/trade. While there is no tremendous depth in any one category, these categories exist across countries, thus allowing comparative analysis. Furthermore, source documents are fully cited for every table or chart. While these data are drawn from many fairly common and available statistical sources, they have nonetheless been presented in a very readable and user friendly format. This information may be useful for undergraduate students doing some comparative policy analysis or examining development trends. A keyword index is included.

450. **Society at a Glance: OECD Social Indicators.** Paris: OECD, 2003. 83 p. ISBN 92-64-19797-4.

These data and charts, provided by the Organisation for Economic Co-Operation and Development, are part of the OECD's effort to provide updated lists of social indicators "on whether our societies are getting more or less unequal, healthy, dependent and cohesive" (p. 3). The charts, tables and explanatory material cover such important subject areas as age, employment, unemployment, working mothers, educational attainment, public social expenditure, child poverty, potential years of life lost, low birth weight, health-adjusted life expectancy, responsibility for financing health care, suicide, juvenile crime, teenage births, and more. Each of the thirty topics includes a definition and indication of how the item is measured, a discussion of the evidence and its explanations, and two or three accompanying charts, graphs, or tables.

451. United Nations Development Program. **Human Development Report 2002: Deepening Democracy in a Fragmented World.** New York: Oxford University Press, 2002. 277 p. index. $22.95. ISBN 0-19-521915-5.

Each annual *Human Development Report* from the UNDP includes an introductory essay that attempts to summarize trends affecting development. In 2002 the *Report* focuses on the links between democratic governance and development. There are five narrative chapters that address various aspects of these links, and statistical tables are interspersed among each of these. The set of human development indicators that is common to all of the *Reports* begins after these narrative chapters. The "Human Development Index" ranks 173 countries according to their capacity for human development; this capacity is determined by a set of factors, including life expectancy at birth; adult literacy rate; combined elementary, secondary, and tertiary education enrollment ratio; and GDP per capita. Other indicators of human development, such as gender inequality in education and victims of crime, are presented in a series of statistical tables. The *Report* includes a short glossary of terms and a topical index.

452. **Vital Signs: The Trends that Are Shaping Our Future.** New York: W. W. Norton, 1992– . annual. ISSN 1075-0576.

Produced by the Worldwatch Institute, in cooperation with the United Nations Environment Programme, this handbook covers environmental, economic, and social indicators from around the world. In the 2003 edition, there are two parts. Part 1 includes sections with trend data on food, energy and atmosphere, economy, transportation and communication, health and social, and the military. Each of these, in turn, has three or four subtopics. "Health and Social Trends" includes subsections on population growth, the HIV/AIDS pandemic, and cigarette production. On any particular subtopic, there is a page of text describing the worldwide trend and an accompanying page of tables or charts documenting it. Part 2 is devoted to "special features" and has chapters on environment, economy, resource economics, health and social features, and military and governance. The "economy" chapter covers the growing rich-poor divide, the gap in CEO-worker pay, and severe weather. The "health and social features" chapter addresses drops in the number of refugees as well as the popularity gain of alternative medicine, inequitable maternal deaths, mortality and consumption patterns, and increases in orphans due to AIDS. Overall, this is an interesting overview of, among other things, social and economic indicators that may be of interest to sociology students and general readers.

453. World Bank. **World Development Report 2004: Making Services Work for Poor People.** New York: Oxford University Press, 2003. 271 p. $26.00. ISBN 0-8213-5537-6.

This long-standing series from the World Bank is similar to the UNDP's *Human Development Report* in that each annual edition focuses on a particular issue. The 2004 *World Development Report* looks at the provision of social services to poor people throughout the world through ten narrative chapters. Several of the chapters look at the various stakeholders involved in providing services to the poor, while others look at specific services such as basic education; health and nutrition services; and drinking water, sanitation, and electricity. Statistical tables, charts, and graphs are used to illustrate the points in each chapter. The book concludes with a series of tables on selected world development indicators, including economic, health, and social variables.

454. **World Economic Factbook.** 10th ed. London: Euromonitor, 2002. 453 p. $520.00. ISBN 1-84264-234-0.

This is a useful compendium of social and economic indicators for 204 countries. Each entry consists of a narrative overview that focuses on political and economic conditions, together with a tabular representation of major indicators (e.g., death rate, birth rate, life expectancy, age analysis, etc.). Data are provided for 1999, 2000, and 2001. The entries are prefaced by a series of tables which show the countries ranked by various criteria.

Web Sites and Research Centers

455. **Social Indicators: Statistics Division, United Nations Department of Economic and Social Affairs.** Available: http://unstats.un.org/unsd/demo graphic/social/default.htm (Accessed: March 8, 2004).

The UN's Social Indicators Web site features tables on population, youth and elderly populations, human settlements, water supply and sanitation, housing, health, childbearing, education, illiteracy, income and economic activity, and unemployment. The data contained in each table vary by country. In addition to this set of indicators, the site also links to the general statistical program of the Department of Economic and Social Affairs.

456. **Social Indicators Department: German Social Science Infrastructure Services (GESIS).** Available: http://www.gesis.org/en/social_monitoring/ social_indicators/index.htm (Accessed: March 8, 2004).

The *Social Indicators* Web site features access to the various research programs and publications associated with GESIS. Chief among these are the *German System of Social Indicators*, which provides online access to time-series data on population, health, the environment, and other topics; the *Social Indicators Information Service*, which consists of German-language releases of current research; and, the *Data Report*, which provides a detailed set of social, political, and economic statistics in German.

457. **The Social Indicators Site: Canadian Council on Social Development (CCSD).** Available: http://www.ccsd.ca/soc_ind.html (Accessed: March 8, 2004).

In addition to providing information about the dated symposium hosted by the Canadian Council on Social Development, this site features a "Social Indicators Launchpad." The Launchpad consists of links to various international sources of social indicators, as well as to CCSD's own research on Canadians.

Social Networks and Social Support

Handbooks and Yearbooks

458. Scott, John. **Social Network Analysis: A Handbook.** 2d ed. London; Thousand Oaks, CA: Sage, 2000. 208 p. index. ISBN 0-7619-6338-3.

This second edition is intended to appeal both to newcomers to social network analysis and more advanced specialists in the field. In all, there are eight chapters updating and addressing key issues and techniques in the area: networks and relations; development of social network analysis; handling relational data; points, lines, and density; centrality and centralization; components, cores, and cliques; positions, roles, and clusters; and dimensions and displays. Each chapter, in turn, has a number of subtopics. The appendix has been revised from the first edition and includes descriptions of various social network packages (computer programs) that are available for data analysis. Scott reviews the main features of the four major packages currently available: GRADAP, STRUCTURE, UCINET, and PAJEK. A bibliography is provided, as is a very modest index.

Web Sites and Research Centers

459. **International Network for Social Network Analysis (INSNA).** Available: http://www.sfu.ca/~insna/ (Accessed: March 17, 2004).

The INSNA is the most important specialized organization in this field. Its Web site provides not only general information about the organization, but also extensive information on relevant journals (e.g., *Social Networks* and the electronic *Journal of Social Structure*), texts, research centers, relevant courses, online bibliographies for social networks and policy networks, conferences, PowerPoint presentations, graduate programs, and Web sites, to name just some of its many features. SOCNET, the organization's discussion listserv, is also fully described and available. There is also an extensive list of social network software, as well as a list of hot topics with links to relevant Web sites. This is an excellent Web site with numerous resources.

Social Problems

General

Handbooks and Yearbooks

460. Kaelber, Lutz, and Walter Carroll, comps and eds. **Instructor's Resource Manual on Social Problems.** Washington, DC: American Sociological Association, 2001. 158 p. (ASA Resource Materials for Teaching).

Social problems classes are ubiquitous as sociology offerings, and they are frequently demeaned as being "problem of the week" courses with little theoretical or disciplinary rigor. However, as the editors and contributors to this manual demonstrate, that stereotype is not true. The course syllabi presented in this manual reinforce the idea and practice that social problems can only be fully analyzed if understood as part of broader social structures and relationships (p. 4). As is pointed out, these classes foster critical thinking and attempt to instill the "sociological imagination" and our ability to see personal or individual troubles as social issues. Included here are thirteen syllabi, as well as an assortment of assignments, exercises, and policy guidelines. There is also a list of Web sites for social problems classes, and a list of the contributors and their departmental and university affiliations. The introductory essay on the teaching of social problems is quite good and is accompanied by a list of references. Overall, this handbook may be useful to anyone teaching or preparing to teach a social problems course, including graduate students, part-time faculty, or full-time faculty.

Dictionaries and Encyclopedias

461. Kronwetter, Michael. **Encyclopedia of Modern American Social Issues.** Santa Barbara, CA: ABC-CLIO, 1997. 328 p. index. ISBN 0-87436-779-4.

Though not exclusively about social problems, this encyclopedia nonetheless identifies and explores a wide range of ongoing controversial social issues in American life. According to the author, these are issues that have been dominant during the twentieth century and promise to continue being so. Entries cover political, economic, cultural, scientific, legal, and medical issues. Many classic controversies are included, such as gun control, the death penalty, welfare reform, legalized gambling, religion in the schools, abortion, flag burning, school choice, race and prejudice, crime, and television violence, among others. While some entries are more definitional in scope, others provide balanced and fairly extensive overviews of hotly debated topics. An historical context is provided in some cases, and texts or partial texts of key documents are reproduced in others (e.g., the Universal Declaration of Human Rights). There are also some entries for and references to famous legal cases, such as the *Bakke* case (reverse discrimination). Throughout the encyclopedia, the writing is excellent and the goal is clearly to introduce the reader to the scope and importance of the topic. Statistics are kept to a minimum on the theory that they may soon become outdated anyway. The clarity of the overview of the topics more than compensates. This work would be best suited for students and general readers. A detailed name/subject index provides additional access to the entries, which are arranged alphabetically by topic.

462. Roth, John K., ed. **Encyclopedia of Social Issues.** New York: Marshall Cavendish, 1997. 6v. ISBN 0-7614-0568-2 (set).

Aimed at a popular audience, the approximately 1,500 entries in this encyclopedia touch on virtually any remotely topical social issue or social problem that one might be interested in. Ranging from a paragraph to five pages, the entries provide a simple and readable overview of a topic and why it might be considered an issue. In fact, the topics covered include legislation (e.g., the Animal Welfare Act), court cases (e.g., *Brown v. Board of Education*), organizations (e.g., Accuracy in Media), individuals (e.g., George H. W. Bush), events (e.g., the Vietnam War), and a vast array of subjects. Many photographs and an occasional chart are included with the text, and entries are sometimes accompanied by suggested readings. The last volume includes a supplemental listing of entries arranged under the thirty-plus broad, core subjects of the encyclopedia. These core subjects are the ones receiving the longest essays of approximately 3,500 words. There is also a supplementary bibliography for thirty core topics; an annotated "Mediagraphy" of recommended books, music, and films/television programs; and a "Timeline of Major Twentieth Century Court Rulings and Legislation." An extensive subject index includes topics, people, legislation, court cases, organizations, and landmark events. This would be suitable for general users, K–12 students, and some college undergraduates. For readers trying to supplement their historical and cultural literacy, this could be a handy reference tool.

Web Sites and Research Centers

463. **Society for the Study of Social Problems (SSSP).** Available: http://www.sssp1.org/ (Accessed: March 8, 2004).

Like its sister organizations in clinical and applied sociology, the SSSP is devoted to applying "critical, social, and humanistic perspectives to the study of vital social problems" (Web page). The site includes the usual information about the annual meeting, membership, awards and scholarships, the organization newsletter, job announcements, and related links. The organization also includes "special problems divisions" that focus on over a dozen noteworthy problem areas, including education, health policy, poverty, crime, environment, family, sexual behavior, conflict, and more. The organization's journal, *Social Problems*, is also fully described.

Alcoholism and Drug Abuse

Handbooks and Yearbooks

464. Bellenir, Karen, ed. **Drug Abuse Sourcebook.** Detroit, MI: Omnigraphics, 2000. 629 p. index. (Health Reference Series). ISBN 0-7808-0242-X.

This is a wide-ranging guide to information and resources on drug abuse, reflecting the diversity of causes, consequences, interventions, and treatments related to the problem. Included here are descriptions of abused drugs, the causes and health consequences of addiction, prevention strategies, treatment programs, key terms, important organizations, and more. The information is presented in sixty-nine chapters under seven major categories: drug use and abuse, the nature of addiction, drugs of abuse, recent research on drug-related health risks, treatment issues, prevention issues, and additional help and information. Specific chapters describe particular drugs, physiological causes and manifestations of abuse, treatment programs, ethical issues, prevention research, workplace effects, and much more. The last section includes glossaries of terms, an annotated guide of resources for parents, annotated directories of self-help groups and federal agencies, a listing of federal drug data sources, a directory of Drug Enforcement Administration (DEA) division offices, and a directory of the primary state agencies for all states. Information from each chapter is drawn or excerpted from reputable sources, such as the National Institute on Drug Abuse (NIDA), the Harvard Mental Health Letter, the Drug Enforcement Administration, and other government and private agencies and publications. A subject index is provided.

465. Zerning, Gerald et al., eds. **Handbook of Alcoholism.** Boca Raton, FL: CRC Press, 2000. 492 p. index. $119.95. ISBN 0-8493-7801-X.

Featuring an international list of contributors, this handbook includes over forty chapters addressing alcoholism from multiple perspectives. The chapters are divided into sections for patient care, research, and useful data and definitions. Within section 1, chapters are further grouped by themes: screening and diagnosis, acute treatment, treatment of alcohol abuse and dependence, and treatment of nonpsychiatric alcohol-related disorders. Some of these related disorders include those of the liver, kidney, nervous system, immune system, endocrine system, skin, and more. Section 2, on research, includes chapters on such topics as epidemiology, heritability, behavioral pharmacology, and meta-analysis of pharmacotherapeutic trials, among others. Section 3 on data and definitions includes chapters on calculating blood alcohol levels, drug interactions, and harmful daily alcohol consumption, DSM-IV and ICD-10 definitions of alcohol-related conditions. Also included are chapters listing psychometric test instruments (with copies of most instruments included), useful Internet addresses, and abbreviations used. There is a substantial subject index that includes proper names for drugs, organizations, and research instruments.

Dictionaries and Encyclopedias

466. **Encyclopedia of Drugs, Alcohol, and Addictive Behavior.** 2d ed. Rosalyn Carson-DeWitt, ed. New York: Macmillan Reference USA, 2000. 4v. $475.00. ISBN 0-02-865541-9 (set).

While the first edition of this encyclopedia focused on drug and alcohol abuse, this second edition has expanded to include other forms and manifestations of addictive behavior, such as compulsive gambling. The focus of these volumes is on the diagnosis, causes, consequences, and treatment of varieties of addictive behavior. Included here are essays on various drugs; physiological, genetic, social, and psychological factors in addiction; research organizations; support groups (e.g., Adult Children of Alcoholics, Al-Anon); consequences of addiction (personal, familial, social, economic); diagnostic and research instruments; patterns of abuse; and much more. The essays are written by experts on the topics, and they can range from less than one page in length to over ten pages. The entries are accompanied by *see also* references to related terms found elsewhere in the encyclopedia, as well as a bibliography of references. The final volume includes appendices, three of which are directories of poison control centers, federal and state drug resources, and state treatment and prevention programs. Two other appendices present an overview of federal attempts to control the drug problem, and schedules of controlled substances. A substantial subject index includes organizational names, acronyms, titles, and personal names. Social, psychological, and physiological research on addictive behavior is well represented here.

467. O'Brien, Robert, Morris Chafetz, and Sidney Cohen. **The Encyclopedia of Understanding Alcohol and Other Drugs.** New York: Facts on File, 1999. 2v. (Facts on File Library of Health and Living). $214.50. ISBN 0-8160-3970-4 (set).

The content in these volumes varies between presenting dictionary entries and encyclopedia-length essays on hundreds of terms. Included are definitions or descriptions of drugs, concepts, medical or psychological conditions, organizations, key individuals, theories, legislation, and more. Entries can range from a sentence to multiple pages. Tables, charts, graphs, maps, document excerpts, or brief lists of references complement some of the entries. Drug names are extensively covered. There are also entries on various countries, their experiences with drug and alcohol abuse, and their approaches to treatment. Volume 2 includes a glossary of terms, numerous appendices, an organization directory, a bibliography, and an extensive index. The six appendices cover some source documents on alcohol and drug addiction, including some historical documents, as well as research reports and health alerts on contemporary issues. These documents originate from private, state, and federal organizations and can include newsletters, health advisories, short booklets, articles, and more. The final appendix includes alcohol and drug usage statistics. There is a wealth of information in these appendices, though it would have been useful to have some indication of their organization, which at first glance appears somewhat random. Nonetheless, these volumes constitute a tremendous resource.

Web Sites and Research Centers

468. **Sociology of Health: Drugs.** Available: http://www2.fmg.uva.nl/sociosite/topics/health.html#DRUGS (Accessed: November 11, 2003).

Part of the Dutch sociology Web site, *SocioSite*, this page includes numerous Web links on drugs, alcohol, and tobacco. This site is international in scope and includes Web pages on drug policy, the debate over legalization of certain drugs, addiction research, self-help groups, and more.

Homelessness

Bibliographies

469. Klinker, Susanne, and Suzanne Fitzpatrick. **A Bibliography of Single Homelessness Research.** Bristol, United Kingdom: Policy Press, 2000. 81 p. ISBN 1-86134-256-X.

This work complements two other monographic research reports on the issue of single homelessness in Britain. Covering research since 1990, this bibliography includes hundreds of unannotated bibliographic citations to books, book chapters, and journal articles. These are arranged alphabetically by author under eight subject chapters: general homelessness, legal framework, extent of homelessness, groups of homeless people, aspects of life affected by homelessness, responses to homelessness, research methods, and selected international literature. The section on affected groups includes such categories as asylum seekers, ethnic minorities, older people, runaways, survivors of sexual abuse, and more. Similarly, the aspects of life treated in that chapter cover health, housing, benefits, employment, education, family, crime, and others. Responses to homelessness include topics like accommodation, services, prevention, business involvement, and more. The international citations include both research on other countries, and research that is comparative in nature. Though citations are not annotated, they are accompanied by lists of keywords reflecting their content. Appended is a directory of relevant British organizations. Overall, this is a solid, academically oriented list of research sources focusing primarily on British homelessness.

470. Kutais, B. G., and Tatiana Shohov, eds. **Homelessness: A Guide to the Literature.** 2d ed. Commack, NY: Nova Science Publishers, 1999. 230 p. index. $69.00. ISBN 1-56072-701-2.

There are well over 1,000 entries in this bibliography arranged under seven major subject categories: general, social legislation, social issues; housing policy, shelters; homeless children and the aged; mental illness and psychological issues; urban poverty; welfare, health issues; and alcohol and drug abuse. Within these chapters, there are entries for books, popular magazine articles, scholarly journal articles, newspaper articles, government documents, congressional hearings, and more. Arrangement of the entries themselves is alphabetical by author or, lacking that, by title. Some entries have annotations or brief descriptive excerpts from the source itself, though many do not. Books have complete bibliographic citations and also include subject headings and ISBN numbers. In all, this is a fascinating array of sources. However, some needed attention to detail is lacking. For example, titles beginning with the articles "a" or "the" are alphabetized by those words. Furthermore, the citations, titles, and text of the entries are undifferentiated and somewhat difficult to scan. Also, while a detailed subject index would help access sources, the included index is somewhat spare. An author index is included, however. Despite its unfriendly layout and quirky arrangement, a diligent researcher should find some useful resources here.

471. Nordquist, Joan, comp. **Homelessness in the United States: A Bibliography.** Santa Cruz, CA: Reference and Research Services, 2001. 80 p. (Contemporary Social Issues: A Bibliographic Series, no. 61). $20.00. ISBN 1-89068-20-6.

Included here are over 800 sources looking at many facets of homelessness from a variety of policy and theoretical perspectives. Articles, books, book chapters, dissertations, Web sites, and pamphlets comprise the citations. The unannotated entries are drawn from both mainstream and more critically oriented databases and indexes, thus giving the bibliography a breadth of analytical perspectives. The entries are arranged into sixteen subject chapters: theoretical works, descriptive studies, families, children, children and education, women, youth, veterans, housing, health, substance abuse, health and medical care, AIDS, attitudes towards the homeless, testimonials, literary collections, resources (i.e., bibliographies and directories), and Web sites. Most of these chapters have subsections for books and articles, with entries arranged alphabetically by author in each category. As with other titles in this series, this is a thoughtfully constructed bibliography of valuable sources on the topic.

Handbooks and Yearbooks

472. Hombs, Mary Ellen. **American Homelessness: A Reference Handbook.** 3d ed. Santa Barbara, CA: ABC-CLIO, 2001. 299 p. index. (Contemporary World Issues). $45.00. ISBN 1-57607-247-9.

Now in its third edition, this book nonetheless reports a worsening of homelessness. This suggests how intractable the problem is within current policy approaches, which are discussed within this volume. Overall, this handbook is similar in structure to other titles in the series in that it provides a wide variety of information to explore the problem. There are nine chapters: introduction; chronology; biographical sketches; facts and statistics; documents and reports; legislation on homeless assistance; homelessness and the law; directory of organizations, associations, and government agencies; and selected print and nonprint resources. The documents and reports include excerpts from United States, Canadian, British, Australian, and European reports and statements on homelessness. As well, the chapters on statistics, legislation, organizations, and the law are also international in scope. Each chapter is accompanied by a list of references, and the final chapter includes an annotated bibliography of books and films/videos, as well as a list of relevant databases. A glossary of key terms is included, as is a detailed name/subject index. This provides a solid overview of many features of the problem and would make an excellent resource for students and general readers.

Web Sites and Research Centers

473. **National Coalition for the Homeless.** Available: http://www.nationalhomeless.org/ (Accessed: December 29, 2004).

This organization focuses on homelessness both as a social and policy issue. There are Web pages dealing with housing justice, economic justice, health care justice, civil rights, public education, policy advocacy, and technical assistance. In addition, there are breaking news stories and hot topics, with many of the latter covering current or proposed legislation and policy initiatives (e.g., voter registration for the homeless). Links to Internet resources and K–12 educational materials are also included. Besides the political and legislative materials, one can also find commentary on social and cultural responses to and explanations of homelessness, as well as personal stories of homeless individuals that personalize and put a human face on a growing social problem.

474. **National Law Center on Homelessness and Poverty.** Available: http://www.nlchp.org (Accessed: December 29, 2004).

Primarily an advocacy group, this organization focuses on policy issues that may impact efforts to eliminate homelessness. The Web site includes pages on housing, income, education, and civil rights, as well as links to fact sheets, state laws, and other Web sites dealing with homelessness issues and policies. Other specific issues addressed include voting rights and criminalization. While not explicitly sociological in focus, the site nonetheless lends itself to such analysis. There are numerous links to other sites and documents.

Rape, Sexual Assault, and Harassment

Bibliographies

475. Nordquist, Joan, comp. **Violence Against Women—International Aspects: A Bibliography.** Santa Cruz, CA: Reference and Research Services, 1998. 64 p. (Contemporary Social Issues: A Bibliographic Series, no. 49). $20.00. ISBN 0-937855-96-0.

Drawn from both mainstream and alternative periodical indexes and databases, this bibliography includes references to almost 700 books, articles, book chapters, pamphlets, government documents, dissertations, and other materials on the issue of violence against women. The focus is on countries and regions other than the United States. The chapters alternate between a topical focus and a country or world region focus and include: violence against women; violence against women and war; Europe; Australia, New Zealand, Oceania; Asia; sexual exploitation, violence and prostitution: the trafficking of women and children; India; genital mutilation; Middle East; Latin America; and testimonials. Each chapter has separate lists, arranged by author, for books or articles. Some chapters have a country/region index at the end, though the references do not always seem to match the country or region indicated. Most sources date from the early 1990s onward, though works from the mid- to late-1980s are not uncommon. At the end of the bibliography is a "Resources" chapter with separate listings for bibliographies and Web sites. The importance of these topics, along with the breadth of critical sources consulted and listed, makes this a valuable bibliography, despite the lack of annotations.

Web Sites and Research Centers

476. Sexual Harassment, Rape, Domestic Violence, Abuse. Available: http://www2.fmg.uva.nl/sociosite/topics/men.html#HARRASSMENT   (Accessed: December 29, 2004).

Part of *SocioSite*, a Dutch Web site on sociology, this page includes links to numerous Web pages on rape, marital rape, battering, domestic violence, rape prevention, men's violence prevention, husband battering, sexual harassment, and much more.

Suicide

Dictionaries and Encyclopedias

477. Evans, Glen, and Norman L. Farberow. **The Encyclopedia of Suicide.** 2d ed. New York: Facts on File, 2003. 329 p. ISBN 0-8160-4525-9.

During the 1990s, suicide accounted for eight million deaths worldwide and 300,000 in the United States. It is, of course, a private, self-destructive act. Yet it is also a major public health concern and of profound sociological interest, as reflected in Émile Durkheim's landmark work on the subject. This encyclopedia includes fairly concise entries on the full range of topics that relate to suicide. There are entries here on theories of suicide, key issues (e.g., unemployment and suicide), famous individuals, important books, drugs, key organizations, cultural groups and nationalities (e.g., Eskimos, Muslims, Native Americans, Holland), states and state laws, important journals, psychological tests, and much more. This second edition has also been updated to include entries on topics of more recent interest, such as suicide bombers, suicide by copy, mass suicide, and school violence and suicide, among others. Two appendices provide directories of national and international organizations and agencies (both public and private), and of suicide prevention and crisis intervention agencies in the United States. A third appendix includes international data for suicide rates per 100,000 individuals. A concise bibliography is included, as is a detailed subject index. The concise entries and straightforward prose make this well suited to general readers and high school and undergraduate students.

Web Sites and Research Centers

478. Suicide. Available: http://www.trinity.edu/~mkearl/death-su.html (Accessed: December 29, 2004).

This is a sociologically oriented Web page with data, analysis, sociological theories, links to important related sites, and more. It is part of the Web site *A Sociological Tour through Cyberspace*, and it contains a wealth of thought-provoking information. There are data for other countries, as well as U.S. data broken down by age, gender, and race, among other categories. The author is careful not to offer simplistic explanations of the causes of and variations in suicide rates and instead explores features of a more complex sociological analysis. There is also some information on Émile Durkheim and his pathbreaking analysis of suicide. Numerous links to other Web sites are provided, including sites for more data, suicide prevention, and sociological literature reviews on suicide.

479. **Suicide Research Consortium.** Available: http://www.nimh.gov/research/suicide.cfm (Accessed: April 12, 2004).

Sponsored by the National Institute of Mental Health, the consortium "coordinates program development in suicide research across the Institute, identifies gaps in the scientific knowledge base on suicide across the life span, stimulates and monitors extramural research on suicide, keeps abreast of scientific developments in suicidology and public policy issues related to suicide surveillance, prevention and treatment, and disseminates science-based information on suicidology to the public, media, and policy makers" (Web page). There are links to research, statistics, policy statements, reports, fact sheets, research reviews, reviews of research instruments, and more. The site also includes links to those in crisis who may be seeking help.

Violence

Bibliographies

480. Nordquist, Joan, comp. **Hate Crimes: A Bibliography.** Santa Cruz, CA: Reference and Research Services, 2002. 72 p. (Contemporary Social Issues, no. 66). $20.00. ISBN 1-892068-30-3.

Over 600 books, articles, documents, pamphlets, and dissertations are identified in this recent bibliography. As with other titles in the series, this bibliography draws references from a variety of mainstream and alternative indexes, abstracts, and other sources. The unannotated references are arranged alphabetically by author under fifteen chapters, with subsections for books and articles. Topics covered include: hate crimes—general; race, ethnicity, religion and hate crimes; gays, lesbians, transsexuals and hate crimes; gender and hate crimes; the disables and hate crimes; the victim—psychological aspects; offenders—psychological aspects; hate groups; hate crimes in schools and colleges; hate crimes on the Internet; hate crimes in other countries; hate crimes and the law; hate crimes and law enforcement; statistics; and resources. The resources chapter includes bibliographies and Internet sources covering organizations, resource sites on the Internet, and online publications. Publication dates range from the 1990s through 2002. The thoughtful arrangement and broad search for relevant citations more than compensate for the lack of annotations.

481. Rachia, I. M., ed. **Youth Violence: A Selective Bibliography with Abstracts.** Huntington, NY: Nova Science, 1999. 166 p. index. $49.00. (Social Issues Bibliography Series, no. 1). ISBN 1-56072-716-3.

The causes and consequences of youth violence and its growth are clearly of sociological interest. School shootings, metal detectors in schools, and gang violence are just some of the visible indicators of the problem. This partially annotated bibliography is an attempt to get at some of the recent literature on this compelling subject. Approximately 1,500 citations are arranged alphabetically by title under six major chapters: school violence, guns and youth violence, juvenile delinquency—crime and violence, youth gangs and violence, campus violence, and dating and violence, and periodical and Web sites. Citations include books, state and federal documents, organization reports, magazine and journal articles, films, and more. Sources span the twentieth century and focus on the United States and, to a much lesser degree, other countries (with some citations in other languages). Some entries have abstracts, though most only include subject headings. While this topic is compelling, the bibliography appears to be a database print of common card catalog data. The layout does not invite scrutiny, and there is no rationale for what is included. A supplementary title index is provided, though a subject index would have been more useful. Overall, the bibliography could be valuable to a researcher in this subject area, but one will have to work harder to extract useful material.

Handbooks and Yearbooks

482. Aspel, Joyce, and Helen Fein, eds. **Teaching about Genocide: An Interdisciplinary Guidebook with Syllabi for College and University Teachers.** 2d ed. Washington, DC: American Sociological Association, 2002. 214 p. (ASA Resource Materials for Teaching).

Included here are twenty-one syllabi and related teaching resources on genocide. The syllabi differ in a number of respects, reflecting the approaches of those in the field who study the problem. As the editor notes in discussing these approaches, some teacher/scholars like to focus on particular cases of genocide and learn all they can about those. Others prefer to take a more comparative approach and look at the common features of many cases. Furthermore, the approaches to studying the problem may be either discipline-specific or more interdisciplinary, contemporary or more historical. The syllabi here reflect a little bit of all of this. They are arranged under five categories: Armenian genocide; holocaust; genocide and holocaust; genocide; and genocide, human rights, and international affairs. The scholars who contributed these syllabi come from history, sociology, political science, theater and drama, psychology, law, anthropology, and philosophy. There is an initial essay on teaching about genocide. Appended is a select list of Web sites on genocide.

Dictionaries and Encyclopedias

483. Gottesman, Ronald, ed. **Violence in America: An Encyclopedia.** New York: Scribner, 1999. 3v. $375.00. ISBN 0-684-80487-5 (set).

Violence is construed broadly in this multivolume set, encompassing direct and indirect violence, legal and illegal violence, physical and emotional or psychological violence, and deliberate or unintentional violence. By doing this, the editors hope to examine both why and how violence "permeates" American society. The 595 entries are arranged alphabetically by topic. However, they do fall into three different categories in terms of their scope. Thirty essays range from 5,000 to 12,000 words and cover core topics of broad theoretical, cultural, and historical sweep. Another 200 essays range from 1,000 to 5,000 words and focus on "more circumscribed topics." Finally, there are 365 informational entries of 500 to 1,000 words on persons, places, and events. Entries include *see also* references and bibliographies, as well as sidebar articles or charts, and the occasional photograph. There is also a chronology covering from 1622 to 1999, as well as an interesting essay overview of violence in the United States. A list of organizations, publications, and Web sites is appended, along with a substantial and thorough index.

Web Sites and Research Centers

484. **National Center for Injury Prevention and Control: Division of Violence Prevention.** Available: http://www.cdc.gov/ncipc/dvp/dvp.htm (Accessed: April 14, 2004).

This center, and its Division of Violence Prevention, is a service of the Centers for Disease Control and Prevention. This site provides a wide variety of information on violence, reflecting the division's attention to such issues as child maltreatment, intimate partner violence, sexual violence, suicide, and youth violence. One can find here data on violence, clearinghouses for information and resources (e.g., sexual violence, youth violence, violence against women), a description of the National Violent Death Reporting System, intervention projects, World Heath Organization data, violence prevention organizations, and a study on the epidemiology of violent deaths in the world. There are also numerous publications available full text online. One can also access and search the site's online Web-based Injury Statistics Query and Reporting System (WISCRS), from which data can be searched and reported using a wide range of demographic and injury/cause of death variables.

Socialization, Gender Roles, and Social Psychology

Bibliographies

485. Nordquist, Joan, comp. **Queer Theory: A Bibliography.** Santa Cruz, CA: Reference and Research Services, 1997. 64 p. (Social Theory, no. 48). $15.00. ISBN 0-9378-5595-2.

The bibliographies in Nordquist's *Social Theory* series provide references on many critical and cutting-edge theories and theorists in the social sciences. This bibliography addresses the fairly recent theoretical and practical developments in work on homosexuality, gender, and lesbianism. Queer theory was intended as a corrective to perceived deficiencies in the conceptualization of gays and lesbians in more mainstream theories on gender. Included here are over 600 books and articles arranged into six chapters: queer theory (including lesbian, bisexual, transsexual, and race perspectives); queer theory in the academy; queer theory and the academic disciplines (including sociology, psychology, language, history literature, art, architecture, music, film, drama); queer politics; testimonials; and bibliographies. Most of these chapters or subtopics are further subdivided into sections for books or articles, with entries then listed alphabetically by author. Articles are drawn from literature searches in many mainstream and alternative indexes or databases, such as *Sociological Abstracts*, the *Social Sciences Citation Index, The Left Index*, and *Alternative Press Index*. None of the citations are accompanied by annotations or abstracts.

Indexes, Abstracts, and Databases

486. **Sexual Diversity Studies: Gay, Lesbian, Bisexual, and Transgender Abstracts.** [electronic resource]. Baltimore, MD: National Information Services Corp., 2002– . updated monthly (online); quarterly (CD-ROM). Available: http://www.nisc.com/Frame/contact-f.htm (Accessed: April 13, 2004).

This database continues and includes the content from the *Gay and Lesbian Abstracts*. Its coverage extends back to 1977 and it cites a wide variety of material, including journal articles, books, book chapters, dissertations, Web sites, popular magazine articles, and more. There are over 70,000 records in the database at this point, with a little over half having abstracts. Topics covered can include queer studies, homophobia, partner abuse, religion and spirituality, and much more. Excluded are citations to HIV/AIDS that are medical in nature; these citations are best found in other databases (e.g., Medline). The database is available both on the Web, through National Information Service Corp.'s BiblioLine search engine, and on CD-ROM.

Handbooks and Yearbooks

487. **American Men and Women: Demographics of the Sexes.** Ithaca, NY: New Strategist Publications, 2000. 440 p. index. $89.95. ISBN 1-885070-29-2.

Though intended as a marketing reference book, this handbook nonetheless has a wide variety of statistical and demographic information relating to sex roles. There are hundreds of tables and charts spread out among nine subject chapters: attitudes and behavior, education, health, income, labor force, living arrangements, population, spending, and wealth. Data are drawn from both government sources (e.g., Bureau of the Census, National Center for Education Statistics) and nongovernment sources (e.g., the General Social Survey). The tables of data have been repackaged quite well for easy use and readability, and most are preceded by a brief discussion of the findings. The data themselves touch on a lot of interesting aspects of sex and gender differences, including educational attainment, two-career families, immigration, spending habits, health differences, poverty, income differences and distribution, and more. There are even some attitudinal survey results on levels of trust, happiness, belief in traditional sex roles, and religious beliefs, among others. Appended are a subject index, a glossary of terms, a directory of data sources (with Web sites or phone numbers), and a bibliography of sources. While virtually all of this information is available from the Internet or from existing print sources, this handbook provides a useful service by assembling interesting data into a readable format. Undergraduate sociology students studying sex roles and gender may find this valuable.

488. Gilbert, Daniel T., Susan T. Fiske, and Gardner Lindzey, eds. **Handbook of Social Psychology.** 4th ed. Boston: McGraw Hill, 1998. 2v. index. $185.00. ISBN 0-19-521376-9.

Now in its fourth edition, this handbook reflects both changes and continuity in the field of social psychology. The editors argue that the core of the field is still well reflected in the content of these volumes' thirty-seven chapters. Yet the understandable evolution of the field, and its research base, has led to the inclusion of some seemingly new topics. In some cases these are subjects that have been part of the field, but now deserve separate treatment. As well, most of the contributing authors are new. The seventeen chapters comprising the first volume are divided into four parts: historical perspectives, methodological perspectives, intrapersonal phenomena, and personal phenomena. After the historical and methodological articles, there are such topics as attitude change, motivation, emotions, the self, and social development in childhood, among others. The twenty chapters in volume 2 are organized into four parts as well: interpersonal phenomena, collective phenomena, interdisciplinary perspectives, and emerging perspectives. These chapters cover such topics as social influence, aggression, altruism, stereotyping, social stigma, intergroup relations, health behavior, understanding organizations, evolutionary social psychology, and much more. Overall, these essays are for specialists, not beginners. For that audience, this is a valuable work. As with the last edition, chapters are accompanied by a lengthy list of references. Both name and subject indexes are included.

489. Ore, Tracy E., comp. and ed. **The Sociology of Sexuality and Sexual Orientation.** 4th ed. Washington, DC: American Sociological Association, 2002. 255 p. (ASA Resource Materials for Teaching).

First and foremost, this handbook includes thirty syllabi from various instructors who teach sociology courses on sexuality and gender. In fact, these syllabi are divided into two sections: more general courses on sexuality, and courses on specific topics in the field. The latter include syllabi on such interesting subjects as the sociology of the sex industry; social movements; and religion, homosexuality, and society, among others. Throughout, the syllabi have been reformatted (e.g., class dates are replaced by numbered weeks) to make them more easily scanned and compared. In addition to the syllabi, there are five introductory essays or articles on various considerations in teaching this subject, including the classroom environment, homophobia, and multicultural considerations. There are separate sections in the handbook for assignments and exercises, as well as instructional resources (e.g., reading lists, films, relevant journals). Teaching this subject has its own pedagogical challenges, and this handbook can help new and experienced instructors better meet them.

490. Stalp, Marybeth C., ed. **Teaching Sociological Concepts and the Sociology of Gender.** Washington, DC: American Sociological Association, 2000. 133 p. (ASA Resource Materials for Teaching).

Unlike most other volumes in this American Sociological Association series, this one does not include course syllabi. Rather, its focus is on kinds of in-class and out-of-class activities to explore the effect of gender on social relationships and the classroom experience itself. These instructional ideas are arranged into five main sections or parts. Part 1, the gendered self, includes activities (e.g., interviews, journals, autobiography) for students to explore the role of gender in their own lives. Part 2, gendered learning, includes over twenty in-class exercises to explore the connection of gender to such issues as identity, equity, violence, the hidden curriculum, sex roles, the marriage contract, political leadership, and much more. Part 3, gendered writing, includes over a dozen paper and writing projects of various kinds. Part 4, gendered conversations, includes activities to explore gender in the classroom. Part 5 identifies Web sites, books, and articles as additional resources or sources of information.

491. Stewart, Chuck. **Gay and Lesbian Issues: A Reference Handbook.** Santa Barbara, CA: ABC-CLIO, 2003. 403 p. index. $45.00. (Contemporary World Issues). ISBN 1-85109-372-9.

Gay and lesbian issues relate to numerous important specialties in sociology, including social movements, gender roles, crime, abuse, social inequality, social policy, and much more. All of these areas are touched on in this new volume in the Contemporary World Issues series. Overall, there are seven chapters. The first is a history of the gay rights movement, dating to the nineteenth century in Germany. The second chapter, on problems and controversies, address such issues as AIDS, hate crimes, marriage, public attitudes, schools, and more. Chapter 3 is a chronology of events going back centuries, while chapter 4 includes biographical sketches of important individuals, both academics and activists (e.g., Martin Duberman, Barney Frank, Holly Near, Susan B. Anthony, Sappho). Chapter 5 includes key document excerpts, court case summaries, laws, and notable quotations. Chapter 6 is a directory of organizations and associations, primarily in the United States and Canada. This listing is broken down by categories, such as family, media, minority, educational, religious, and so on. Finally, there is a selective list of print and nonprint resources that are briefly annotated. A glossary of key terms is appended, as is a fairly detailed index that includes subjects, names, titles, and court cases. As with other titles in this series, this is an excellent overview aimed at students and general readers.

Dictionaries and Encyclopedias

492. Clement, Priscilla Ferguson, and Jacqueline S. Reinier, eds. **Boyhood in America: An Encyclopedia.** Santa Barbara, CA: ABC-CLIO, 2001. 2v. index. $185.00. ISBN 1-57607-215-0.

This encyclopedia examines the various cultural features, myths, and themes found in boyhood in America. While many popular topics are covered, each is written by a scholar in that area and reflects the state of what is known on that subject. The encyclopedia is not only historical in coverage, but also multicultural, with entries on Caucasian, African American, Native American, Asian American, and Hispanic boys. Entries can run up to four or five pages and address such topics as competition, baseball, the 4-H clubs, immigrants, apprenticeships, books and reading, the Civil War, video games, juvenile courts, the slave trade, newsboys, skateboarding, abuse, the YMCA, and much more. References for further reading accompany each entry. There are also *see* and *see also* references to preferred and related terms found elsewhere in the encyclopedia. Overall, the essays are well written and help to pull together the scattered and relatively scarce scholarly research on boyhood. There is an extensive bibliography appended, as well as a subject/name index.

493. **Encyclopedia of Lesbian and Gay Histories and Cultures.** Bonnie Zimmerman and George E. Haggerty, eds. New York: Garland, 2000. 2v. index. $295.00. ISBN 0-8153-3354-4.

Each volume of this two-volume set has a separate editor and focus. Volume 1 is subtitled *Lesbian Histories and Cultures: An Encyclopedia*, while volume 2 is subtitled *Gay Histories and Cultures: An Encyclopedia*. The approximately 1,000 entries found in each volume range from one to five pages in length and include suggested bibliographies for further reading and *see also* references for related entries. Topically, the entries touch on virtually every subject specialization within sociology, not to mention other social sciences, the humanities, and the health sciences. Entries include key concepts, organizations, social groups, movements, geographic locations, health conditions, theory, and much more. There is an outline of all entries found in the front of each volume; entries are categorized under one of more than two dozen broad categories in each volume, including sociology, cultural identities, politics, law, AIDS, education, economics, and theory, among others. Dozens of authors contributed the entries for each volume, and their names and brief biographies are found in the front of each volume. Additional access to the contents of each volume is provided by a detailed subject/name/title index.

494. Forman-Brunell, Miriam, ed. **Girlhood in America: An Encyclopedia.** Santa Barbara, CA: ABC-CLIO, 2001. 2v. index. $185.00. ISBN 1-57607-206-1.

If boyhood has been somewhat understudied as a research topic, then girlhood suffers from even more neglect. The 120 entries in this encyclopedia are both historical and multicultural in their coverage. In reading the entries, one is struck by the breadth of perspectives they represent. Girlhood is addressed in an incredibly wide variety of ways, including such topics as advice books, Barbie©, babysitting, body image, acquaintance rape, consumer culture, Catholic girls, domestic service, enslaved girls of African descent, Girl Scouts, mathematics and science, slumber parties, suicidal behavior, teen pregnancy, and much more. The essays, written by one of a hundred contributing scholars, can be as long as five pages and are accompanied by some photographs and references for further reading. Entries are well written and would be appropriate for interested general readers and scholars alike. Appended are an extensive bibliography and a fairly detailed name/subject index.

495. The Gale Encyclopedia of Childhood and Adolescence. Jerome Kagan, ed. Detroit, MI: Gale, 1998. 752 p. index. $140.00. ISBN 0-8103-9884-2.

The focus here is on developmental aspects of childhood and adolescence. Consequently, this encyclopedia does include a significant amount of information on biological and physiological aspects of child development. However, many entries and parts of entries also elaborate upon social and cultural factors influencing development. For example, the entry for "adolescence" talks about not only the physiological markers of adolescence, but also the social, emotional, and cultural factors related to it. Similarly, terms such as "gender identity" are given broad treatment that includes significant social scientific findings. Throughout, the encyclopedia provides entries ranging from a few paragraphs to a few pages, and each entry is accompanied by suggestions for further study that can include books, articles, media, and organizations. Some entries include highlighted information on some specific aspect of the topic. There are also a significant number of entries on well-known individuals who have contributed to our understanding of childhood and adolescence, such as Jean Piaget and Erik Erikson. Entries may also cover research instruments, standardized tests, drugs, health conditions, and more. *See* references are used to direct the user to the correct entry, and terms found elsewhere in the encyclopedia are in boldface. A bibliography and a name/subject index are also provided.

496. Lerner, Jacqueline V., and Richard M. Lerner, eds. **Adolescence in America: An Encyclopedia.** Santa Barbara, CA: ABC-CLIO, 2001. 2v. $185.00. ISBN 1-57607-205-3.

Adolescence is a period of profound change, both physiologically and socially. The entries in this encyclopedia address many of the physiological and psychological features of adolescence, as well as the social relationships and institutional settings in which adolescents develop and that have a significant influence on that development. Adolescent development is an interesting interaction of these biological and social processes, and these areas are explored in this work. There are upwards of 200 entries in this encyclopedia arranged alphabetically by topic. Some entries address biological features of adolescence, such as changes in body fat, acne, menarche, and hormone changes of puberty, among others. Other entries focus on family interactions and processes that may influence adolescents, such as maternal employment, parent-adolescent relations, child-rearing styles, or adoption. Still other entries address social problems or risk factors of adolescence, such as smoking, alcohol abuse, eating disorders, depression, sexual abuse, or drug abuse. Many entries deal with adolescents in institutions besides the family, such as schools, the workplace, or welfare agencies. Experts drawn from the related social and behavioral sciences write the essays, and they are clearly written for a general readership. Every essay is accompanied by *see also* references to related terms in the encyclopedia, as well as a list of references and suggestions for further reading. A substantial bibliography is appended, as is a detailed subject/name index.

497. Manstead, Antony S. R., and Miles Hewstone, eds. **The Blackwell Encyclopedia of Social Psychology.** Oxford, United Kingdom: Blackwell, 1999. 694 p. index. $123.95. ISBN 0-631-18146-6.

This is a reprint of the 1996 edition, which is also now available as an electronic book from netLibrary (Boulder, CO: NetLibrary, 2001; ISBN 0-631-22774-1). It provides a comprehensive collection of signed entries on "all key topics in social psychology" (p. xv) and is intended for students, faculty, and researchers. Four different types of entries are included, with each type varying in length and in the length of its accompanying bibliography. There are 93 "feature items" with 3,000-word essays and approximately 10 bibliographic references. The entries for 101 "major items" are less extensive, with 1,000-word essays and 5 bibliographic references. Then there are 64 "glossary items" that are approximately 200 words in length, have brief explanations, and cite 2 bibliographic references. Finally, there are 90 glossary items with 50-word definitions. Many entries include *see also* references to terms defined elsewhere in the encyclopedia. Within entries, words defined elsewhere are in capital letters. There is a detailed subject index with extensive subheadings, providing specific additional access to the entries. Throughout, the writing is clear and relatively jargon-free, whenever possible.

Web Sites and Research Centers

498. **Gender and Society.** Available: http://www.trinity.edu/~mkearl/gender. html (Accessed: December 29, 2004).

As we are reminded here, gender is a social construct and reflects dominant social values and priorities in the roles and rewards for women. This site covers issues relating to the women's roles, economic and social inequality, public opinion data on women's roles (e.g., Gallup polls, the General Social Survey), and numerous related links to women's history, which is integral to understanding women's roles in society. There are also Web links to data and analysis on women's social roles in other cultures, in politics and government, in education, and in other areas.

499. **Social Psychology Network.** Available: http://www.socialpsychology.org/ (Accessed: April 25, 2004).

This is a truly impressive Web site, with electronic links to and descriptive information on a variety of resources in social psychology and its specializations. The categories of information include: links to relevant Web sites within the various specialty areas in social psychology; guides to social psychology PhD programs; links to online research studies or surveys in social psychology; lists of journals by specialty, with links to their Web pages and author guidelines; biographical information on and links to the home pages of social psychologists; lists of textbooks in social psychology; links to Web pages for varieties of social psychology courses; online resources to assist instruction in social psychology; links to relevant organizations (e.g., the Society for Personality and Social Psychology); directions on joining various listservs and electronic discussion forums; and more. Despite the large amount of information contained here, the site is intuitively organized and easy to navigate.

500. **Society for Experimental Social Psychology (SESP).** Available: http://www.sesp.org/ (Accessed: April 25, 2004).

With approximately 750 members, the SESP holds an annual conference, gives awards for distinguished research and dissertations, provides listings of specialists in the subject area (courtesy of the Social Psychology Network), and links to the Social Psychology Network's search engine for information on psychology and social psychology-related resources.

501. **Society for Personality and Social Psychology (SPSP).** Available: http://www.spsp.org/ (Accessed: April 25, 2004).

Included here is information on the society (with 3,500 members), its publications (*Personality and Social Psychology Bulletin; Personality and Social Psychology Review*), its annual conference, its diversity programs, its research/travel awards, and more. In addition, there are directions on how to join the e-mail listserv discussion list for this society and related ones. There are also links to related organizations, journals, and Web pages, as well as directories of psychologists, teaching resources, and more.

502. **Society of Australasian Social Psychologists (SASP).** Available: http://www.psy.mf.edu.au/SASP/ (Accessed: December 9, 2004).

This is the new Web site for the SASP. It includes a constitution, online copies of society newsletters, links to officers, links to other professional societies (e.g., the Australian Psychological Society, the New Zealand Psychological Society), an online membership form, a membership directory, conference information, and information for post-graduates and teaching fellowship applicants.

Sociological Practice

Handbooks and Yearbooks

503. Fritz, Jan Marie, comp. and ed. **The Clinical Sociology Resource Book.** 5th ed. Washington, DC: American Sociological Association, 2001. 148 p. $19.00.

Cooperatively put out by the American Sociological Association and the Sociological Practice Association, this is a resource book for faculty and program developers in the area of clinical sociology. The first two chapters include an overview of the field and a guide to developing a successful clinical sociology program. The remaining chapters provide course syllabi for over twenty undergraduate and graduate courses that could be taught in a clinical sociology program. The course outlines are offered by various faculty members from around the country. They generally include the usual features of a course syllabus, such as a course description, course requirements, required readings, class schedule, and assignments, among others. At the end, there is an annotated list of favorite Web sites, as well as biographies of the contributors. If this can be updated regularly, it will be useful to faculty interested in developing clinical sociology programs or improving their course offerings.

Dictionaries and Encyclopedias

504. Alcock, Peter, Angus Erskine, and Margaret May, eds. **The Blackwell Dictionary of Social Policy.** Malden, MA: Blackwell, 2002. 290 p. index. $69.95. LC 2002-66414. ISBN 0-631-21846-7.

Knowing that there are many social science–related dictionaries, the editors attempted to focus this work more narrowly on social policy terms. While the intended audience is policy specialists in the United Kingdom, this does not reduce the dictionary's value for those studying policy in other countries. Excluded from the dictionary are organizations, statutes, or government reports, and more narrow technical terms within an applied policy specialty. However, key individuals in the history of the field are included, as are some prominent social policies (e.g., National Health Insurance) or research projects (e.g., British Household Panel Survey). Entries range from a paragraph to a few pages. There are *see* references to preferred or related terms, and the entries themselves use all capital letters to indicate terms defined elsewhere in the dictionary. A modest subject index is provided.

Web Sites and Research Centers

505. **Social Policy Virtual Library.** Available: http://www.social-policy.org/ (Accessed: March 4, 2004).

This is a tremendously rich Web site for data, links, and resources on policy issues. Included among its information categories are statistics and databases, bibliographies and library search engines, directories of organizations, descriptions of journals, Internet Web sites and search engines, and much more. There are also listings of academic departments, employment and funding opportunities, and online dictionaries, books and study aids. Coverage is international in scope.

506. **Society for Applied Sociology (SAS).** Available: http://www.appliedsoc. org/ (Accessed: March 4, 2004).

This is an international organization for those "interested in applying sociological knowledge" (home page) and exploring the relationship between theory and practice. The site includes statements on bylaws, ethics, and membership procedures, as well information on the annual meeting and related conferences. There is also descriptive information on the society's monographic publications and journals (i.e., the *Journal of Applied Sociology*, and *Social Insight*), association awards, speaker lists, accreditation, an archive (of past officers, meetings, and award recipients), job opportunities, a few posted papers, and more. Links to other Web sites are also provided.

507. **Sociological Practice Association.** Available: http://www.socpractice.org/ (Accessed: March 8, 2004).

Begun in 1978 as the Clinical Practice Association, the organization changed to its current designation in 1986. Its Web site includes certification requirements, ethical standards, bylaws, membership information, conference information, information about the journal *Sociological Practice*, and links to a few other organizational Web sites.

508. **SPA: The UK Social Policy Association.** Available: http://www.york.ac.uk/depts/spsw/spa/ (Accessed: March 11, 2004).

This is a fairly robust Web site, including information on conferences, membership, the SPA's e-mail listserv, publications (including numerous journals), links to other Web sites, news stories (via Social Policy Net), grants for events (e.g., conferences, workshops), links to other organizations (e.g., the European Social Policy Analysis Network), and more.

Sociology of Education

Bibliographies

509. Nordquist, Joan, comp. **Inequities in American Education: Race, Class and Gender Issues. A Bibliography.** Santa Cruz, CA: Reference and Research Services, 2002. 68 p. (Contemporary Social Issues: A Bibliographic Series, no. 65). $20.00pa. ISBN 1-892068-28-1.

The causes and consequences of unequal educational outcomes are some of the most fundamental issues in the sociology of education. This excellent bibliography addresses these issues and more, and includes numerous sources reflecting a fairly critical perspective. Included are bibliographic citations for more than 600 books, book chapters, pamphlets, journal articles, dissertations, and government documents on unequal education. These references are drawn from a variety of mainstream and alternative indexes, databases, and bibliographies, with sources published primarily from the late 1990s through 2002. The entries are divided into ten chapters: minorities—problems; minorities—solutions and successful programs; class and economic issues: the poor—problems; class and economic issues: the poor—solutions and successful programs; class and economic problems: school funding disparities—problems; class and economic problems: fiscal equity—solutions and reforms; class and economic issues: fiscal equity and achievement; gender issues—problems; gender issues—solutions and successful programs; and Internet resources. Many of these chapters are subdivided into books and articles, with citations then arranged alphabetically by author. Nordquist has done a superb job of scouring the literature for critical sources on this important topic, and she has addressed not only race, ethnicity, and gender, but also more structural causes of inequality. The list of relevant Web sites, for both organizations and publications, is excellent. Overall, the bibliography is invaluable and reflects the obvious care with which appropriate sources have been identified.

Indexes, Abstracts, and Databases

510. **Sociology of Education Abstracts.** Vol. 1– , No. 1– . Abingdon, Oxfordshire, United Kingdom: Carfax Publishing Company, 1965– . quarterly. $1,039/yr. ISSN 0038-0415. Available: http://www.tandf.co.uk/era/default.asp (Accessed: April 25, 2004).

This is probably the major resource, along with the ERIC database and *Sociological Abstracts*, for identifying book and journal literature in the sociology of education. It has two main strengths. First, it covers relevant literature published worldwide. Second, many of the 150–200 word abstracts are written by educational sociologists, including members of the editorial board. Works from a variety of theoretical perspectives in the sociology of education are represented, with particularly good coverage of British, Australian, and American scholarship. While the abstracts are not evaluative, they are well written and particularly descriptive. Other abstracts are either full or, in some cases, abbreviated versions of the author's abstract. Approximately 600 items each year are abstracted. Each issue includes both author and subject indexes, with cumulative indexes in the last issue of each volume. The contents are also available online through the Taylor and Francis database, *Educational Research Abstracts Online*.

Handbooks and Yearbooks

511. Hallinan, Maureen T., ed. **Handbook of the Sociology of Education.** New York: Kluwer Academic/Plenum Publishers, 2000. 588 p. index. $120.00. ISBN 0-3064-6238-9.

The articles included here represent, according to Hallinan, some of the best models of future theoretical development and empirical research in the sociology of education. They are arranged under six key themes within the sociology of education: theoretical and methodological orientations, development and expansion of education, the study of access to schooling, the study of school organization, the study of school outcomes, and policy implications of research in the sociology of education. There is an international group of authors, including such well-known names as Maureen Hallinan, Robert Dreeben, Randal Collins, Valerie Lee, and Adam Gamoran, among others. The twenty-four articles do touch on key topics in the sociology of education, but they are not reviews or overviews of these themes. Rather, they present new empirical research or explore new theoretical insights. In fact, the writing is fairly sophisticated and assumes a significant familiarity with literature in sociology and educational sociology. Consequently, this handbook would be most beneficial to advanced students and researchers in the field. These articles provide compelling new insights into traditional research questions, as well as raising new ones. Author and subject indexes are provided.

Dictionaries and Encyclopedias

512. Levinson, David L., Peter W. Cookson, and Alan R. Sadovnik, eds. **Education and Sociology: An Encyclopedia.** New York, Routledge, 2002. 734 p. index. $165.00. ISBN 0-8153-1615-1.

Since the 1970s, the sociology of education has undergone a virtual revolution. Scholars in the field have begun to ask fundamentally new questions about the relationship of schooling and society: what were the origins of mass compulsory schooling; was schooling an institution of democratic opportunity or social control; to what extent does schooling provide or restrict opportunity; what knowledge is taught, how is this decided, who decides it, and does this serve everyone's interests equally; how do we explain the persistence of educational inequality? These and other provocative questions are addressed throughout this volume.

The encyclopedia's ninety-one entries are arranged alphabetically by topic and dealt with in depth. The topics covered include both mainstream, albeit important, topics in the sociology of education (e.g., inequality, curriculum, tracking), as well as more recent issues and approaches in the field. The latter include entries on cultural capital, social reproduction theory, and code theory, among others. The authors of the entries are an impressive list of many of the most respected educational sociologists today, including Hugh Meehan, Maureen Hallinan, Jeanne Ballantine, Christopher Hurn, Amy Stewart Wells, Michael Apple, Sara Delamont, Philip Wexler, Ivor Goodson, and more. Teachers and students in the sociology of education, educational policy, and the foundations of education should find this an excellent resource.

513. Saha, Lawrence J., ed. **International Encyclopedia of the Sociology of Education.** Oxford, United Kingdom; New York: Pergamon, 1997. 961 p. $266.00. ISBN 0-08042-990-4.

Good sociological analysis, not limited just to a narrowly defined "sociology of education," is infused throughout this encyclopedia's research and writing on various educational topics. It includes almost 150 entries arranged under 10 broad categories or sections: theories; sociological fields in the study of education (e.g., curriculum, administration, special education, sex education, religious education), research traditions (e.g., quantitative, qualitative, action research, participatory research, content analysis, biographical research, education production functions), the school as a social system, the structure of educational systems, school processes, family and schooling, teachers, youth in schools, and educational policy and change. Each of these categories includes numerous, lengthy essays on important subtopics in that broad area. For example, the section on youth includes chapters on adolescence, youth culture, youth and leisure, youth unemployment, aggression and socialization, student perceptions of classrooms, and more. Similarly, the section on theories covers a wide variety of theoretical perspectives in the sociology of education and in sociology generally that might apply to education. These include reproduction theory, resistance theory, and postmodernism in education, as well as gender theory, hermeneutics, Marxism, and phenomenology, among others. Essays range from five to ten pages in length and are accompanied by a valuable list of references. The authors are a distinguished collection of international scholars, including such names as Carnoy, Biddle, Oakes, Luke, Hallinan, Davies, Dweck, Altbach, Natriello, Sadker, Weiler, and Burbules, among notable others. A name index and a substantial subject index are appended.

Web Sites and Research Centers

514. The Centre for Educational Sociology. Available: http://www.ed.ac. uk/ces/ (Accessed: April 25, 2004).

Affiliated with the University of Edinburgh, the Centre has been in existence for thirty years and has an impressive list of research activities and publications. Its areas of interest include transitions from school to work, early intervention programs, school leavers, gender and performance, and much more. The Web site describes current and past research projects conducted by the Centre, with links to the Web pages for many of those projects. There are also pages with year-by-year listings of publications and presentations by the Centre's faculty and staff, covering back to 1969. Also provided is information on the Centre's consulting services and its conferences. There is much full-text information available, including updates on research projects and recent presentations. An example of the latter includes a presentation by educational sociologist Adam Gamoran, with text and slides available on the Web site. The Centre's director, Jenny Ozga, is well known and respected in the field. In all, this is an informative Web site on an ambitious and productive research center in educational sociology.

515. Education Policy Analysis Archives. Available: http://epaa.asu.edu/epaa/ (Accessed: April 25, 2004).

This is the Web site for an online, peer-reviewed scholarly journal that focuses on a broad range of policy issues of sociological interest (e.g., educational reform, educational inequality). The site tells one how to subscribe and submit articles to the journal. Both full articles and abstracts are available online. There is a related e-mail listserv that announces newly available articles.

516. National Center for Education Statistics. Available: http://nces.ed.gov/ (Accessed: December 29, 2004).

This is arguably the single best Web source for readily accessible data on schooling at all levels. It includes online versions of major print data sources, such as the *Digest of Education Statistics*, *The Condition of Education*, and *Projections of Education Statistics*, among others. Beyond that, there are tables of quick facts, as well as links to recent reports on major issues like school crime or the status of the education of African Americans. One can also find data from the Nation's Report Card, otherwise known as the NAEP (National Assessment of Educational Progress), as well as the *School District Demographics* page (nces.ed.gov/surveys/sdds/), which integrates school district and demographic data drawn from the Census and other sources. There is a wealth of data at this site that is potentially relevant to educational sociologists.

517. **Ontario Institute for Studies in Education.** Available: http://www.oise. utoronto.ca/ (Accessed: December 29, 2004).

OISE is a major research center devoted to a broad spectrum of educational studies, including the sociology of education, critical pedagogy, critical curriculum studies, and women's studies. It is affiliated with the University of Toronto and publishes the journal *Curriculum Inquiry*, as well as the journal *Resources for Feminist Research*, among others. OISE is the University's graduate department of education.

518. **School District Demographics.** Available: http://nces.ed.gov/surveys/ sdds/ (Accessed: April 16, 2004).

This superb online statistical resource allows individuals to see demographic and Census data organized by school district. In fact, the data requests are user-driven, allowing one to assemble whatever data they want, given the parameters of the database. One can also compare two different school districts, in different states if one prefers, on a common set of variables. These variables include sex and age, household ownership, educational attainment of the population twenty-five and older, rent, per capita income, value of houses, and poverty status, among others. Additional search options allow the user to assemble and display data differently. These data may not be robust enough by themselves for faculty research, but students should be able to make good use of this site. Both 2000 and 1990 Census data are available.

519. **The Section on Sociology of Education.** Available: http://www.asanet. org/soe/ (Accessed: April 25, 2004).

Within the American Sociological Association, there are almost four dozen interest group sections, including this one on the sociology of education. The site provides a listserv, as well as current and back issues of its newsletter. There is also a list of officers, links to publications and Web sites (e.g., the National Center for Education Statistics), descriptions of Willard Waller Award winners for lifetime contributions to the field, sociology of education syllabi, related sociology and education Web sites, data sources, job and funding opportunities, and more. Along with the American Educational Research Association's Division G interest group, the Social Context of Education, this is one of the more important support groups for the study of educational sociology.

520. **Social Context of Education.** Available: http://www.aera.net/divisions/g/ (Accessed: April 25, 2004).

The Social Context of Education is an interest group section (Division G) of the American Educational Research Association (AERA). Included here are calls for Division G-related papers for the annual AERA conference, a history of the founding of the Division, an archive of past newsletters, descriptions of award-winning dissertations, calls for nominations for the upcoming dissertation award, an annual report, a listserv, and more. There are also links to the main AERA Web site. Along with the American Sociological Association's Section on Sociology of Education, this is one of the more important support groups for educational sociology.

Sociology of Organizations and Groups

Handbooks and Yearbooks

521. Bird, Donna C., ed. **Organizational Sociology: A Handbook of Syllabi and Other Teaching Resources.** Washington, DC: American Sociological Association, 1998. 135 p. (ASA Resource Materials for Teaching).

The American Sociological Association has produced a series of these handbooks intended to help graduate teaching assistants, part-time faculty, or full-time faculty in their teaching of various subjects in the discipline. The handbook collects syllabi from a handful of faculty around the country on the area of focus, which in this case is organizational sociology. Though not noted on the title page, this is in fact a second edition of this work. The book includes five sections: undergraduate syllabi (eleven); graduate syllabi (seven); class exercises and assignments; a resource listing of articles, books, and Web sites; and a list of contributors. Courses range from an applied to a more theoretical focus, with course titles including complex organizations; organizational culture; organizational theory; macro organizational theory; and formal organizations and bureaucracy, among others. Beyond its intended audience of instructors, this may appeal to students interested in this specialization and the various lists of required or optional readings.

522. Fields, Dail L. **Taking the Measure of Work: A Guide to Validated Scales for Organizational Research and Diagnosis.** Thousand Oaks, CA: Sage, 2002. 327 p. index. $72.95. ISBN 0-7619-2425-6.

Books like this are invaluable. A fundamental issue confronting many doing research is identifying appropriate research instruments with which to collect data. Rather than construct one's own, the researcher might be better off finding an existing instrument that is valid and reliable at capturing those data. That is what this book does. It identifies and describes dozens of research instruments, which are arranged under ten subject categories: job satisfaction, organizational commitment, job characteristics, job stress, job roles, organizational justice, work-family conflict, person-organization fit, workplace behaviors, and workplace values. Every category has at least ten or twelve instruments listed.

523. **Research in the Sociology of Organizations.** Vol. 1– . Greenwich, CT: JAI Press, 1982– . annual. ISSN 0733-558X.

This annual, edited collection presents approximately eight articles per issue that focus on particular issues or themes in the field. Past volumes have addressed such topics as networks in and around organizations, social psychological processes in organizations, labor relations and unions, deviance in and of organizations, cross-cultural analysis of organizations, structuring participation in organizations, and organizations in the European tradition, to name a few. Contributors are drawn from the fields of sociology, psychology, business, administration, organizational behavior, and related specialties.

Web Sites and Research Centers

524. **Center for Collaborative Organizations.** Available: http://www.work teams.unt.edu/ (Accessed: February 24, 2004).

Housed at the University of North Texas, this center is rooted in the industrial organizational psychology program at the university. The site is multifaceted, including such features as: collaborate work assessment tools; conference, workshop, and distance learning opportunities; a collaborative work systems consortium; change management consultation; research project descriptions (with full reports available for purchase); newsletters, bibliographies, and other publications; links to related sites; and more.

525. **Center for the Study of Group Processes.** Available: http://www.uiowa. edu/~grpproc (Accessed: December 24, 2004).

Established in 1992, the center not only supports multidisciplinary research in group processes, but also maintains a research laboratory and Web site, attracts visiting scholars, promotes conferences and workshops, and more. It also publishes the electronic journal *Current Research on Social Psychology*.

526. **SocioSite: Sociology of Organization.** Available: http://www2.fmg.uva. nl/sociosite/topics/organization.html (Accessed: February 24, 2004).

Part of the *SocioSite* Web site, this page has extensive links and many full-text documents relating to the sociology of organizations. The page is subdivided into categories for organizations, organizational learning, virtual organizations, intranet, mailing lists/listservs in organizational theory, journals, and professional associations. The links in the "organizations" section do not all work, nor do those that do work always connect to the entire full text of the documents. Nonetheless, this is a robust Web site with numerous leads and relevant full text.

Sociology of Religion

Indexes, Abstracts, and Databases

527. **ATLA Religion Database.** [electronic resource]. New York: Ovid Technologies. Available: http://www.atla.com/products/catalogs/databases/catalogs_rdb.html (Accessed: March 8, 2004).

This is a database of over a million records and is the online equivalent of a number of print or electronic products from the American Theological Library Association. It includes the contents from two versions of the *Religion Index*, one for periodical and one for multiauthor works, as well as the *Index to Book Reviews in Religion*. Included here are citations to journal articles, book reviews, and chapters or essays in edited collections. Though the database currently covers items dating back to 1949, it is in the process of retrospectively including older sources dating to early in the nineteenth century. Various disciplinary approaches to religion are found here, including sociology. For example, simple searches on sociology and Émile Durkheim, Max Weber, or Karl Marx retrieve 157, 329, and 55 citations, respectively. Religion and alienation retrieves 213 citations. Furthermore, the journal *Sociology of Religion* has 652 articles cited here. Other journals, such as the *Journal for the Scientific Study of Religion*, are indexed as well. In short, this is a fruitful database for identifying sociologically related research on religion. It is available online from a number of major vendors, including NISC, Ovid, OCLC, Cambridge Scientific, and EBSCO, and is also available on CD-ROM and in MARC format for mounting on library Web sites.

Handbooks and Yearbooks

528. Lewis, James R. **Cults in America: A Reference Handbook.** Santa Barbara, CA: ABC-CLIO, 1998. 232 p. index. (Contemporary World Issues). $39.50. LC 98-29089. ISBN 1-57607-031-X.

Sociologists of religion, sociologists of social movements, and students of religion will all find material of interest in this handbook. The first chapter presents an overview of academic analyses of the cult phenomenon, a controversial topic since at least the early 1970s (p. xi). Lewis introduces the diversity of cults with brief case studies of the Heaven's Gate and Northeast Kingdom movements, and uses these examples to highlight social anxieties regarding cultist movements. The chapter also provides historical background on cults, noting that the contemporary "brainwashing debate" was foreshadowed by social responses to the Mormon Church, and discusses the anticult movement, "deprogramming," and "cult withdrawal syndrome." Lewis analyzes cult stereotypes and looks at how the media treats cults, and then considers why cults appeal to people and what social processes are at work in cult environments. Chapter 2 provides a chronology of "religious conflicts in the United States that were raised by the presence of minority religions," as well as significant cult developments in foreign countries. In the same vein, Chapter 3 presents brief descriptions of controversial minority religious movements such as Christian Science, Raelian Movement International, and Black Muslims. Chapter 4 situates these movements in the legal environment, providing descriptions of major court cases, pieces of legislation, and government action. Chapter 5 includes several documents pertaining to cults, including a "Resolution on Pseudo-Religious Cults" from the National PTA Convention, as well as statistical tables depicting trends in cult movements and other topics. The remaining chapters list academic and religious organizations and print and nonprint resources for further exploration of the topic. An index provides additional access to entries found in the book.

529. Parker, Philip M. **Religious Cultures of the World: A Statistical Reference.** Westport, CT: Greenwood Press, 1997. 144 p. index. (Cross-Cultural Statistical Encyclopedia of the World, vol. 1). $72.95. ISBN 0-3132-9768-1.

While the primary focus here is on cross-cultural consumer studies, there is nonetheless much of interest to sociologists and other social scientists. The author has compiled cross-cultural data on approximately 400 religious groups and some 300 variables across those groups. Variables related to marketing and economics are covered in many of the chapters. However, chapters 4 and 5 include primarily social and demographic variables, as well as "cultural resources," broken down by religious group. Elsewhere, the author discusses at length the difficulties in comparing religious cultures, and he provides detailed explanations of the methodological measures he took to generate the quantitative data he presents. A selected bibliography is attached, as are indexes for countries and subject. This work would be suitable for advanced students or researchers in the sociology of religion.

530. Utter, Glenn H., and John W. Storey. **The Religious Right: A Reference Handbook.** 2d ed. Santa Barbara, CA: ABC-CLIO, 2001. 382 p. index. (Contemporary World Issues). $45.00. ISBN 1-5760-7212-6.

The emergence and development of the religious right could be of tremendous interest not only to sociologists of religion, but also to those studying social movements and political sociology. The fact that this handbook is now in its second edition speaks to the subject's ongoing relevance in social science and policy debates. As with other titles in this series, this handbook is divided into a number of common chapters: an introduction (including a history), chronology, biographical sketches, survey data and quotations, directory of organizations, selected print resources, and selected nonprint resources. The biographies are one to two pages long, and the survey data are taken from sources such as the General Social Survey or Gallup polls and include both tabular data and explanations. The quotations are a bit more idiosyncratic and are not accompanied by any sort of analysis or contextualization. The organization directory includes a paragraph description of each organization, along with addresses, phone numbers and, in some cases, Web site addresses. All of the print and nonprint resources are annotated. Throughout, there is a strong thread looking at the linkage between religion and politics. A thorough index is provided. Overall, this work is well suited to students and general readers alike.

Dictionaries and Encyclopedias

531. Swatos, William H., Jr., ed. **Encyclopedia of Religion and Society.** Walnut Creek, CA: Alta Mira Press, 1998. 590 p. ISBN 0-7619-8956-0.

This primarily focuses on twentieth-century social science perspectives on religion, including sociology, anthropology, and psychology. There are paragraph to multipage entries on major theories, theorists, concepts, people, and organizations. For example, one can find entries on feminist theory, gerontology, postmodernism, death and dying, globalization, and numerous other large fields of study within the social sciences. Specific, topical issues are also covered, such as homosexuality/bisexuality, human rights, poverty, and abortion. There are also entries on many religions, both mainstream (e.g., Roman Catholicism) and "new" religions (e.g., Unification Church, Scientology). Major classical social scientists, such as Émile Durkheim, Max Weber, Sigmund Freud, and Karl Marx, are covered, as are other and more contemporary writers with social science views on religions (e.g., Erik Erikson, Milton Yinger, George Homans). Entries are accompanied by bibliographic references, and *see* references are used to direct users to preferred terms. There is an extensive index that includes subjects, names, titles, and organizations.

Web Sites and Research Centers

532. **American Religion Data Archive.** Available: http://www.thearda.com (Accessed: March 1, 2004).

Supported by the Lily Endowment, this Web site collects and makes accessible quantitative data on a wide variety of aspects of religion in this country. These data include such subjects as "churches and church membership, religious professionals, and religious groups." Data from the General Social Survey related to religion are found here as well. The Web site allows users to search and subset existing data and even generate maps or reports from those data. Also, a bank of questions from other surveys on religion is maintained and searchable, allowing a user to create a survey questionnaire to suit their specific needs. There is also a newsletter, links to related Web sites, and much more. In short, this is a superb data source for sociologists of religion.

533. **Hartford Institute for Religion Research.** Available: http://www.hartfordinstitute.org/ (Accessed: March 1, 2004).

This is a multifaceted Web site on the social scientific study of religion that is devoted to conducting and disseminating research, as well as offering education and consultation. Provided by the Hartford Seminary, the Web site includes subsections for the sociology of religion, organizational studies, descriptions and resources on various research areas (including women, family, church growth, and homosexuality), resources for congregations, a bookshelf page for suggested readings, and more. The sociology subsection not only explains the focus, history, and varying research and theoretical interests of this specialty, but also includes online syllabi, bibliographies, research resources, articles, and professional associations. The Web site is very well constructed and full of valuable information that leads to other sources.

534. **Weberian Sociology of Religion.** Available: http://www.ne.jp/asahi/ moriyuki/abukuma/ (Accessed: June 28, 2004).

Included here is information on Max Weber and his work on the sociology of religion, Web versions of his major texts, information on Christianity and Japanese religions, and more.

Sociology of Sport and Leisure

Bibliographies

535. Cox, Richard William. **International Sport: A Bibliography, 2000 Including Index to Sports History Journals, Conference Proceedings, and Essay Collection.** London; Portland, OR: F. Cass, 2003. 78 p. (Sports Reference Series). $39.50. ISBN 0-7146-5364-0.

Most of this bibliography of over 860 sources on sport does not appear to be especially sociological, but rather seems to be a list of books on sports or sport in certain countries. However, many of the entries do deal with historical, cultural, and social aspects of sport, as well as gender issues related to sport. So, while not explicitly labeled as "sociological," many of the sources do lend themselves to such an analysis. This is an unannotated classified bibliography, with the entries arranged under such broad categories as reference works, individual sports, collective biographical studies, sport in ancient civilizations, and sport in individual countries (broken down by country). The "reference works" section is somewhat misleading in that it has subsections not only for dictionaries and encyclopedias, but also for books and articles on various aspects of sport. These can include research methods, historiography, and general histories of sport. Both books and journal articles can be cited under these sections. The entries under specific sports or specific countries can branch into cultural aspects of such sports, as well as their importance to and development in a specific country's cultural history. There is an accompanying author index, and index to the contents of specific journal issues, and an index to the contents of essay collections. Not everything here is useful, but there are some worthwhile citations.

Indexes, Abstracts, and Databases

536. **Physical Education Index.** [electronic resource]. Bethesda, MD: Cambridge Scientific Abstracts, 1970– . monthly updates. Available: http://md2.csa. com/csa/factsheets/pei.shtml (Accessed: April 18, 2004).

Though indexing articles primarily in the areas of sports, fitness, exercise physiology, sports medicine, coaching, and related areas, this Web site also identifies sources relating to sport sociology and sport psychology. Approximately 875 journals are scanned for references, and 96 of these are considered core journals for the database and index. Records for some dissertations are included as well. Coverage goes back to 1970, and the citations are now accompanied by abstracts (since 2001). There are over 200,000 records in the database, with approximately 12,000 added a year, which are arranged in the index by title under an extensive list of subject headings. Over and above the headings for sports psychology and sports sociology, one can also look under more specific topics (e.g., lifestyle, leisure, demographics, eating disorders, attitudes). Records include the author, article title, source/journal title, volume, date, pages, abstracts and, more recently, author e-mail addresses, among other fields. Overall, this is a highly research-oriented database with coverage that should be of interest to sport sociologists. There is also a print equivalent index that is updated quarterly.

537. **SPORT Discus.** [electronic resource]. New York: Ovid, 1975– . quarterly updates. Available: http://www.ovid.com/site/catalog/DataBase/153.jsp?top=2& mid=3&bottom=7&subsection=10 (Accessed: April 18, 2004).

The Sport Discus database is one of the most important research databases for the fields of health and physical education and sports studies, which are not particularly well covered in mainstream education databases. It indexes articles in approximately 2,000 sports journals, covering such topics as fitness, coaching, exercise physiology, biomechanics, and more. Also covered are topics related to sport psychology, sport sociology, leisure, and attitudes and behaviors relating to sport. There are also citations and abstracts for upwards of 50,000 monographs, dissertations, and conference proceedings. Over 25,000 documents are added to the database each year, with the database now totaling over 650,000 records. Subject searching of the database is aided by the use of the *SPORT Thesaurus*, which is built into the database's subject search function and is also available in print form. One can search the database readily by keyword, author, title, or subject, or one can customize a search using any of the many indexed or limit fields. The database now selectively covers literature from 1930 to the present. It is a product of the Sport Information Resource Centre in Canada, and is made available by SilverPlatter (now Ovid) on its Web site through its WebSPIRS software interface. There are other online versions available (e.g., from EBSCO), as well as CD-ROM versions; it is also searchable through the Dialog database service.

Handbooks and Yearbooks

538. Coakley, Jay, and Eric Dunning, eds. **Handbook of Sports Studies.** London: Sage, 2000. 570 p. index. $141.00. ISBN 0-8039-7552-X.

The editors argue that the sociological study of sports is expanding, and this handbook is a reflection of the state-of-the-art of this growing area of research. They have assembled forty-four essays on a variety of topics and arranged them into four major parts: (1) major perspectives in the sociology of sport, (2) cross-disciplinary differences and connections, (3) key topics, and (4) sport and society research around the globe. The first part has essays on major sociological theories that are often used by those in the field, including functionalism, Marxism, cultural studies, feminist theories, interpretive theories, figurational sociology, and post-structuralism. The second part has chapters covering other social science disciplines and their contributions to broader social science views of sports. Part 3, which covers key topics, includes chapters on such issues as gender, education, media, nationalism, violence, doping, emotions, social control, doping in sports, disability, and much more. Finally, part 4 has essays on the current state of sport and society research in twelve countries or regions of the world. While the essays on particular countries or regions are fairly short (i.e., three or four pages), the other essays can range from ten to twenty or more pages and are accompanied by references. The list of contributing authors is international in scope, and these authors are drawn primarily from sociology, sports studies, and sports specializations within related social science disciplines. A subject index is included.

Dictionaries and Encyclopedias

539. Cashmore, Ellis. **Sports Culture: An A–Z Guide.** London; New York: Routledge/Taylor & Francis, 2002. 482 p. (Routledge World Referenc Series). $31.95. ISBN 0-415-28555-0.

This is a unique work on the cultural features of sports that includes entries on sports organizations (e.g., FIFA, ESPN), landmark individuals (e.g., media mogul Rupert Murdoch, superagent Mark McCormack, Roone Arledge, Florence Griffith Joyner), theories (e.g., Marxism, postmodernism), concepts (e.g., psyching, racism), events (e.g., the Munich disaster), legislation (e.g., Title IX), publications (e.g., *A Season on the Brink*), films (e.g., *Field of Dreams*), social issues (e.g., drugs in sports, eating disorders), and much more. This work acknowledges the cultural importance and ubiquitousness of sports. Beyond this, however, the entries also examine sports critically and socially, rather than just descriptively. Thus, this encyclopedia/guide treats sports as a social institution, not unlike other major social institutions. The author has written all but 17 of the 174 entries, which are typically two to five pages long. Entries include cross-references to terms defined elsewhere, and they are accompanied by a brief list of references for further reading. There is an extensive subject index that includes names and titles. Overall, this is fascinating reading and clearly sociological in its definition of and approach to sports culture.

World Wide Web/Internet Sites

540. **SIRC: A World of Sport Information.** Available: http://www.sirc.ca (Accessed: April 25, 2004).

The Sport Information Resource Centre (SIRC) is one of the two major providers, along with the *Physical Education Index*, of bibliographic information on sports. Its database, *Sport Discus*, is available on the Internet and CD-ROM through multiple vendors, such as SilverPlatter, EBSCO, Ovid, and Dialog. The Web site exists mainly to support the database, but it also provides a conference calendar, a service—SportQuest—that provides links to related sites, SIRCExpress (its document delivery service), and a directory of relevant publishers. One can also sign up for e-mail updates.

541. **Sport in Society.** Available: http://www.sportinsociety.org/index2.html (Accessed: April 18, 2004).

Part of Northeastern University, the Center for the Study of Sport in Society is one of the most important centers focusing on the sociology of sport. It also supports research into other aspects of sports, such as business and journalism. Among its other activities, the center publishes the *Journal of Sport and Social Issues*. The center participates in or sponsors such programs as Athletes in Service to America, Disability in Sport, Mentors in Violence Prevention (MVP) Program, National Consortium for Academics and Sports, Project Teamwork (violence prevention), and Urban Youth Sports. All of these programs are described and linked to from the Web site. There is also a description of the Center's well-known publication, the *Racial and Gender Report Card*, as well as links to related Web sites. One can also find information on awards, student-athlete day, a hall of fame, outreach activities, and much more.

Stratification and Inequality

Handbooks and Yearbooks

542. Kaul, Chandrika, and Valerie Tomaselli-Moschovitis, eds. **Statistical Handbook on Poverty in the Developing World.** Phoenix, AZ: Oryx Press, 1999. 425 p. index. $69.95. ISBN 1-57356-249-1.

The stated intent of this source is to assemble a wide variety of legitimate statistics documenting the extent and correlates of poverty in developing countries. This is important not only because of the widespread problem of poverty in an otherwise abundant world, but also because of the varieties of causes and consequences of this poverty. This handbook draws data from a number of sources (e.g., World Bank, United Nations, UNICEF) and presents it in readable form. Tables are clearly laid out and data sources are all noted. The data themselves are arranged into a number of subjects reflecting the causes and consequences of poverty. These include: poverty measures, economics, demographics, health, AIDS, education, nutrition and food supply, women and poverty, children and poverty, cities, and policy. Each topic can have anywhere from three to sixteen data tables. Education, for example, includes data on illiteracy, children not expected to reach grade five, public education expenditure as a percent of GNP, and more. Most of the data are broken down by country, though sometimes by world region. There is a somewhat quirky subject index (e.g., a table on the percent of households consuming iodized salt is indexed only under "percent" and "households"). While some of these data may be find-able separately, this compilation is valuable in providing ready access to statistics on a critically important topic.

543. **Poverty in the United States.** Washington, DC: U.S. Dept. of Commerce, Bureau of the Census: For sale by the Supt. of Docs., U.S. GPO, 1985– . annual.

This is an annual statistical publication from the Bureau of the Census and is part of the Current Population Reports series. The 2002 edition (released in September, 2003) is available online at the Census Web site (www.census.gov/hhes/www/poverty02.html), along with information such as a press briefing, a press release, and poverty highlights that include text, graphs, and detailed tables. As stated in the introduction, "this report illustrates how poverty rates vary by selected characteristics—age, race and Hispanic origin, nativity, family composition, work experience, and geography" (2002 ed., p. 1). Current and historical data are presented in a variety of formats. Appended are definitions and explanations, time series estimates of poverty, and discussion of the source and accuracy of estimates, as well as additional data tables. Previous editions, dating back to 1995, are also available at the Census site (http://www.census.gov/prod/www/abs/poverty.html; accessed: April 18, 2004).

Dictionaries and Encyclopedias

544. Gordon, David, and Paul Spicker, eds. **The International Glossary on Poverty.** London; New York: Zed Books, 1999. 162 p. $17.50. ISBN 1-85649-688-0 (pbk.).

The term "glossary" does not do this book justice. It is truly a multidisciplinary and comparative dictionary of poverty. Collectively, its international list of contributors treat poverty as a "heterogeneous" concept, which is reflected in the approximately 200 terms discussed here. Each definition or short essay is a paragraph to a couple of pages long. Entries can address concepts (e.g., contextual poverty), statistical measures (e.g., TIP-curves), and proper names of poverty measures (e.g., Malawi Poverty Profile), and many of these entries are accompanied by a list of references. There are also cross-references to terms found elsewhere in the glossary. While the entries are predominantly influenced by Western research orientations towards poverty, the book is nonetheless comparative and mindful of the value of broader conceptions of poverty. Two brief but interesting articles are included with the glossary: one asking "Do Poverty Definitions Matter?"; and the other discussing clusters of meaning in definitions of poverty. This should be a valuable resource for undergraduate and graduate students delving into poverty definitions, concepts, and research, especially in a comparative context.

Web Sites and Research Centers

545. **CROP: Comparative Research Programme on Poverty.** Available: http://www.crop.org (Acccessed: April 25, 2004).

Initiated by the International Social Science Council in 1992, *CROP* provides a network for international researchers in the area of poverty. It fosters research towards the end of understanding and reducing poverty, and some of its ongoing projects address poverty and law, poverty and elite perceptions, poverty and the state, and poverty and water, among others. The site also mentions CROP's various publications, including reviews, annual reports, newsletters, and a poverty research series. There is also a discussion forum or listserv that one can register to join, as well as links to other Web sites of interest.

546. Explorations in Social Inequality. Available: http://www.trinity.edu/~ mkearl/strat.html (Accessed: April 18, 2004).

Part of the Web site *A Sociological Tour through Cyberspace*, these pages document not only the extent of inequality in the United States, but also the varieties of theoretical explanations and analyses of this fact. After an initial review of the worsening of income inequality, the site launches into competing theoretical explanations for these facts and existing research studies trying to analyze its causes and consequences.

547. Institute for Research on Poverty (IRP). Available: http://www.ssc. wisc.edu/irp/ (Accessed: April 18, 2004).

Located at the University of Wisconsin, this institute was started in the 1960s to study the "causes and cures of poverty." It was begun under the auspices of the U.S. Office of Economic Opportunity. The center has been involved in studying some of the most compelling issues related to poverty and inequality, including welfare reform, low-wage labor markets, education and poverty, health and poverty, child support, child and family well-being, and more. The center also publishes research reports, discussion papers, and a newsletter, among others, and will make available reprints of articles and abstracts of books written by affiliated staff members. There are extensive links to other Web sites addressing issues related to poverty and inequality. The IRP also gives grants and sponsors workshops and conferences to promote its research agenda. Overall, this is an excellent site for scholars and public policy experts in the areas of poverty and inequality.

548. Joint Center for Poverty Research. Available: http://www.jcpr.org/ (Accessed: April 18, 2004).

Jointly sponsored by Northwestern University and the University of Chicago, this site includes a wealth of research, data analysis, and policy discussions on poverty, its causes, its consequences, and the impact of public policies addressing it. Major features of this site include working papers, policy briefs, a newsletter, and other research. Many of the current policy briefs deal with welfare, the transition from welfare to work, and the effect on families and female-headed families, among other issues. Older briefs cover a wider range of poverty-related research that has policy implications. Also included here are announcements of events and conferences, descriptions of funding opportunities, lists of available publications, links to other Web sites, a new classroom section with reading lists, and much more. In short, this is a superb policy-related site dealing with poverty in the United States.

549. **Poverty.** Available: http://www.census.gov/hhes/www/poverty.html (Accessed: April 18, 2004).

This U.S. Census Bureau Web site includes data and discussion on poverty, its measurement, and the populations affected. There are links to the Current Population Survey and the latest edition of *Poverty in the United States* (see above), the Survey of Income and Program Participation (SIPP), the decennial census, recent poverty measurement research, related research centers, and more.

550. **A Profile of the Working Poor, 2000.** Available: http://www.bls.gov/cps/cpswp2000.htm (Accessed: April 18, 2004).

Also in print form under the same title, this Bureau of Labor Statistics document presents data describing the relationship between poverty status and level of involvement in the labor force. After defining what constitutes being classified as working poor, the document analyzes the data according to a variety of demographic variables, including age, gender, ethnicity, educational attainment, unrelated individuals, and labor market problems. Initial overviews of the findings from the data are followed by definitions of terms and the various data tables.

551. **Social Inequality and Classes.** Available: http://www2.fmg.uva.nl/sociosite/topics/inequality.html (Accessed: April 18, 2004).

Inequality, classes, stratification, poverty, social movements, and socialism are all covered in this subsection of the *SocioSite* Web site, which is hosted by the University of Amsterdam. Information on these areas includes archives of discussion lists, newsgroups, book summaries, book excerpts, bibliographies, position papers, links to other Web sites, and more. The materials cited or linked are international in scope, making this site a good gateway to diverse data on and approaches to class, stratification, poverty, and inequality.

Theory

Bibliographies

552. Clark, Michael. **Michel Foucault, An Annotated Bibliography: Tool Kit for a New Age.** New York: Garland, 1983. 608 p. index. (Garland Bibliographies of Modern Critics and Critical Schools, vol. 4; Garland Reference Library of the Humanities, vol. 350). ISBN 0-8240-9253-8.

Though not current, this bibliography is comprehensive through the early 1980s and, consequently, is a major resource for scholars of Foucault and poststructuralism. It includes over 2,500 published items through 1981, with additional major items for 1982 and 1983. Also included are sources found in the national bibliographies of France, Germany, the United States, and Great Britain. References span the social sciences and humanities and may be in any of seven languages. The descriptive annotations, however, are all in English. There are three major parts to the bibliography: primary works, secondary works, and background works. "Primary Works" is arranged chronologically and is comprised of five subchapters: books and collections of essays; prefaces, translations, and books edited; essays and review articles; reviews; and interviews, miscellaneous. "Secondary Works" is arranged alphabetically by author and also has five subchapters: books and collections of essays, special journal issues; essays and review articles; reviews; dissertations; and miscellaneous. Finally, the "Background Works" chapter includes sections for books and essays in which Foucault is discussed, though he may not be a major focus of the item. The book provides a brief biography of Foucault, as well as a lengthy introduction. There are also five indexes covering authors, book titles, article titles, journals, and topics.

553. Deegan, Mary Jo, ed. **Women in Sociology: A Bio-Bibliographical Sourcebook.** New York: Greenwood Press, 1991. 468 p. index. $79.50. ISBN 0-313-26085.

Deegan's work documents "the lives and work of founding women in sociology" (p. 6), covering the 150 years from 1840 through 1990. It includes discussion about both their lives and their "social thought." There are fifty-one women covered, including such notable names as Hannah Arendt, Jane Addams, Charlotte Perkins Gilman, Helena Lopata, Alva Myrdal, Alice Rossi, and Helen Lynd. The women sociologists ultimately included in this work were identified through either the recommendations of other sociologists or extensive research; all met at least one of five criteria to be considered a sociologist. The introduction discusses these criteria, as well as these women's place in the historical development of sociology. The essays themselves are anywhere from five to ten pages, with an additional few pages of references. All of the essays include sections for a biography, major themes in that sociologist's work, and critiques. There are also accompanying bibliographies of works by and about the individual and her work. Name and subject indexes are appended.

554. Egan, David R., and Melinda A. Egan. **V. I. Lenin: An Annotated Bibliography of English-Language Sources to 1980.** Metuchen, NJ: Scarecrow Press, 1982. 482 p. $50.00. ISBN 0-8108-1526-5.

Almost 3,000 English-language sources about V. I. Lenin are included in this bibliography. Covering a wide range of political perspectives, they are drawn from "books, essays, chapters from general studies, periodical articles, reminiscences, interviews, addresses, doctoral dissertations, reviews of major Lenin studies, and introductions to Lenin's works" (p. vii). Lenin's writing is excluded, but little else is. This bibliography is international in scope, including many Soviet-era interpretations of Lenin's work.

The entries are arranged alphabetically by author under an extensive number of chapters and subtopics. Books and essays have Library of Congress call numbers, and the contents of anthologies are listed. The annotations are descriptive, and there are author and subject indexes. This is an excellent source for those interested in both Leninist theory and practice and revolutionary social change.

555. Eubanks, Cecil L. **Karl Marx and Frederich Engels: An Analytical Bibliography.** 2d ed. New York: Garland, 1984. 299 p. index. (Garland Reference Library of Social Science, vol. 100). ISBN 0-8240-9293-7.

This second edition adds 1,000 new entries to the first edition (1977). Its purpose remains the same: to be a comprehensive listing of various editions and translations of the writings of Marx and Engels and to provide a comprehensive listing of works dealing with or elaborating upon their writings. Books, articles, monographs, book chapters, and dissertations are included. Marxist-Leninist literature is considered too derivative and is therefore excluded. The entries are arranged into four sections: the works of Marx and Engels (with separate listings for each author's individual and collected works, as well as their joint works), books on Marx and Engels, articles on Marx and Engels, and dissertations on Marx and Engels. Within each section, entries are arranged alphabetically by author. There are two introductory bibliographic essays (from both editions) that are quite useful, as well as newly added subject indexes to books, articles, and dissertations. Since it is now a bit dated, this is no longer a comprehensive bibliography of secondary works on Marx and Engels. However, it remains an important guide to many classic analyses of their work. Furthermore, the comprehensive listing of primary works by Marx and Engels is as valuable as ever. Graduate students and faculty will find this most useful.

556. Kivisto, Peter, and William H. Swatos, Jr. **Max Weber: A Bio-Bibliography.** New York: Greenwood Press, 1988. 267 p. index. (Bio-Bibliographies in Sociology, no. 2). $73.95. ISBN 0-313-25794-9.

Both English translations of Weber's work and a "comprehensive, annotated bibliography of secondary literature" (p. 8) are included in this bibliography. Textbooks and book reviews (of primary and secondary works) are excluded, while dissertations and theses are included selectively. Overall, the book has two parts. Part 1 includes a biographical essay, an essay on Weber's reception in Anglo-American sociology, and a discussion of various Weber archives. Part 2, the largest, includes seven chapters. The first of these lists Weber's works in English translation, along with notes describing additional features of the edition or translation. The next chapter lists collections "on and out of Weber's work" (p. 58). The 764 books, chapters, and articles cited in the last five chapters focus on different subjects concerning Weber and his work: biography and intellectual history; methodology; religion; politics and social classes; and modernity, rationalization, and bureaucracy. All entries in these chapters receive brief, descriptive annotations. There is an author index, including editors and individuals mentioned in abstracts, and a name/subject index. This is an essential research tool for advanced students and faculty researching Weber.

557. Kurtz, Lester R. **Evaluating Chicago Sociology: A Guide to the Literature, with an Annotated Bibliography.** Chicago: University of Chicago Press, 1984. 303 p. index. (The Heritage of Sociology). ISBN 0-226-46476-8.

This is an analysis of and guide to further research on the Chicago school and its place in American sociology. The first part of the book is an overview of the Chicago school's development, key individuals, philosophical foundations, theoretical perspectives, areas of research, and approaches to social change and collective behavior.

The second half of the book is a bibliography on the Chicago school, its members, and their works, including writings of the members themselves. There are more than 1,000 books, articles, dissertations, and so on, arranged alphabetically by author. Most entries are annotated and all were published before 1983. A name/subject index is included.

558. LaPointe, Francois H. **Georg Lukacs and His Critics: An International Bibliography with Annotations (1910–1982).** Westport, CT: Greenwood Press, 1983. 403 p. index. ISBN 0-313-23891-X.

Lukacs, a Hungarian social theorist, is considered an important figure in the development of Marxist theory. Not surprisingly, his work has generated a considerable secondary literature. Though somewhat dated, this partially annotated bibliography is a comprehensive guide to that literature for items published through the end of 1982. References in many languages are included, adding to the bibliography's value. There are approximately 2,000 entries arranged into four parts. Part 1 includes references to books and reviews, with subdivisions for books in English, German, French, Italian, Spanish, and other languages. If the books were reviewed, references to the reviews are included. Some books are extensively abstracted and may even include a list of chapters. An additional section lists special issues of journals devoted to Lukacs; the constituent articles are listed. Part 2 covers dissertations and theses on Lukacs done worldwide; abstracts from **Dissertation Abstracts International** are included for some of these. Part 3 lists essays and articles on Lukacs, with a further breakdown by language (English, German, French, Italian, Spanish, other). Part 4 lists items in which Lukacs is compared to other theorists. This section is arranged alphabetically by the names of the other theorists, with references listed under those names. There is an index for authors and editors, though there is unfortunately no subject index.

559. Perrin, Robert G. **Herbert Spencer: A Primary and Secondary Bibliography.** New York: Garland, 1993. 1005 p. index. (Garland Reference Library of the Humanities, vol. 1061). $80.00. ISBN 0-8240-4597-1.

Spencer is one of the important nineteenth-century sociologists, best known for incorporating Darwinism and natural selection into his views on societal evolution. This bibliography is an extensive guide to works both by and about Spencer. It is organized into two major sections. Section 1 lists works by Spencer and includes correspondence, manuscripts, books, pamphlets, articles, and letters. The second section cites books, articles, reviews, and dissertations about Spencer. These are organized into chapters by subject, including categories for biographical and general studies, philosophy—religion, philosophy—ethics, biology, psychology, economics, politics and political science, sociology and social thought, education, art/literature/style, music, and miscellaneous. Virtually all entries, except dissertations, receive brief, descriptive annotations. In all, more than 2,000 primary and secondary sources are cited. A lengthy introductory chapter provides an overview of Spencer's life and work. Supplementary material includes a chronology of Spencer's life, a list of periodicals cited, and a name index.

560. Schultz, William R., and Lewis L. B. Fried. **Jacques Derrida: An Annotated Primary and Secondary Bibliography.** New York: Garland, 1992. 882 p. index. (Garland Bibliographies of Modern Critics and Critical Schools, vol. 18; Garland Reference Library of the Humanities, vol. 1319). $50.00. ISBN 0-8240-4872-5.

Though most influential in the area of literary criticism, deconstructionism has had an impact in the social sciences too, as seen for example in some of the work of sociologist Anthony Giddens. This is a comprehensive guide to over 4,000 works by and about deconstructionism's principal exponent, French philosopher Jacques Derrida. The guide is divided into major sections for primary and secondary sources. Primary sources are further subdivided into books and chapters, articles, interviews, and reviews and translations by Derrida. Both the book and article sections include subsections for works in different languages (i.e., English, French, German, Italian, or Japanese). Many, though not all, of these primary sources are briefly annotated. The secondary sources are subdivided into sections for books, chapters, articles, dissertations, reviews, and background articles and reviews. As in the section for primary sources, books, chapters, and articles are further subdivided by language. Most of these sources are annotated. The introduction includes a useful overview of the controversial nature of Derrida's work, as well as a categorization and discussion of many issues addressed in the secondary literature. Author and name indexes are provided.

561. Sica, Alan. **Max Weber: A Comprehensive Bibliography.** New Brunswick, NJ: Transaction Publishers, 2004. 334 p. index. $69.95. ISBN 0-7658-0209-0.

With almost 4,900 entries, this is easily the most comprehensive, predominantly English-language bibliography of works by and about Max Weber. Sica states that he has taken particular pains to check the accuracy of the references comprising the bibliography. Online indexes are terrific search tools, he acknowledges, but they often have introduced or reproduced bibliographic errors into the cited literature. Sica implies that the buck stops here and that this bibliography can serve as a definitive and correct listing of Weber citations, given the parameters of the bibliography. The bulk of the bibliography is in the final chapter of works on Weber, "Comprehensive Weber Bibliography of Works in English." However, earlier chapters cover: Weber's works in English translation, reviews of Weber's major works in English translation,

Weber's works in German and English-language reviews, selected reviews of Weberiana (i.e., works on Weber), selected dissertations and theses relating to Weber or his ideas, and Weber on rationality and rationalization processes (primary and secondary sources are in English). In all of these chapters, entries are arranged alphabetically by author. Sica justifies this arrangement by suggesting that (1) a subject category breakdown would require extensive cross-referencing, thus vastly expanding the size of the book, and (2) an author arrangement assembles all of an author's citations together, capitalizing on the fact that Weber scholars often devote careers to such work. Weber is a core figure in sociological thought, and for advanced researchers interested in his ideas this is a critical research tool.

562. Simich, Jerry L., and Rick Tilman. **Thorstein Veblen: A Reference Guide.** Boston: G. K. Hall, 1985. 240 p. index. ISBN 0-8161-8358-9.

This is a comprehensive annotated bibliography of books, portions or chapters of books, articles, reviews, dissertations, and other sources on Veblen written between 1891 and 1982. Both English-language and some foreign-language sources are included. The entries are arranged first chronologically, then alphabetically by author. Within each year, the entries are numbered; the combination year/entry number is used in the index. The descriptive annotations are generally a paragraph long and well written. The editors also provide a selective list of major writings by Veblen; they do not explain why more of Veblen's work is not cited. There is a thorough author/title index that also includes personal names as subjects and a selective number of other subject headings.

563. **Social Theory: A Bibliographic Series.** Santa Cruz, CA: Reference and Research Services, 1986– . quarterly. $55/year. ISSN 0887-3577.

All of the bibliographies in Joan Nordquist's **Social Theory** series are arranged similarly. They typically are 70 pages long and include approximately 500 unannotated references to books, articles, reviews, and other sources by and about the theorist or theory. In some cases, works in languages other than English are also cited. The bibliographies on theorists are typically organized into four sections. Section 1 usually cites books written by the theorist, while section 2 lists the theorist's articles or essays. Sections 3 and 4 cite books and articles about the theorist, respectively. In some of the bibliographies, the different sections are accompanied by their own keyword indexes. Classic and contemporary theorists covered include Max Weber, Émile Durkheim, Antonio Gramsci, Hannah Arendt, W.E.B. Du Bois, Louis Althusser, Simone De Beauvoir, Talcott Parsons, Rosa Luxemburg, Emma Goldman, Theodor Adorno, Max Horkheimer, Jean Baudrillard, Jean-Francois Lyotard, Michel Foucault, Pierre Bourdieu, Jacques Derrida, Hans-Georg Gadamer, Frederic Jameson, Herbert Marcuse, John Rawls, Maurice Merleau-Ponty, and Julia Kristeva. There are also bibliographies in this series on different contemporary theories in the various social sciences, including feminism, postmodernism, queer theory, postcolonialism, ecofeminist theory, radical ecological theory, deconstructionism, and more. These are important bibliographies not only because they provide access to the literature by and about traditional and contemporary theorists, but also because they span a wide range of theoretical and ideological positions.

564. Steinhauer, Kurt, comp. **Hegel: Bibliography.** New York: Bowker, 1981. 896 p. index. ISBN 3-598-03184-X.

Admittedly, this bibliography on Hegel and the philosophy of German idealism is not for everyone. But for those interested, for example, in fully understanding the roots of Marxist theory, this could be valuable. There are over 12,000 entries, representing a variety of countries and languages. Citations are, for the most part, in the language of origin.

The main body of the bibliography has two sections: works by Hegel and secondary sources on his work. The primary sources are arranged by complete works, selected works, single editions, and correspondence. Secondary sources are arranged chronologically from 1802 through 1975.

There are an author/editor/translator index, a keyword index, and a list of periodicals and series. Effective use of this bibliography would require knowledge of German. A follow-up volume by Steinhauer, *Hegel Bibliography, Pt. 2: Background Material on the International Reception of Hegel Within the Context of the History of Philosophy*, was published by K. G. Saur in 1998 and covers literature from 1976–1991.

Handbooks and Yearbooks

565. LeMoyne, Terri, comp. and ed. **Resource Book for Teaching Sociological Theory.** Washington, DC: American Sociological Association, 2001. 235 p. (ASA Resource Materials for Teaching).

Theory is a critically important component of any sociology curriculum. Consequently, it is not surprising that the ASA presents a resource handbook for those teaching the class. Like others in the series, this volume includes copies of syllabi from various sociologists around the country. The syllabi cover both classical and modern theory, at both the undergraduate and graduate level. There are also syllabi focusing on postmodern theory. Beyond the class syllabi, this handbook provides lots of additional and useful material for instructional purposes. For example, there are reviews of a handful of classic sociological theory texts. There are also sections on class handouts and study guides (e.g., on functionalism), journal article critiques (i.e., how to do them), paper assignments, exams, novel teaching ideas and activities, other important topics (e.g., theory Web sites), and a bibliography. Generally, this handbook is more robust and includes a wider variety of material than others in this series. Furthermore, students of theory may find it as useful as faculty tinkering with their theory courses.

566. Rasmussen, David M., ed. **Handbook of Critical Theory.** Oxford, United Kingdom: Blackwell, 1996. 426 p. index. $102.95. ISBN 0-631-18379-5.

Included here are sixteen essays providing critical analyses and overviews of the various theories and theorists that comprise the history and current state of critical theory. Among the theorists and schools covered are the Institute of Social Research and the Frankfurt School, Jurgen Habermas, Theodor Adorno, Max Horkheimer, Michel Foucault, Karl-Otto Apel, post-structuralism, and postmodernism, among others. The chapters fall under sections for philosophy and history; social science, discourse ethics, and justice; law and democracy; civil society and autonomy; pragmatics, psychoanalysis, and aesthetics; and postmodernism, critique, and the pathology of the social. A final chapter provides a bibliography of the primary writings of the Institute of Social Research and important critical theorists, as well as secondary writings on aspects of critical theory. There is a thorough subject index. This is a sophisticated treatment of critical theory and is suitable for specialized graduate students, researchers, and faculty. A 1999 paperback edition is also available.

567. Ritzer, George, and Barry Smart, eds. **Handbook of Social Theory.** Thousand Oaks, CA: Sage Publications, 2001. 552 p. index. $141.00. ISBN 0-7619-5840-1.

Defining what constitutes sociological or social theory is problematic. The authors of this work do not want to define a "canon" of acceptable social science theories that would constrain intellectual exploration and freedom. Instead, they present essays on virtually every significant social theory one might need to be conversant with in discussions of theory. The thirty-nine essays are arranged into three major parts or sections: classical social theory, contemporary social theory, and issues in social theory. Classical social theory includes essays on the expected theorists, such as Marx, Durkheim, Weber, Mead, Mannheim and others. The section on contemporary social theory is more wide ranging and includes essays on theorists (e.g., Parson, Nietzsche, Habermas, Foucault), theories (e.g., phenomenology, functionalism, rational choice, social exchange, ethnomethodology, conflict theory, postmodernism), and some ongoing debates (e.g., structure and agency). Finally, the social issues section covers topics such as cultural studies, globalization, postsocial relations, sexualities, and more. An international team of sociologists contributes the essays, which are approximately ten to twelve pages long. Each essay is accompanied by an extensive list of references. There is a detailed name/subject index. Overall, the entries are well written, fairly sophisticated, and best suited to advanced undergraduate and graduate students with significant grounding in theory.

Dictionaries and Encyclopedias

568. Bottomore, Tom, ed. **A Dictionary of Marxist Thought.** 2d ed. Oxford, United Kingdom: Blackwell, 1991. 647 p. index. ISBN 0-631-16481-2.

This second edition enlarges upon the first (1983) by adding almost fifty new entries and expanding or revising numerous others. The entries are written by a stellar group of contributors, including Bottomore, David McLellan, Ralph Miliband, Ernest Mandel, Paul Sweezy, John Rex, David Harvey, Istvan Meszaros, Russell Jacoby, and Immanuel Wallerstein, among others. Some of the new entries address Marxism in various countries or regions, analytical

Marxism, liberation theology, market socialism, dependency theory, modernism and postmodernism, and even particular works (e.g., Antonio Gramsci's *Prison Notebooks*). The lengthy, signed definitions are accompanied by brief bibliographies of suggested readings. The dictionary also includes biographies of well-known contributors to Marxist thought; newly added biographies treat Jurgen Habermas, Raymond Williams, Nicos Poulantzas, and Joan Robinson, to name a few. The definitions are mostly self-explanatory, though they do include cross-references to terms defined elsewhere. While clearly written, the essays vary in difficulty, with entries in economics and philosophy often presuming some background knowledge. There are appended bibliographies of the cited works of Marx, Engels, and others. A thorough name/subject index is included.

569.   Carver, Terrell. **A Marx Dictionary.** Totowa, NJ: Barnes and Noble, 1987. 164 p. index. ISBN 0-389-20684-9.

Karl Marx is one of the major, founding theorists of sociology. However, it is not an easy matter for sociology students to become conversant with his ideas, which are often quite complex. This dictionary is intended to render Marx more understandable to undergraduate students by straightforwardly discussing sixteen central concepts in his work. Those concepts are: alienation, base and superstructure, capitalism, class, communism, dialectic, exploitation, fetishism of commodities, ideology, labor, materialism, mode of production, revolution, science, state, and value. For each concept, there is a three to ten page essay discussing its origin and meaning in Marx's work. The essays also cite key works where Marx developed the concept and they highlight in boldface terms that are treated elsewhere in the dictionary. There are also suggestions for further reading that include both works by Marx, with relevant page references, and secondary sources about that particular concept. Carver also provides an introductory historical overview of Marx's life and works. Supplements include a bibliographical essay of works by and about Marx, a bibliography of Marx's writings, and a subject index.

There is no disputing the importance of these sixteen concepts in Marx's work. While the essays are very well written, they are probably best suited not for introductory course "students" but for upper-level undergraduates in sociological theory, social change, or social stratification.

570.   Payne, Michael, ed. **A Dictionary of Cultural and Critical Theory.** Oxford, United Kingdom: Blackwell, 1996. 644 p. $108.95. ISBN 0-631-17197-5.

This is excellent guide to the concepts, theories, and theorists within cultural and critical theory. Sociologists may be particularly interested in the essays on such topics as modernity, structuralism, postmodernism, phenomenology, poststructuralism, race-class-gender analysis, alienation, deconstruction, base and superstructure, Marxism and Marxist criticism, social formation, subcultures, and other concepts. In addition, there are biographical essays on important theorists, such as Marx, Derrida, Habermas, Lyotard, Lukacs, Arendt, Baudrillard, De Beauvior, Gramsci, and more. All essays are signed and range in length from a few paragraphs to seven multicolumn pages. Within essays, concepts and individuals defined elsewhere in the dictionary are capitalized. Each essay is accompanied by a brief author/title list of suggested readings; a complete bibliography is found in the back of the volume. An introductory essay provides a broad overview and categorization of theorists and theories. There is also a subject index for additional access to the entries. The concepts dealt with here are not for beginners, but for more advanced students of cultural and critical theory.

571. Turner, Bryan S., ed. **The Blackwell Companion to Social Theory.** Oxford, United Kingdom: Blackwell, 1996. 484 p. index. $31.95. ISBN 0-631-18401-5.

Focusing on recent developments in social theory, this volume is a collection of introductory essays providing overviews of a variety of contemporary theories. The fifteen signed essays fall under five categories: foundations; actions, actors, systems; the micro-macro problem; historical and comparative sociology; and the nature of the social. Within these categories are essays on such topics as classical social theory, critical theory, systems theory, structuralism, rational choice theory, theories of action and praxis, historical sociology, feminist social theory, cultural sociology, psychoanalysis and social theory, postmodern theory, sociology of time and space, and social theory and the public sphere. While the focus is contemporary theory, there is some effort to connect these theories to their classical sociological roots (where appropriate). These essays are thought provoking and well written. However, they presume enough knowledge that their appropriate audience would be advanced students and faculty. A subject index helps in tracking down particular concepts and theorists mentioned throughout the volume.

Web Sites and Research Centers

572. **ASA Section on Marxist Sociology.** Available: http://csf.colorado.edu/psn/marxist-sociology/index.html (Accessed: April 4, 2004).

This is one of the American Sociological Association's almost four-dozen sections or interest groups. The section on Marxist Sociology is interested in varieties of ways of researching, teaching, and applying Marxist theory in contemporary societies. This site includes not only a statement about the section and its vision, but also instructions on joining the e-mail list, lists of officers and some members, links to other Web sites on Marxism and the writings of Marx and Engels, some current newsletters, and the section's bylaws.

573. **Dead Sociologists Index.** Available: http://www2.pfeiffer.edu/~lridener/DSS/INDEX.HTML (Accessed: April 4, 2004).

Information about and writings by sixteen of the major sociologists in the history of the field are covered in this Web site. Those sociologists are Comte, Durkheim, Marx, Spencer, Simmel, Weber, Veblen, Cooley, Mead, Park, Pareto, Thomas, Du Bois, Addams, Martineau, and Sorokin. For each sociologist there is information about the person, a summary of his or her major ideas, and excerpts from some original works. Much of the information about the sociologist and his or her ideas is drawn from Lewis Coser's *Masters of Sociological Thought* (2d ed., 1977) and Don Martindale's *The Nature and Types of Sociological Theory*. The Web site also includes numerous newly added links to topical Web sites in sociology, the American Sociological Association, the National Science Foundation, and the Internet Scout Report (Social Sciences and Humanities Division), which selected this as a noteworthy Internet site. Also linked is a social theory course syllabus that includes recommended readings written by these theorists. The Web page author is a faculty member at Baylor University.

574. **The Durkheim Pages.** Available: http://www.relst.uiuc.edu/durkheim/ (Accessed: April 4, 2004).

This Web site includes: a biography of Durkheim, full text of some of Durkheim's works, critical summaries of his major works, reviews of recent book and articles on Durkheim, a time line of important events for Durkheim and the Third French Republic, a biographical dictionary of his antecedents and contemporaries, a glossary of important terms, bibliographies of primary and secondary works, a list of lectures Durkheim gave at Bordeaux and Paris, a list of Durkheim scholars, directions on how to subscribe to the Durkheim listserv, and information on how to subscribe to the print annual, *Durkheimian Studies*.

575. **Famous Sociologists.** Available: http://www.pscw.uva.nl/sociosite/topics/ sociologists.html (Accessed: April 5, 2004).

This is another subsection of the Dutch sociology Web site, *SocioSite*, that includes such items as texts, sections from or summaries of texts, a curriculum vitae, biographies, full-text articles, conference papers, bibliographies, lists of related Web sites, and Internet discussion lists by and about ninety well-known living and dead sociologists. Along with classic theorists such as Weber, Marx, and Durkheim, one also finds information about more contemporary theorists such as Pierre Bourdieu, Jean Baudrillard, Anthony Giddens, Claus Offe, Immanuel Wallerstein, and Paul Willis, among others.

576. **Georg Simmel Online.** Available: http://socio.ch/sim/index_sim.htm (Accessed: April 4, 2004).

Part of the Sociology in Switzerland Web site, *Simmel Online* includes texts by and about Simmel and his work. Much of the material here is in German. However, there are numerous works by and about Simmel that are in English or are translated into English. Some biographical and contextual information about Simmel is reproduced from Lewis Coser's *Masters of Sociological Thought* (1977).

577. **The MarX-Files.** Available: http://www.appstate.edu/~stanovskydj/ marxfiles.html (Accessed: April 4, 2004).

The author of this site is a lecturer at Appalachian State University, and this Web page provides support to courses he teaches there, in particular "Marx for Beginners" and "Marx's *Capital*." This site has links not only to the full text of works by Marx and Engels, but also to explanatory texts on these works; biographical works on Marx and Engels; related libraries, archives, books and journals; labor and left resources; and an assortment of other links to cultural manifestations of left politics and culture (e.g., films, plays, etc.).

578. **The Marxists.org Internet Archive.** Available: http://www.marxists.org (Accessed: April 4, 2004).

Sponsored by the Marxists Internet Archive (MIA), this site includes long and short biographies on Marxist writers, histories of selective Marxist movements (with numerous links to texts), a selective subject index (also with extensive links), an online encyclopedia, links to information on reference (i.e., relevant) writers, and a "learning Marxism" section or beginner's guide to Marxism. There is also a search engine that allows one to search for certain authors on the various pages within the Web site, and a new subscription e-mail newsletter.

579. **The Mead Project.** Available: http://spartan.ac.brocku.ca/~lward/ (Accessed: April 4, 2004).

Sponsored by the Sociology Department at Brock University, this site has a stated goal of revitalizing work on George Herbert Mead. To foster this, the site includes biographical information, texts of writings, career time lines, bibliographies and other materials on not only George Herbert Mead, but also John Dewey, James Baldwin, W. I. Thomas, Charles Horton Cooley, William James, and Edward Sapir. For each of these individuals, there is at least a list of some writings, a number of which are available full text on the Web site. Finally, there are also links to other social and natural scientists, for whom selective full text of their writings is available.

580. **Norbert Elias and Process Sociology.** Available: http://www.usyd.edu.au/su/social/elias/elias.html (Accessed: April 4, 2004).

Elias is known not only for his work in process sociology, but also in historical sociology and sociological theory. Though pages vary as to when they have been modified (i.e., 1998 to 2001), this site has information on the Elias-I listserv, upcoming (i.e., past) conferences, and calls for papers, copies of Elias-related research in progress and papers/presentations, descriptions of Elias readers and biographies, copies of mid-1990s issues of *Figurations* (a newsletter on Elias), some Elias writings, bibliographies, and more. While numerous pages are dated, most links work and the Web site can provide useful information and leads on Elias.

581. **Society for the Study of Symbolic Interactionism.** Available: http://sun.soci.niu.edu/~sssi (Accessed: April 4, 2004).

There is a variety of information here related to symbolic interactionism and, more generally, qualitative research. The site describes how to access the SSSITALK discussion list and provides an archive of recent traffic. There is also information on the annual Couch-Stone Symposium (with thematically related papers on symbolic interactionism), the SSSI annual conference, teaching resources (e.g., syllabi on symbolic interactionism and qualitative research, books of interest), the journal *Symbolic Interaction*, and links to other qualitative research and symbolic interactionist Web sites. Finally, there is information on the officers, awards, annual meetings, and how to join.

582. **Sociological Theories and Perspectives.** Available: http://www2.fmg. uva.nl/sociosite/topics/theory.html (Accessed: April 4, 2004).

A subsection of the Dutch *Sociosite* Web site, this guides the visitor to other Web sites that are categorized under fourteen theories, perspectives, sociological specialties, or methodologies. The topics are: anomie, chaos theory, ethnomethodology, game theory, interaction, knowledge, sociologists, marxism, network, rational choice, sociobiology, sociolinguistics, time, and methodology. For each, anywhere from one to ten Web sites are identified. These can include such things as important texts, interviews, biographies of theorists, dissertations, articles, conference papers, organizations, and links to many more related sites. The "knowledge" category identifies sites relating to the sociology of knowledge. Across all sites, a variety of types of information is identified, including theses, book chapters, bibliographies, newsletters, organization Web sites, interviews, and more.

583. **Verstehen: Max Weber's HomePage.** Available: http://www.faculty.rsu. edu/~felwell/Theorists/Weber/Whome.htm (Acccessed: April 13, 2004).

Notably, this site summarizes Weber's thoughts on key concepts in his (and others') writings. These include such topics as the Protestant ethic, bureaucracy, ideal type, authority, rationalization, Karl Marx, and more. In clarifying and summarizing these concepts or issues, the Web site's creator, a faculty member at Rogers State University, also cites source theory books where the explanation can be found. These sources include some of the classic theory textbooks by Lewis Coser, Hans Gerth and C. Wright Mills, and Raymond Aron. The site also includes small quotes from Weber, larger excerpts from some of his primary works, and links to similar Web pages on other important theorists (e.g., Karl Marx, T. Robert Malthus, Émile Durkheim, C. Wright Mills, Robert Merton, and Gerhard Lenski).

Urban Sociology and Community Studies

Indexes, Abstracts, and Databases

584. **Index to Current Urban Documents (ICUD).** [electronic resource]. Westport, CT: Greenwood Press, 1972– . Available: http://www.urbdocs.com/ (Accessed: April 25, 2004).

The *Index to Current Urban Documents* indexes seemingly obscure publications from local governments and other agencies on a variety of topics relating to urban life, services, and management. Some county, state, and other government-related publications are included as well. Approximately 2,400 documents are added each year from approximately 500 cities in the United States and Canada. *ICUD* supports several search features, including browse by topic and browse by municipality. Depending on the subscription package, the indexed citations include the agency's URL and may link to pdf versions of the documents. The online version of *ICUD* currently begins with volume 29 (2000/2001) of the corresponding print index. For the print volumes 1 through 28, most citations match with documents that are held in the Urban Documents Microfiche Collection; these documents are contributed by dozens of libraries and agencies. The order number for the document, and the number of fiche it occupies, is included with the citations. Various subscription packages are available. The full-subscription option includes online access to both the index and to pdf copies of the documents, as well as paper and CD-ROM copies of the index. A regional subscription includes online, print, and CD-ROM versions of the index, along with pdf copies of documents for a designated region (e.g., New England, Mid Atlantic, etc.). Institutions may also subscribe to the index alone. Copies of the print volumes 1 through 28, along with the microfiche documents, are available for purchase.

585. **Sage Urban Studies Abstracts.** Vol. 1– , No. 1– . Thousand Oaks, CA: Sage, 1973– . quarterly. $797/yr. ISSN 0090-5747. Available: http://www.sagepub.com/journal.aspx?pid=160 (Accessed: March 4, 2004).

Approximately 300 books, book chapters, journal articles, government publications, and other items are abstracted in each issue. Entries are arranged alphabetically by author under fifteen chapter headings, which include such topics as trends in urban policy, urban history, urban planning, urban and regional economics, urban development, crime, social services, social issues, theory and research, education, politics, and more. Besides a paragraph-long abstract, each citation also includes up to five subject headings that are used in the subject index. This index provides significant coverage of numerous sociological concepts, including race, ethnicity, gender, socioeconomic status, social mobility, and social networks. Besides the subject index, an author index is also provided, and both are cumulated in the last issue of each volume. A source list cites all of the journals from which citations were drawn.

Handbooks and Yearbooks

586. UN Department of Economic and Social Affairs Population Division. **World Urbanization Prospects: The 2001 Revision.** New York: United Nations, 2002. 321 p. $37.50. ISBN 92-1-151371-5.

This United Nations source provides both data and analysis of trends in urban and rural population growth, regional population growth, urbanization patterns, population growth in cities, the distribution of population, and more. There are approximately one hundred tables, charts, and and figures illustrating these trends, and many of the tables are retrospective to 1950. These data are part of a biannual UN project to publish the trends in urban and rural population growth "of all countries in the world and of their major urban agglomerations" (p. 1). Data sources for all tables and charts are cited in a separate chapter. Seventeen supplementary annex tables of data are also provided.

Dictionaries and Encyclopedias

587. Christensen, Karen, and David Levinson, eds. **Encyclopedia of Community: From the Village to the Virtual World.** Thousand Oaks, CA: Sage, 2003. 4v. 1839 p. index. $595.00. ISBN 0-7619-2598-8.

Included in this award-winning reference book are some 500 signed articles, arranged alphabetically, on the wide variety of topics that relate to the idea of community. In fact, one of the strengths of this encyclopedia is its consideration of diverse perspectives on many of the topics provided here. The articles can run to a number of pages and may also include sidebar articles on particular subtopics or relevant documents. They also include a list of references for further reading. Throughout, *see* references are used to refer the reader to preferred terms found elsewhere in the encyclopedia. There is also a supplemental topical guide to the entries. Among other features, a master bibliography is appended.

588. Ember, Melvin, and Carol R. Ember, eds. **Encyclopedia of Urban Cultures: Cities and Cultures Around the World.** Danbury, CT: Grolier, 2002. 4v. index. $399.00. ISBN 0-71725-698-7.

The focus here is on the cultural features of 240 of the world's major cities. The analysis and discussion of these cities is from the perspective of the social sciences, including urban anthropology, sociology, political science, geography, and history. Articles on the cities include the same categories: orientation (e.g., location, population, distinctive features), history, infrastructure, cultural and social life (e.g., ethnic/class/religious diversity, family, and other support systems), quality of life, and future of the city. Most of these sections have standard subsections as well, making for "maximum comparability." Each article is accompanied by a bibliography of recommended readings. The first volume begins with sixteen thematic essays on important issues in the study of cities, including the origins of cities, migration and cities, cities and religious institutions, health and disease in urban areas, urbanization in different regions, and more. Volume 4 includes appendices that (1) list cities alphabetically, by country, and by region of the world, (2) provide some statistical tables, and (3) list Web sites that provide data. A list of contributors is also provided, as is a substantial index.

589. Shumsky, Neil Larry, ed. **Encyclopedia of Urban America: The Cities and Suburbs.** Santa Barbara, CA: ABC-CLIO, 1998. 2v. 974 p. index. $175.00. ISBN 0-87436-846-4.

The editor acknowledges what is apparent in this volume: it is an "eclectic" and "idiosyncratic" collection of articles that is, nonetheless, very compelling. There are approximately 500 essay entries here contributed by some 300 separate authors. The topics covered range from multipage histories of well-known cities and suburbs to essays on social science–related topics. The latter include such interesting issues as race riots, the Chicago school of sociology, desegregation, bohemians, basketball, organized crime, planned communities, population growth, suburbanization, unions, social structure of cities, and much more. For sociology students, the list of potentially interesting essays is seemingly endless. Also included are biographies on well-known individuals. Essays run from one to seven pages and are accompanied by *see also* and bibliographic references. An overall selected bibliography, arranged under eight broad categories, is provided, as is a listing of entries under major subject categories. The extensive subject/name/title index provides detailed access to the entries. This would be a useful source and good starting point for sociology students and general readers.

590. Van Vliet, Willem, ed. **The Encyclopedia of Housing.** Thousand Oaks, CA: Sage, 1998. 712 p. index. $216.00. ISBN 0-7619-1332-7.

This encyclopedia attempts to "bridge the gap" between various disciplinary approaches to housing and housing studies. One can find here essays not only on economic planning, the housing industry, and federal housing policies, but also affordability, slums, segregation, single-parent households, drugs and public housing, and much more. The entries vary in length from a paragraph to multiple pages, but most include *see also* references to related terms, as well as bibliographies for further reading. Entries cover issues or controversies, key words or concepts in the field, organizations, different population groups, and legislation. Organization or association entries include contact names, phone and fax numbers, and addresses. Appended is a list of core or nodal entries, which in turn cross-reference satellite entries; a list of organizations; a list of periodicals; and major federal legislation and executive orders authorizing HUD programs. The three indexes provided are for contributors, authors cited, and subject. This is a detailed guide that covers many social policy and technical aspects of housing.

Web Sites and Research Centers

591. **American Planning Association (APA).** Available: http://www.planning. org/ (Accessed: March 3, 2004).

The APA is a public policy and research organization involved in urban, rural, suburban, and regional planning. Its site includes, among other things, descriptions of the various applied research projects in which they are engaged, as well as links to and descriptions of community-oriented projects, conferences, publications, legislation, policy issues and guides, and much more. Topics of interest include homelessness, housing, neighborhood collaborative planning, preservation of historic and cultural resources, sustainability, and subsidized housing, among others.

592. **The Community Web.** Available: http://www.commurb.org/ (Accessed: March 1, 2004).

This is the Web site of the American Sociology Association's interest-group section of Community and Urban Sociology. It includes not only information on the interest group, its officers, its history, its newsletter, and new journal, but also articles, listserv digests on special themes, convention information, awards, and more. The notice board includes news and views, conference information, new book titles, teaching related information, and links to some members' home pages.

593. **Cyburbia.** Available: http://www.cyburbia.org/ (Accessed: March 3, 2004).

Sponsored by the Department of Urban and Regional Planning at the University of Buffalo, this site provides a number of interesting features. For example, it presents planning-related news stories and articles, with links to the site's listserv so that participants can discuss the story and its implications for the planning community. Stories can relate to such topics as immigrant settlement, fostering community, migrant settlement patterns, and residential density, among others. There is an extensive planning resource directory that provides links to Web sites arranged under more than a dozen topical areas. A *Cyburbia*-sponsored forum or bulletin board is also provided, with an extensive number of discussions on planning-related topics.

594. **Urban Institute.** Available: http://www.urban.org (Accessed: March 1, 2004).

A "nonpartisan economic and social policy organization," the Urban Institute provides research and analysis of compelling issues of urban social policy concern. Reports included here are on such topics as minority high school graduation rates, single mothers, working families and children, lack of health insurance, housing discrimination, teens and welfare reform, and much more. A synopsis of each report is available, with a link to the text of the full report. The *Institute* also provides access to research and analysis by broad research topic, including education, criminal justice, children, adolescents, immigration, race and gender, ethnicity, and many more areas. On all topics covered on this Web site, the current policy options and proposals are analyzed and critiqued. A directory and description of other policy centers, with a link to the Web site, is also provided, among other things.

Women's Studies

Guides

595. Olson, Hope A. **Information Sources in Women's Studies and Feminism.** Munchen: K. G. Saur, 2002. 189 p. index. $89.00. ISBN 3-598-24440-1.

This guide is designed to direct researchers to the best starting point for research on the topic of women's studies and feminism. The book is divided into three sections: "Issues of Form," which covers archival materials, serials, electronic resources and "gray" literature and other formats likely to be encountered; "Issues of Information Access," which discusses library collection development policies and practices, and the organization of research materials in indexes and abstracts, online catalogs, and other print and electronic research tools; and "Issues of Diversity," which discusses information useful for diverse groups, specifically lesbians, and the HIV/AIDS population. The book includes information useful for researching sociological aspects of women's studies and each of the chapters is signed and includes information on author affiliation, detailed footnotes, references, further-reading lists, and organization contact information. The book concludes with an insightful essay on global information technologies.

Bibliographies

596. Hofstetter, Eleanore O. **Women in Global Migration, 1945–2000: A Comprehensive Multidisciplinary Bibliography.** Westport, CT: Greenwood Press, 2001. 535 p. index. $109.95. ISBN 0-313-31810-7.

This source offers a comprehensive listing of women immigrants around the world since 1945. With over 5,000 entries this bibliography covers the multidisciplinary research on this topic. Each chapter has a brief introduction followed by the entries for that subject, with the listing for sociology sources being one of the most extensive (130 pages). Other chapters relevant to the field of sociology include economics, education, and psychology. The source offers two separate indexes, one set up by nationality, religion, and ethnic group; and the other by receiving country or region.

597. Krikos, Linda, and Cindy Ingold. **Women's Studies: A Recommended Bibliography.** 3d ed. Westport, CT: Libraries Unlimited, 2004. 875 p. index. $120.00. ISBN 1-56308-566-6.

Krikos and Ingold present an extensive bibliography that taps into the multidisciplinary, international world of literature in feminism and women's studies from 1985 to 1999. Divided into nineteen subject areas, the entries here are detailed, evaluative, and include comparisons to other works on the topic. Core titles and essential out-of-print titles are also listed. This is an excellent source for scholars conducting literature reviews in the area of women's studies and feminism, as well as a useful tool for library collection development.

Indexes, Abstracts, and Databases

598. **Contemporary Women's Issues.** [electronic resource]. Farmington Hills, MI: Thomson Gale, 1992– . weekly. Available: http://www.gale.com/pdf/facts/rdscwi.pdf (Accessed: June 28, 2004).

This is a multidisciplinary, international, full-text database comprised of relevant content from English-language periodicals and journals, "gray" literature, and the alternative press. It brings together ephemera such as newsletters and other types of organizational literature that can be hard to come by, and includes NGO (nongovernmental organizations associated with the United Nations) research reports. It includes coverage of sociological issues in women's lives such as domestic violence, employment/workplace, and gender issues.

599. **GenderWatch.** [electronic resource]. Ann Arbor: ProQuest Company. 1970– . quarterly. ISSN 1520-0655. Available: http://www.proquest.com/ products/pt-product-genderwatch.shtml (Accessed: June 28, 2004).

The purpose of this full-text, international, and interdisciplinary database is to cover the impact of gender issues (such as the evolution of the women's movement and changes in gender roles) on numerous subject areas. Indexed and abstracted publications include over 170 academic journals and magazines, newspapers, newsletters, regional publications, books, and government documents; as well as content form nonmainstream publications such as pamphlets, conference proceedings, and NGO research reports. Among the topics relevant to sociology are: careers and the workplace, family studies, public policy, and women's and gender studies.

600. **Women Studies Abstracts.**Vol. 1– , No. 1– . Rush, NY: Rush Publishing, 1972– . quarterly, with annual cumulations. $240/yr. (institutions). ISSN 0049-7835.

Approximately 400 or more books and articles are cited and selectively annotated in each quarterly issue. References are listed alphabetically by author under some thirty key categories, including such sociological areas as: education and socialization, sex roles, family, violence against women, prejudice and sex discrimination, employment, sexuality, society, interpersonal relations, and more. Most abstracts come from either the source journal or from an abstractor. For other references, a brief, descriptive phrase or sentence accompanies the citation. A separate section lists media and book reviews, which are also abstracted. Each issue of the index lists the specific journals and issues that were scanned for references. There are also author and subject indexes, which are cumulated in the last issue of each volume. Also available online as part of the database Women's Studies International (see below).

601. **Women's Studies Index.** Vol. 1– . New York: G. K. Hall, 1989– . annual. $175/yr. ISSN 1058-8369.

Over eighty popular and scholarly journals, mostly American, are scanned each year for the articles cited here. The references themselves are arranged by title under an extensive alphabetical list of subjects and authors. Library of Congress subject headings are used, with *see* and *see also* references to other terms. There are also specific subject headings for book, film, music, play, and video reviews. Among the sociological headings are such terms as "class differences," "divorce," "family structure," "family roles," "aging," "sexuality," "gender differences," "race relations," "postmodernism," and "poverty." In fact, most sociological specialties are reflected in the many and varied subject headings. The journals indexed, as well as their specific volumes and issues, are noted in a "List of Periodicals Indexed." There is also a list of subscription addresses for these journals.

602. **Women's Studies International.** [electronic resource]. Baltimore, MD: NISC International, 1972 and earlier. quarterly. Available: http://www.nisc.com/ frame/NISC_products-f.htm (Accessed: June 28, 2004).

This database, which includes bibliographic citations and abstracts, indexes women's studies materials from around the world, including nearly 800 journals, newspapers, newsletters, books and book chapters, theses and dissertations, organization Web sites and documents. Feminist research in many subject areas is covered, including sociology and related topics such as psychology, political/social activism, employment and workplace harassment, and social welfare and socioeconomics. *Women's Studies International* is comprised of information found in *Women Studies Abstracts* (1984–present); Women's Studies Database (1972–present); Women Studies Librarian, four files from the University of Wisconsin: *New Books on Women and Feminism (1987–present), WAVE: Women's Audiovisuals in English: A Guide to Nonprint Resources in Women's Studies (1985–1990), Women, Race and Ethnicity: A Bibliography (1970–1990)*, and *The History of Women and Science, Health and Technology: A Bibliographic Guide to the Professions and Disciplines (1970–1995)*; MEDLINE Subset on Women (1964–present); *Women of Color and Southern Women: A Bibliography of Social Science Research (1975–1995)*; and *Women's Health and Development: An Annotated Bibliography (1995).*

Handbooks and Yearbooks

603. **American Women: Who They Are and How They Live.** Ithaca, NY: New Strategist Publications, 2002. 413 p. index. $89.95. ISBN 1-885070-42-X.

By repackaging the 2000 U.S. Census data this resource presents the racial composition, age, size, and distribution of women in the United States. Other statistics are also presented from such branches of the federal government as the Bureau of Labor Statistics and the National Center for Health Statistics. This handbook is comprised of ten sections: attitudes and behavior, business, education, health, income, labor force, living arrangements, population, spending, and wealth; and makes use of statistical tables to further enhance the text. The logical arrangement of the data makes this an effortless way to access U.S. Census and other federal government agency statistics.

604. **The World's Women 2000: Trends and Statistics.** New York: United Nations, 2000. 180 p. $16.95. ISBN 92-1-161428-7.

This statistical handbook is international in scope and of sociological interest as it covers the social and economic roles of women throughout the world. It includes comparative data and analysis on a range of topics dealing with the lives of women in political, economic, and social settings. Two previous editions of this resource were first published in 1991, and again in 1995. This 2000 edition includes six topical chapters that are very similar to those in the previous volumes: population, women and men in families, health, education and communication, work, and human rights and political decision making. Within chapters, highly readable prose is interspersed with tables and charts to give succinct overviews of the topic. Chapters do include subsections to help focus the analysis. For example, the chapter on health has sections on life expectancy, the health of children and adolescents, reproductive health, HIV infection and AIDS, and the health of an aging population. Appended to each chapter are bibliographic notes and tables of data. Also included for each volume is a list of the statistical sources consulted. A more detailed and extensive version of these data are available on a United Nations' CD-ROM source, Women's Indicators and Statistics database (Wistat).

Dictionaries and Encyclopedias

605. Gamble, Sarah, ed. **The Routledge Critical Dictionary of Feminism and Postfeminism.** New York: Routledge, 2000. index. $22.95. ISBN 0415925185.

In part 1 of this single-volume dictionary, "Feminism: Its History and Cultural Context," key concepts, theories, and individuals in feminism and postfeminism are covered in an essay-style format, followed by a select bibliography of further reading. Critical essays of interest to researchers in sociology may include "Feminism and Gender," "Feminism and New Technologies," and "Feminism and Popular Culture," among other chapters. Throughout the essay, text names and terms are highlighted to facilitate further research in part 2, "A–Z of Key Themes and Major Figures," where definitions are arranged alphabetically and range in length from a paragraph to a full page.

606. Walter, Lynn, ed. **The Greenwood Encyclopedia of Women's Issues Worldwide.** Westport, CT: Greenwood Press, 2003. index. $550.00. ISBN 0313327874 (set).

This six-volume set, divided into the regions of Asia and Oceania, Central and South America, Europe, Middle East and North Africa, North America and the Caribbean, and Sub-Saharan Africa, documents the current issues and challenges for women in more than 130 of the world's most populated countries. The set contains a glossary of terms and a comprehensive index in the final volume. The signed entries are arranged alphabetically by countries within the volume's region, and include maps, photos, statistical tables, and charts that enhance the text. The chapters are thorough in their coverage of each country and include such subheadings of interest to sociologists such as family and sexuality, social and government programs, working conditions, health issues, and violence against women. Each entry concludes with an extensive listing of further research resources: suggested readings and bibliographies, organization information, Web sites, and videos and films.

607. Kramarae, Chris, and Spender, Dale, eds. **Routledge International Encyclopedia of Women.** New York: Routledge, 2000. index. $695.00. ISBN 0-415-92088-4.

The four volumes in this set are arranged alphabetically by topic. Topics include education—globalization, economy—global restructuring, and sociology. Chapters often include subsections to help focus the research on a particular aspect of a topic or issue. The signed entries include *see also* references to facilitate further in-depth research, and also a listing of references and further readings are provided. More than 600 scholars have contributed articles that illuminate the issues surrounding feminism and the status of women worldwide. A useful alphabetical list of articles at the beginning of each volume and a topical list of articles for the set at the beginning of volume 1 are also key features of this accessible and easy-to-use encyclopedia.

608. McFadden, Margaret, ed. **Women's Issues: Ready Reference.** Pasadena, CA: Salem Press, 1997. 3v. index. $331.00. ISBN 0-89356-765-5 (set).

This three-volume set is comprised of 696 entries, arranged alphabetically, dated, and signed by the article author, on topics such as people, events, organizations, and issues, as well as definitions for subject-relevant terminology. A unique feature of this source is the use of the "relevant issues," "significance," and "areas of achievement" headings that appear at the beginning of many of the articles, this helps to put information into context. The articles cover topics that pertain to women in the United States and Canada, many of which are relevant to the field of sociology, and are enhanced by photographs, charts, tables, and other graphic illustrations. Articles that are longer than 1,250 words include a bibliography, and articles that are longer than 2,500 words include annotations. Also featured are useful lists and appendices. This resource makes use of *see also* references to facilitate thorough research on the topics covered.

609. Tierney, Helen, ed. **Women's Studies Encyclopedia.** New York: Greenwood Press, 1999. 3v. index. $356.95 (set). ISBN 0-313-29620-2 (set).

These three volumes focus on recent feminist research dealing with a broad range of topics and from diverse disciplinary perspectives. Some 425 scholars have contributed over 700 alphabetically arranged articles. Typical entries are fairly substantial, ranging from 750 to 1,500 words, and the intended audience is anyone studying women's or social issues at the university, public or high school level. This new edition of Tierney's encyclopedia includes an expanded coverage of a number of issues, such as violence against women, and the majority of articles now include more extensive bibliographies. Each volume includes a selected bibliography and a combined name/title/subject index. Also available electronically from Greenwood Electronic Media (www.gem.green wood.com).

World Wide Web/Internet Sites

610. **Feminism and Women's Issues.** Available: http://www2.fmg.uva.nl/ sociosite/topics/women.html (Accessed: May 17, 2004).

A subsection of the *SocioSite* Internet site, this resource provides links to a variety of other Web sites on women's issues, feminism, sexual harassment, women's history, and more. This site is international in scope, and features a guide to discussion lists and news groups, as well as full-text journals and magazines, online bibliographies, associations and networks, and academic institutions; links to other major directories on women's studies and feminism, such as that found on *Yahoo!*, are also provided. Links to the *Feminism and Women's Issues* page are provided from the broader *SocioSite* sociological subjects page, under the headings "Feminism," "Sexism," and "Women Issues," and the *Feminism and Women's Issues* home page also includes links to information on gender and queer studies, masculinity and men's issues, and family and children.

AUTHOR/TITLE INDEX

Numbers refer to entry numbers

223

SUBJECT INDEX

Numbers refer to entry numbers